THE PRESS IN AFRICA

THE PRESS IN AFRICA

COMMUNICATIONS PAST AND PRESENT

by

ROSALYNDE AINSLIE

WALKER AND COMPANY · *New York*

The author is grateful to M. Mathieu Ekani Onambélé
for allowing her to quote from the manuscript of his
book on the Press in Africa, South of the Sahara. This
material appears on pp. 130 and 225.

Library of Congress Catalog Number: 67–23083
First published in the United States of America in 1967
by Walker and Company, a division of Walker Publishing
Company, Inc.

PRINTED AND BOUND IN GREAT BRITAIN

CONTENTS

CONTENTS

CHAPTER I

INTRODUCTION

UNTIL AFRICA IS in uncontested control of its own communications, the struggle for full independence will still not be won. For he who controls communications controls more than the means to transmit messages. He has in his hands a terrible power, the power to create for his audience an image of the world, and, more important still, an image of itself. Not least of the humiliations of colonial peoples was the fact that this power was in the hands of foreigners.

And yet today in independent Africa, it is a curious fact that telecommunications are still dependent upon Europe, and that the mass media are still largely at the mercy of foreign interests. Newspapers are financed from London, or Paris, or Johannesburg; television programmes must be bought from London or Paris or New York; the strongest radio beams in Africa are those of non-African stations. And all the media require the services of foreign-owned international news agencies for the collection of news. As the mass media develop throughout the continent, this tendency towards foreign influence and control is not diminishing but increasing, in all countries where the government itself has not intervened to reverse it.

How significant is this tendency? How important is a strong and independent communications system to Africa today? What kind of communications, and what kind of mass media has the continent inherited from the past? What attitudes do African leaders have towards their development in the future?

From the moment when modern Africa first found a united voice, at the All-African Peoples Conference in Accra in 1958, the vision of an independent African system of news collection and distribution has excited the continent's journalists and political leaders. It was at the time a representative of the African National Congress of South Africa who put forward the proposal for an All-African News Agency; but he was not alone in his concern, for one of the first acts of independent Ghana had been the establishment of the Ghana News Agency in 1957, and the Middle East News Agency in Cairo was already two years old. In the following five years, during which most of Africa north of the Zambesi demanded, and won, political independence, the presence of these two centres of news collection, able to receive and sift international news, and then distribute it directly to large areas of the continent by radio, was of no little importance. During the Algerian war, for instance, Cairo was able to challenge the French version of events with news received from the F.L.N.; during the crisis in the Congo, Ghana could provide a voice for the "Lumumbists" when they had been deprived of all others.

It was at the Conference of Independent African States in Addis Ababa in May 1963, however, that problems of continental communications were for the first time dealt with seriously as problems of African development and unity. The Educational and Cultural Commission of the Organisation of African Unity was charged with the specific tasks of building information media, encouraging exchanges of information, radio and television programmes, and establishing an All-African News Agency. This resolution was couched in terms of developing 'understanding' among African peoples through the projected exchanges. But the following year, when the Heads of State met for the first time in ordinary session in Cairo, they seem to have recognised an even more compelling reason for communication development: that economic development is impossible without it. Accordingly, a new permanent commission of the O.A.U., the Commission on Transport and Communications was set up, proposed by President Kenyatta of Kenya, in order to draw up plans and co-ordinate action for "telecommunications and postal services as well as for air, land and maritime transport."

Independent Africa is now engaged in a vast programme of communications development, involving massive financial investment, technical and professional help from abroad, and training programmes for African telecommunications engineers, journalists and broadcasters. The United Nations, UNESCO, the International Telecommunications Union and many other international organisations are called upon for assistance. And the past few years have seen a succession of specialist conferences inside and outside Africa, dealing with postal agreements, telecommunications development, the establishment of national news agencies, development of television, and the use of radio in education. Parallel with these activities has been the establishment of three Pan-African specialist bodies concerned with the mass media: the African Radio and Television Union (URTNA, founded at Rabat in May 1960), the Union of African News Agencies (founded at Tunis in April 1963), and the Pan-African Union of Journalists (founded in Accra in November 1963).

Why should African states regard communications as of such fundamental importance that they are prepared to devote precious budget allocations to seeing that people who do not yet have adequate homes shall have radios, schools that are short of textbooks shall have television sets, and populations still largely illiterate shall have access to newspapers?

This sense of urgency can only be understood in the light of the political and economic problems that currently face African states—problems that involve the preservation of the state itself, and its future economic survival.

When Africa was unceremoniously carved up by the colonial powers in the nineteenth century, little attention was paid to historical associations or to national and tribal groupings, and not much more to natural geographical barriers. Borders were the offspring of chance, and of negotiations between the imperial powers taking place thousands of miles away in Europe. Colonial policy was of its nature never designed to create a national awareness among the colonial subjects. The loyalties due to the State were focussed upon a foreign metropolitan power; upon the British or the German or the Belgian sovereign, or upon 'la Patrie', which was neither 'le Senegal' nor 'l'Algérie', but 'la France.' Educational policies encouraged the young towards pride not in the culture and historical traditions of Africa, but of Europe. And it was also in the interest of the foreign ruler to leave undisturbed or to encourage internal divisions, such as tribal jealousies, distinctions between chiefs and commoners, between the European-educated and the illiterate, since these all served to hinder the development of national resistance to colonial rule. So the independent countries have inherited internal disruptive tensions, exacerbated after independence by new international pressures. These tensions have broken forth over the past few years into border disputes (between Algeria and Morocco, for instance, Ghana and Togo, Kenya, Ethiopia and Somalia), mutinies (such as in the three territories of East Africa in February 1964), and even successful revolutions.

At the same time, colonialism has left the new States with the equally urgent problem of economic and social development. It is by now a cliché of African political speeches that the chief enemies of the continent are "poverty, ignorance and disease." According to the 1963 UNESCO Yearbook, the rate of illiteracy varied in Africa between 65.1 per cent (Basutoland) and 98.5 per cent (among the so-called non-civilised population of Moçambique): in few of the independent states was the rate lower than 80 per cent.

Throughout the continent endemic diseases such as malaria, bilharzia and trachoma on the one hand, and malnutrition diseases such as kwashiorkor on the other, kill, or reduce human efficiency. But the World Health Organisation's latest figures[1] show that nowhere outside South Africa and the U.A.R. is there more than one doctor per five thousand inhabitants, and in Ethiopia the ratio is as low as one doctor to 96,000. In the United Kingdom, the ratio is one doctor to 910.

African States therefore find themselves obliged to undertake campaigns of national reorientation and propaganda in order simultaneously to project and consolidate the new national identity, to destroy old antagonisms and build a new unity; and to promote urgent national development programmes involving agricultural reform, the establishment of new industries, educational expansion at every level, and vast investment in social and medical services. To both tasks a first essential is a developed system of communications, without which the state is like a body without a nervous system, unable to transmit the instructions of the brain to the members or the needs of the members to the brain.

A campaign for national unity, in one country, might start with a complex process of accustoming village peoples used to looking for authority to their chiefs, to turn instead to a central administration; and persuading a western-orientated minority to accommodate itself to local, indigenous values. And it is explanation and exhortation through the mass media, that would play the key role. The very fact of developed

[1] For 1961.

road, rail and telegraphic contact with the capital would encourage the growth of a national consciousness and this in turn would feed the mass media with news and opinions from remote areas and so help them to reflect the needs and aspirations of the nation as a whole. The same process applies equally to the development of continental communications in the struggle for Pan-African unity.

Similarly, too, no programme for economic and social development can be efficiently planned, let alone executed, without developing sufficient communications first, to enable the needs of the people to reach the planners, and the new plans, the new knowledge and the new equipment to reach the people. But the mass media, if properly used, can do more than this—they can intervene actively to take short cuts, to shoulder burdens for which, otherwise, large trained staffs would be required, and thus help to hasten the natural pace of change into a "great leap forward."

Whether the change to be introduced is a new farming implement, a new food, or a new industrial skill, radio, newspapers, and television can take over the discussion and explanation that must precede the change, and even the demonstration that accompanies it. In the field of more formal education, be it adult literacy, schooling or higher education, radio and television can make the skill of a single teacher available all over the country, to supplement the efforts of teachers or monitors on the spot. In fact, some experts, among them the American Wilbur Schramm who was appointed by UNESCO to write a study of *Mass Media and National Development*,[1] foresee that in the circumstances of the developing countries, where there is hunger for education and a desperate shortage of trained teachers, the mass media can increasingly assumg the role of teacher. If men can learn law or mathematics alone from books, why not from television? We have not yet found the limit of what can be achieved by the media unaided, once a system of feed-back (a check on how well a given lesson has been learnt, for instance, through criticism of written work) can be centrally organised.[2]

On the pace and nature of development will depend the extent to which the media are pressed into the service of

[1] Published by Stanford University Press, 1964.
[2] As it already has been in the Soviet Union.

Government policy. What is established is that mass communications are the indispensable allies of developing societies, and that independent Africa is increasingly conscious of this fact.

The colonial era, naturally, needed communications too, but what it needed was communication with Europe. Roads were built, railways, and internal telegraph systems between main administrative centres. But except where possessions of a single power had common borders (as did the French-ruled territories of West and Equatorial Africa, and the three regions of British East Africa), these systems were not inter-territorial, and tended to stop dead on a frontier. International communications were all with Europe: shipping and airline routes, telegraph and telephone cables. One primary task, recognised by the 1964 resolution of the Organisation of African Unity, is the development of direct inter-African transport and communications.

Internal communication systems geared to purposes of colonial administration, are also no longer adequate for country-wide social development. Modern governments need to be in touch with remote villages as well as with towns, for development campaigns are likely to be needed even more urgently in backward rural areas than in urban ones.

Against so inadequate a background of basic transport and telecommunications, the mass media could hardly be expected to flourish. According to the 1964 edition of the UNESCO handbook *World Communications*, Africa had in 1962 a total of 220 daily newspapers, and 1.2 copies per hundred people; 400 radio transmitters, and 2.3 receivers per hundred people; 25 television transmitters, and .07 television sets per hundred people. Africa had the lowest total circulation of daily newspapers of any region in the world, and the lowest literacy rates. Europe, for comparison, had 23 copies of daily newspapers, 20.6 radio receivers and 7.4 television sets per hundred people. UNESCO has suggested a set of minimum standards, as immediate targets for the developing countries—10 copies of a daily newspaper, 5 radio receivers and 2 television sets per hundred of population—but to reach even these modest standards will be a mammoth task.

The history, and present condition, of news media in various parts of Africa is the subject of later chapters in this book. The general poverty of media and consequent dependence on foreign sources of news and feature material, however, raise problems not simply of the quantity of information available to the people of Africa: but of its quality. If a task of mass media is to help create a new national pride and sense of continental identity, is the blatantly white-racialist French cartoon *Tintin* correct television fare for African children? If a task is to educate the people in the policies of their own governments, to teach them to see the world and themselves from an African standpoint, can African newspapers afford to continue to depend on foreign sources for practically all their international (including inter-African) news?

Africans are constantly accusing foreign newspapers, radio and news agencies of biassed and prejudiced reporting on Africa. The conflict reached crisis point over the Congo, following the Belgian paratroop landings in Stanleyville in November 1964.

The Stanleyville landings and the horrors that accompanied them had provoked in the Western Press a wave of what can only be described, in some cases at least, as racial hysteria. The *New York Times* of November 26th, 1964, came to the solemn editorial conclusion that "the Congo rebels of Stanleyville were savages." Its main news preoccupations were with alleged communist influence among the rebels and the sufferings of white refugees. "China Pledges Aid to Congo Rebels" was the front page story on the following day. A double column picture of the body of Dr. Peter Carlson, the American missionary held as hostage in Stanleyville, was spread across an inside page, beneath it a report entitled "Nun Tells of Savage Beatings by Rebels in Congo—recalls waiting for death as she was forced to parade naked through street." The indignation of African governments at the landings themselves —statements by Presidents Nyerere of Tanzania and Ben Bella of Algeria, of the Ghana and Somalia Governments and the Liberation Committee of the Organisation of African Unity— were given two or three inches each. While the main report from inside the Congo was an 'own correspondent' piece that actually suggested that "the Belgian paratroop intervention might have been provoked by the Communist-trained rebel leaders to arouse an African outcry against white influence." The vagueness of the attributions for these speculations, to

"Congo specialists", or "many long-term residents", appearing not in editorial comment but in a news report, will have done nothing to increase African respect for Western journalism.

Time, a week later (December 4th), allowed itself to be carried away even further on the tide of emotion generated by African 'savagery' and white martyrdom. Carlson's portrait was on the cover, inside were photographs of Carlson's dead body, Carlson with a colleague, Carlson saying grace with his family. The accompanying report made liberal use of emotive words such as 'blood', 'brutality', 'savagery.' The mayor of Stanleyville had "his liver and kidneys eaten raw by a laughing rebel officer." Major Bubu, the officer alleged by "some survivors" to have given the order to fire on hostages, was "a deaf-mute ex-boxer addicted to hemp . . . Bubu's order could not have been a scream, but in its strangled inarticulate ferocity must have expressed precisely the blood-lust of the Simbas."

Times' righteous anger was then extended to condemn all "Black African civilisation—with its elaborate trappings of half a hundred sovereignties, Governments and U.N. delegations" as "largely a pretence", since that civilisation had had the temerity to denounce the parachute rescues as "imperialist aggression."

The excesses of this story were not equalled anywhere in the British Press, though the same stress on the white refugees, who were generously interviewed and photographed, was apparent. The *Daily Telegraph* on November 27th gave a three-quarter double column to 'Congo Rebels kill 20 more whites', and a quarter double column to a picture 'Refugee Collapses at Queen Fabiola's Feet.' On the 28th it thanked Belgium for undertaking the rescue, and the white mercenaries for their part in it. *The Times* and the liberal *Guardian* both agreed that the rescue, though involving a political and moral dilemma, "had to be attempted." No British paper matched the exposures of white atrocities conducted by *Espresso* in Italy or *Der Spiegel* in West Germany, nor reprinted even the regular accounts appearing in (white) South African newspapers which had correspondents travelling with the South African mercenaries, and did a very creditable job on reporting the more grotesque aspects of their mission.

Dr. Conor Cruise O'Brien, then Vice-Chancellor of the University of Ghana, and former United Nations representative in Katanga, was so appalled by the tone of foreign reporting that he complained to the London *Observer* on December 6th. "We are not told," he wrote, "how many African lives were lost as a result of the humanitarian intervention of the Belgian para-commandos. African ears, listening to European radio—including the B.B.C.—heard the detailed reports about Europeans rescued or dead. They heard—so far as I have been able to learn—nothing, not even a global estimate, of how many Africans died when the para-commandos came down, or how many more died when Tshombe's mercenaries entered to mop up in the city which the humanitarian intervention had left open to them."

When eventually some estimates of African deaths were published in January 1965, a *New York Times* News Service figure of 8,600 received barely five column inches in that paper on January 14th. Only in Africa was this shocking total accorded the headlines it undoubtedly deserved: *The People*, an unofficial Government mouthpiece in Uganda, printed the figure across half of its front page on January 16th, over a story two and a half pages long detailing atrocities of the Tshombe forces.

What the reaction in Africa might have been if as much material had been available on crimes against Africans as on crimes against whites, must be left to the imagination: if pictures of the mutilated bodies of African children had been as widely circulated as those of white hostages. The problem of African radio and newspapers, however, was that in spite of the flood of words coming over the tapes they were short of the kind of news that interested them. None of them had a correspondent behind the Simba lines, and the news-agency men were all with the Tshombe forces. There was no one to interview the nationalist leaders on the spot, to talk to the people of Stanleyville on what the war meant to them, as the white refugees were being interviewed daily. Part of the trouble was that none of the journalists there were Africans, let alone local men with a knowledge of local conditions and local languages—here was a simple instance of African poverty in financial resources and trained personnel. But part was also the corresponding fact that not only were the reporters in the Congo not African—they were British, American, French, formed inevitably by their own background, employed by an international news agency whose principal customers are in Europe, America, Australia. It is not necessarily a reflection on the integrity or the professionalism of these reporters to concede that they are likely to view the news from a point of view that is their own and not African. A simple, but revealing instance of the gulf between foreign and African reporting is in the word 'rebel', used to describe the Stanleyville forces by most of the Western news media, including the news agencies. To Africans, these were 'nationalists', 'freedom-fighters', or at least (to the cautious, foreign-owned *Daily Nation* in Nairobi) 'anti-government forces.'

Putting quotations round the word 'rebel' in the Reuter reports—one of the minor tasks of the sub-editorial departments of several African news agencies—is however not enough by way of reorientation of news reports felt to be biassed. The Kenya News Agency withheld all Reuters despatches after Stanleyville, on the ground that they would exacerbate a delicate situation during President Kenyatta's attempt to mediate in the Congo. And it is a remarkable fact that not only at the time when Reuter reports were being held up, but throughout the crisis period, most East African newspapers found their main Congo stories from other than news agency sources. On November 27th, the *Standard* (settler-owned) and *The Nationalist* (owned by the ruling Tanganyika African National Union) in Dar-es-Salaam, and the *Daily Nation* in Nairobi, all used as their main stories local protest demonstrations against the para landings, the denunciation of the Belgian action by President Nyerere, and the statement of the Organisation of African Unity. The *Standard's* headline was "Nyerere on 'Congo Insult'; Action defied all Africa." The agency stories on the rescue of the white hostages, which figured so prominently in British and American papers on the same date, were ignored. *The Nationalist* condemned them as "exceptionally vicious propaganda" and even the edited versions that found their way into the services of the Kenya News Agency and the Voice of Kenya led one Kenya member of Parliament, Mr. Luke Obok, to complain that "we are told about the Tshombe Government and the European hostages. But not one word of the people of Stanleyville who died when the Americans and the Belgians attacked the city."

Conflicts such as these between the African and non-African

view of events, particularly of African events, are the main driving force behind Africa's determination to develop news collection and dissemination facilities of its own.

There are more than twenty national news agencies in Africa today, nearly all of them established since 1960. Not half a dozen of these have their own correspondents abroad, and some of them have only skeletal facilities for handling domestic news. The few newspapers that boast foreign correspondents are nearly all foreign-owned. According to *World Communications*, all African news agencies "rely for world news upon the European, United States, or Soviet news agencies which also report African news to the rest of the world. The exchange of news between African countries is still largely carried out by Reuters and A.F.P., and, to a lesser extent, by D.P.A., U.P.I., Tass and A.P. in that order." This is almost as frustrating to African editors as it would be, say, to British editors if they were suddenly to find that their only access to news, not only of international affairs, but of Britain itself, was via Tass. The British editor would have good reason to feel frustrated. The Soviet Union has a different world outlook from his own, he would argue, its news agency a different basis for the selection and presentation of news: as for the Tass correspondents in Britain, he might add, they are foreigners who seldom move beyond the main cities, and neither fully understand nor sympathise with Britain's aspirations and way of life. Yet that is, basically, the situation of every African editor today. He must see not only the world outside, but his own continent and sometimes even his own country, through someone else's eyes.

Wilbur Schramm describes in his book a remarkable study of the world news flow, conducted in 1961. The contents of three newspapers were analysed in each of thirteen countries, including highly developed and developing nations. The investigators found that foreign news in all cases was dominated by four countries, the United States, the Soviet Union, the United Kingdom and France. At least three of these four "received more attention in the press of Argentina than did nearby Brazil; in the press of Brazil than did nearby Argentina; in the press of India than did nearby Pakistan; in the press of Pakistan than did nearby India; and so forth." Schramm concludes that news flows from the developed to the developing countries; and in particular that it flows from four highly developed countries that *are also the homes of the five world news agencies*: Associated Press and U.P.I. (American), Reuters (British), A.F.P. (French), and Tass (Soviet). His accompanying tables show that not only do these four countries dominate world news, but that one of them, the United States, has a markedly higher proportion of coverage than the other three, United States news forming between 26 per cent and 49 per cent of the total foreign news in the thirty-nine newspapers analysed.

All this evidence contributes to the conclusion that if the mass media are to play the active role in African growth envisaged by the Organisation of African Unity, and not remain at the mercy of a world-image created by others, a massive programme of development is required, on a scale beyond the resources of any single country. African leaders profess little interest in mass media as mere entertainment. When Uganda's delegate to a UNESCO conference on television in Lagos in October 1964 referred contemptuously to European television services as "those gods set up to the entertainment industry" he was expressing a general sentiment. Though he was also touching on a dilemma—how, in view of Africa's continuing dependence on material from Europe and America, to avoid setting up its own gods of entertainment? This is above all a dilemma for the very expensive medium of television.

In accordance with a basically serious approach to the mass media therefore, most African newspapers contain an exceptionally high proportion of political news. Radio is already an important contributor to adult and schools education. And in most countries, the first television sets have been installed in schools and community centres rather than in private homes. Journalists and politicians generally agree on the broad objectives they expect the media to serve: to help forge national and continental unity, encourage economic development, and serve formal and social education. But Africa is a continent ruled not by one but by thirty-five governments, excluding the remaining patches of colonial soil. The independent States, whether democracy is judged according to tolerance of opposition or according to the degree of popular participation in decision-making, range from the dictatorial to the indulgent. The end which the media are expected to serve will therefore vary from country to country, as will the extent of freedom of expression. Broadly, both politicians and journalists can be divided into those who see the Press in a 'revolutionary' role, as the direct instrument of a 'revolutionary' government, and those who see its most important function as that of 'independent' critic and commentator.

President Nkrumah of Ghana is a vehement advocate of the 'revolutionary' theory. He expounded it to the Second Conference of African Journalists in Accra in November 1963: "The truly African revolutionary Press does not exist merely for the purpose of enriching its proprietors or entertaining its readers. It is an integral part of our society, with which its purposes are in consonance. Just as in the capitalist countries the Press represents and carries out the purpose of capitalism, so in revolutionary Africa our revolutionary African Press must present and carry forward our revolutionary purpose. This is to establish a progressive political and economic system upon our continent that will free men from want and every form of injustice, and enable them to work out their social and cultural destinies in peace and at ease."

Algeria, Guinea, Mali and the United Arab Republic, all have a similar view of the place of the Press, and the other mass media, in society: they are servants of a central revolutionary purpose, whose function is to explain and to inspire rather than to criticise. The main problem which this theory has to face, is that of retaining that vitality which ideological conflict can bring to a 'free' Press—how to retain the dialectic of ideas in the absence of an ideological opposition?

The opposing theory, the 'free Press' theory, is expressed by Mr. Kelvin Mlenga, editor of the *Zambia Mail*, formerly the *Central African Mail*, Lusaka, once privately owned and now controlled by the Zambia Government. Mr. Mlenga told a meeting of the Zambia Association for National Affairs in February 1965 that the Nkrumah credo was one he could not accept. "It is my view that a newspaper owned and run by the State for the sole purpose of spreading Government propaganda is valueless. A newspaper must have freedom to disagree—sometimes quite violently—with Government policy . . . It has been said that controversy is the lifeblood of a newspaper. I thoroughly support this view . . . If a Government wants to keep its finger on the pulse of public opinion, it is

vital that there should be a free Press in the country; for it is
only in such a Press that the true feelings of the public can be
portrayed."

The weakness in Mr. Mlenga's argument is that, in assuming
that the Government does not necessarily speak for the people,
he assumes that the Press does. And this obviously depends on
who owns, controls, or runs the newspapers.

Other leaders have taken up positions somewhere between
these two. Mr. Simon Kapwepwe, when Zambian Minister of
Home Affairs in 1964, while upholding the freedom of the
Press, added the qualification that criticism should be
"responsible and constructive." Mr. Tom Mboya in Kenya has
taken a similar line, appreciative of the critical functions of a
free press, while warning that newspapers must be ready
broadly to identify themselves with the aspirations of the
African people.

His warning is directed mainly at foreign-owned newspapers
(there is no indigenously-owned daily in Kenya), which present
the principal difficulty for the advocates of unrestricted freedom
to publish. Some governments, rather than ban the foreign
papers, have attempted to establish their own in competition
(as in Nigeria and Tanzania); but this is ruinously expensive,
and competition is almost inevitably unequal with a powerful
foreign-based group that has established technical and journalistic facilities and experience to draw on. It is not irrelevant
that the Government of a country as developed as New
Zealand, with a more powerful press than any in Africa outside
the Republic and the U.A.R., felt it necessary in 1965 to
bring a bill before Parliament to prevent control of any New
Zealand newspaper from falling into foreign hands.

Should there be free competition between newspapers?
Should newspapers be privately or publicly owned, financed by
advertisement, or by Government? Need there be conflict
between Government and Press? What of radio and television?
Should they be controlled by private capital, public corporation, or by Government directly? How can all the mass media
be enabled effectively to reach not only the educated and the
town-dwellers, but the broad mass of the people? These are
questions to be asked now. The first step towards meaningful
answers is to examine how the media have grown up in Africa;
and what is their situation today.

CHAPTER 2

WEST AFRICA: THE PAST

IN ENGLISH-SPEAKING West Africa, the Press is over 160 years old—as old as the Press in South Africa, and a hundred years older than the Press in East Africa, or in the French-speaking territories. Only in Egypt has it a longer history. And apart from official publications, and a very few missionary papers, it has from the beginning been almost exclusively in African hands. Europeans never settled in West Africa, and even trade in the nineteenth century was conducted by African, and not white, middle men—traders who brought the products of the interior to the trading posts at the coast and on the great rivers —so that the market for a commercial Press serving a foreign merchant community did not exist. Instead the impetus for publication was from the beginning a political one.

A second special circumstance in West Africa was the return of numbers of freed negro slaves from America and the West Indies to settle in the colonies in Liberia (which became the Free State of Liberia in 1847) and Sierra Leone. English-speaking, and in many cases well educated, they brought their experience of political struggle in the Americas, technical knowledge, and a certain amount of capital. These Afro-Americans, and their sons and grandsons with Anglo-Saxon names, acted as a leaven in all sorts of enterprises up and down the coast from Lagos in the south to Monrovia in the north. Thus, after *The Royal Gazette and Sierra Leone Advertiser* (first published in 1801) and *The Royal Gold Coast Gazette* (published from 1822), the first West African newspaper was founded by Charles L. Force, an American negro who arrived in Monrovia in 1826 with a small hand-operated printing press, a gift from the Massachusetts Colonisation Society of Boston. Force started *The Liberia Herald*, a four-page monthly. Unhappily, he died a few months later, and his paper ceased, but in 1830 it was revived by another Afro-American, a former editor of the first negro weekly in the United States, *Freedom's Journal*. *The Herald* survived under various editors until 1862, its last editor being the great West-Indian-born writer and scholar, Edward W. Blyden; and the few early issues which have been preserved show that it was a worthy ancestor for Africa's modern nationalist Press. *The Herald's* motto, printed on its masthead, reads "Freedom is the Brilliant Gift of Heaven", and an editorial in September 1830 attacking local apologists for the slave trade, complains:

"Should the origin of African slavery be enquired for, it must be sought amongst most barbarous nations, and will be found growing out of the most sordid and malignant passions of the human heart; while fraud and violence have in almost every instance been the means by which our slaves were originally procured. Yet are there multitudes in our own enlightened country, in our boasted land of liberty, who, with the book of God in their hands, and a public profession of allegiance to the compassionate Saviour in their mouths, unblushingly stand forth as the advocates of this cruel system." The author goes on to quote the example of Hannibal and other Africans whose names have gone down in European history, to argue that black men deserve no less respect than white.

No one who looks back on this early history can but be impressed with the vigour and the enterprise behind the newspapers all along the coast, which from the mid-nineteenth century sprang up, one after another, most of them short-lived, but each one that died replaced by another, and another. In 1858, Charles Bannerman, the first African editor in the Gold Coast, had no printing press on which to produce his *Accra Herald* (later *The West African Herald*), so he reproduced it in his own hand-writing, and circulated it among the local intelligentsia. A year later, Anglican missionaries at Abeokuta (in what is now the Western Region of Nigeria) started the first vernacular paper, the *Iwe Ihorin*, published in Yoruba, and later in both Yoruba and English. It sold for thirty cowrie shells, and ceased publication only after the press was destroyed during the Egba rising of 1867.[1] But before its demise, *The Anglo-African* had appeared in Lagos, on June 6th, 1863, owned and edited by a West Indian immigrant, Prof. Robert Campbell. It was stiff with elegant prose, formal Victorian-style essays, quotations from the London papers, and a serial entitled

---

[1] The Egba are a Yoruba-speaking people who until 1914 enjoyed nominal autonomy under an "independent" treaty with the British Government.

"We Four Villagers" which opened with the, for Lagos, unlikely sentences: "A clear moon-illumined sky beamed brightly overhead, the air was keen, cold and bracing. Hills and dales were deeply sleeping beneath a well frozen covering of snow." *The Anglo-African* lasted for three years.

Catering as they did for a small European-educated minority, and each the enterprise of a single vocal individual, these papers were very different from the party broadsheets that form the base of the modern Press tradition in Africa. They were political, in that they arose from the need felt by the élite for a voice in public affairs: but they also aimed to instruct, and to entertain, taking as a model (and often quoting extensively from) the London papers of the period. Thus *The African Interpreter and Advocate* of Sierra Leone in February 1867 not only published extracts from the London Press and—remarkably— from *The Cape Argus*, Cape Town, but it had a poet's corner to which local talent freely contributed. "Sir, Please insert the following in your Poet's Corner," writes 'A.C.E.', enclosing a comment in verse on the avarice of the medical profession. But it was also a vehicle for public criticism of the administration, for the same paper publishes a letter complaining of a dangerous road built along a precipice; and of political polemic: "As to the first portion of this wretched effusion," says an editorial in January 1868, "as it appeared in the journal of a notorious political apostate with a proper sense of his own high position and long-tried political consistency . . . " The object of attack is the editor of a rival newspaper, the subject under discussion obscure, but the political emotion obvious enough.

In the Gold Coast, in fact, it was political protest that soon became the dominant theme, mainly directed at colonial officials. J. H. Brew started *The Gold Coast Times* in 1874, and in 1880 at Cape Coast *The Western Echo*, together with Timothy Laing and J. E. Casely Hayford. The names of these three men are still remembered in Ghana today as the originators of a tradition of irreverent political satire that enlivened the country's Press for many years to come. An example of their heavily ironic style is a paragraph from the *Echo* of November 28th, 1885, "It is not generally known," says the report, "that for once in the way a portion of our monies is being expended by our government in a manner certain to benefit us." It seems that "a somewhat peculiar vessel" was being built in

Birkenhead, to repress piracy on the Lagos lagoons. "It is possible of course that piracy may be rife on the lagoons of Lagos," comments the *Echo*, "but we have never heard of there being. Would not the colonial office do well to check such reckless expenditure of public monies for the repression of 'things' which have no existence except in the fertile brains of some official who is hard up for a subject on which to write?" *The Western Echo* died in 1887; but political polemic did not die with it, for *The Gold Coast Methodist*, started by English missionaries, was being edited by a local minister, the Rev. S. R. B. Solomon. Solomon, or Attoh Ahuma as he later called himself, was a militant nationalist who did not hesitate to express himself freely in his paper. Eventually he was dismissed, and joined with another local churchman, the Rev. Eggijir Asaam, to found *The Gold Coast Aborigines* as the organ of the earliest political pressure group in the colony, the Aborigines Rights Protection Society. In announcing itself on 1st January, 1898, the new paper referred to the conflict with the Methodists, with the hope that "*The Gold Coast Aborigines* will honestly undertake what the *Times* (a rival) is requested from certain quarters to leave undone." It also promised to instruct the young in the history of their country. "Most of our youth," remarks the editorial, "are acquainted with the history of England with such precision and to such a degree, that it astounds the Briton, and yet these cannot tell B from a bull's foot in the history of this country." Accordingly, regular articles appeared in the paper on the recent (colonial) history of the Gold Coast and Nigeria, or on the ancient civilisation of Egypt, as an example of African achievement.

The newspaper deathrate was high: Ahuma once lamented the fact that Gold Coast citizens were more anxious to read their paper than pay for it, pleading, "It is earnestly hoped and requested that all subscribers and purchasers will do everything to discourage the almost universal practice of lending for perusal, papers to those individuals who, loudly mourning the want of a local paper, are never known to support the Press, but ever prefer to borrow from their too indulgent and obliging friends." Yet in spite of economic difficulties, and an average life-span of only three or four years per newspaper, the eighteen-nineties were a vital period for the Gold Coast Press. *The Gold Coast People* had been established by James Mensah Sarbah in

1891, and *The Gold Coast Independent* by the Sierra Leonean James Bright Davies in 1895, "to create and foster public opinion in Africa and make it racy of the soil." The *Independent* was an outspoken abuser of Government, calling it on various occasions 'autocratic,' 'astounding,' and even 'revolting.' Its invective was particularly strong after Government had allegedly lured away its only journeyman printer! But the paper's principal strength seems to have been its news, which came from all over West Africa, and covered in detail the regions of the Gold Coast and its neighbouring colonies. A random issue contained items datelined Akropong, Lomé, Cape Coast, Kevitta, Kyebi, Salt Pond and Appam.

Two of the four main papers at the time were being published in Accra, and two at Cape Coast, some 200 miles away. President Nkrumah[1] once described the 'underground' communications between the two centres, explaining that "In those days, there was no proper road between Cape Coast and Accra. ... So those editors and their co-workers worked their clandestine way by canoe along the coast to the capital, Accra. There they ferreted out the latest material that could be used against the colonial Government, and then they paddled their dangerous way back to Cape Coast. All these activities were done at night. It was always a puzzle to the British administration in Accra as to how these newspapers were able to appear in Cape Coast with such 'hot' news so quickly."

By 1880 Lagos too had its organs of protest, voicing grievances, though still in a more sedate and cautious manner than their Gold Coast or Liberian contemporaries. Richard Beale Blaize, editor of *The Lagos Times and Gold Coast Advertiser*, which appeared twice monthly for a period of two years, told readers of his first issue on 10th November, 1880: "Our paper shall not be a medium for the circulation of vulgar personalities, but its columns shall be free and open to those who are polite and dispassionate in their communications." Nigerians then seem to have been as eager to express themselves in print as they are today, for the very first number contains a beguiling letter from T. A. King, The Druggist's, Lagos, which ends: "P.S. If you can allot me a small space in your journal, I shall not fail to communicate occasionally some authenticated information, and shall always subscribe my initials, T.A.K."

[1] In an address to the Second Conference of African Journalists in Accra in 1963.

The Lagos Times quoted 'Opinions of the Press' from Gold Coast, Sierra Leone and London papers. An early number criticises Government in a lengthy editorial for failing to consult the Egba on affairs that affect them, and so bringing about violent conflict. Letters complain of dishonesty among traders, raids against commercial ventures, and acts of lawlessness in the interior. "Thank God," writes Lojueh, Lagos, "there is a public Press in which we can report all mismanagement of things. I have suffered enough, and we do not wish to suffer more; I fear that the present policy of the Administrator will in future give rise to some unpleasantness between this and the Abeokuta Government." But another correspondent finds less comfort in mere words, and ends his communication, "Mr. Editor, I am constrained to stop. Alas for Lagos! Alas for Africa!" Already, the sense of close identification between newspaper and reader that is so remarkable a feature of later popular journalism in Africa is there. And already complaints of administrative ineptitude are beginning to develop into more general formulations of political and race oppression. "How long will this state of things continue," cries another letter-writer, "When will Europeans respect Afric's [*sic*] sons who are qualified and worthy to hold offices of trust and honour? When will Africa be independent?"

The most highly developed political consciousness however, seems still to have been found in Monrovia, where the *Herald* was joined in 1839 by *The Liberian Star*, *The Amulet*, and *Africa's Luminary*. The *Luminary* was published by the Missionary Society of the Methodist Episcopal Church, New York, and was edited by the Rev. John Seys. Seys stood for election as Governor, and after being defeated, published a series of attacks on Government that led to a law-suit against the Mission. Another ambitious editor was Edward J. Roye, who started *The Liberia Sentinel* in 1854, and later became Speaker of the House of Representatives. And another twenty years later, in 1873, came *The Liberia Advocate*, its motto "Christian Liberia, the open door to heathen Africa," and its objects to campaign for the education and conversion of Muslim and tribal Liberians. Perhaps because Liberia was already an independent State, perhaps because so many of its citizens had been born and brought up abroad, often with the hard experience of slavery behind them, Liberians tended to look beyond the borders of their own territory, and to feel a 'missionary' responsibility to all Africa, that on occasion led to a quite extraordinary grasp of the colonial situation as it affected the continent. *The Observer*, Monrovia, for instance, a paper whose origins remain obscure, carried an editorial on July 8th, 1880, which, as a comment on the economics of imperialism, had a sophistication years ahead of its time. It is titled 'The Black and White.'

"On all sides," it reads in part, "the same cry is heard, all the Great Nations of Europe as well as the United States of America seem to evince a more or less ardent desire to divide Africa among themselves. The reasons for this wish are obvious, when we think of the millions of heathen who are sitting in darkness and who would serve as consumers of the refuse and surplus manufactures. Heathen who, if only civilised, would buy up a large quantity of old clothes, condemned guns, bad liquor, *et hoc genus*. And again we must remember that surplus population which could find in Africa congenial homes. Men who are nobodies but who as missionaries and explorers would be lions; men whose genius brings them to the treadmill when exercised at home; but if exercised in Africa would make them wealthy merchants, or great landowners. Nor must we forget the philanthropists of the Jelleby stamp who unmindful of the squalor and wretchedness around them love to spend their time and other people's money in conveying doubtful blessing to the heathen. For these and a thousand other reasons the partition of Africa is a most desirable arrangement. The Negro may have some objection, but a first class English newspaper told us some months ago that savages have no rights which civilised (na)tions were bound to respect; so the objections of the Negroes will doubtless be treated as were those of the Zulus, and because we wear the 'shadowed livery of the burnished sun,' and do not regulate our costumes by the latest Paris fashions, our land is to be divided out by these *soi-disant* Heralds of Civilisation."

Next to Monrovia, then, Lagos remained a little prim. *The Eagle and Lagos Critic*, 1883, was one of four Lagos newspapers started in the 1880's. Its editor, Owen Macaulay, declared his desire to 'infuse' into "the minds of the community the fondness for reading for its own sake," and announced that he did not want "any correspondence bordering on scurrility." He may have had good reason for this severity, but his columns,

though impeccably produced and relatively free of the profusion of proof-reading errors characteristic of later and more
militant publications, are solemn rather than serious. Extracts
from the debates of the "Imperial Parliament—House of
Lords" are followed by complete scorecards and bowling
analyses of a match between the Lagos Criket [sic] Club and
the Combined Team L. and W.H.S.C. Clubs. Letters are
signed 'Amicus,' or 'Nerius and Gaius,' and on the last page is
a column of jokes, the kind from Victorian joke-books featuring
cockneys and chambermaids, that seeks no doubt to lighten
the rather ponderous text.

Within ten years, however, the Lagos scene was to be
transformed by the advent of John Payne Jackson's *The Lagos
Weekly Record*, a frankly nationalist political organ, and the
work of the West Coast's first full-time professional journalist.
Since Jackson has been the subject of a monograph 'John
Jackson, Journalist, Apostle of Humanism,' by Mr. Gwamm of
Ibadan University, and is thus one of the very few early African
newspaper men to have had his life chronicled, it is worth
telling his story in some detail.

Jackson was born in Liberia in about 1847, of Americo-
Liberian parents, and educated at a mission school, where he
learned the art of printing. He came to Lagos in the 1860's,
where he was first employed by a merchant as book-keeper.
He later set up as a 'baracooner,' or Niger trader, on his own.
He married Mary Thompson, whose parents had been
captured as slaves in Ekitiland in the 1840's, and transported to
the West Indies, where she was born. Jackson's trading enterprise failed, and he was compelled to take up employment
again, this time as book-keeper to Richard Beale Blaize, merchant and publisher of the short-lived *Lagos Times*. He was dismissed following a quarrel in 1882, struggled for eight years,
and finally, apparently with Blaize's financial backing, started
The Lagos Weekly Times in March, 1890. But the partners
quarrelled again, nine months later, it seems as a result of
Jackson's "hard-drinking habits," and again he was sacked.

This time, though, Jackson was not left poverty-stricken; and
in addition he had established a reputation, according to
Gwamm, as "a matchless journalist." It is not clear how he
managed to keep control of the paper, but from January 1st,
1891, he was publishing it as *The Lagos Weekly Record*. Now he

could give himself full rein, inveighing against Government, against white men in general, and against the Governors who represented political power in Lagos, in particular. Gwamm quotes from an editorial in the *Record* of March 8th, 1913, on the appointment of Sir Frederick (later Lord) Lugard, as Governor of the newly amalgamated Northern and Southern Nigeria, as an illustration of the power of Jackson's pen.

"His Excellency Sir Frederick Dealtry Lugard, K.C.M.G., C.B., D.S.O., is a disappointment to Southern Nigeria," it begins. "(He is) a man whose walking stick is a pistol and whose thought by day and dream by night are punitive expeditions and military patrols. Stirring tales are told of his negrophobism, his anti-black proclivities, and his distant attitude to all men in general.

"Taking a fancy to salutation by prostration in Northern Nigeria, he was said to have arranged for the Emirs and potentates to do him royal homage by throwing themselves in the dust at his approach and to shout ZAKI!!! in his presence.

"This fancy became contagious and filtered down to petty officials and non-officials until the people of the country were transformed, or transformed themselves into a set of 'human' crocodiles crawling on all fours and dragging prostrate at the approach of any white man . . .

"His Excellency was represented as a man who is enemy of all, friend of none, recognising the white man a little, the black man not at all; and brushing aside the amenities of civilised life; in fact some sort of ogre . . .

"(So) the day of his arrival was beset with orisons and litanies, with inward sighs and upward glances."

Jackson was an active campaigner as well as a writer—he led a delegation of Dahomeian chiefs to Paris in 1894 to protest against the occupation of their country; and he called his home after the Dahomeian warrior, Samadu, who stood out against the French until 1898. He was a signatory to a series of petitions to Government House, and he went himself into the interior to support a land-tenure agitation, not long before his death in 1915—itself apparently a consequence of the adventure. His son, Thomas Horatio, had taken over editorship of the paper the year before, and it survived until 1930.

Gwamm attributes the *Record's* success to Jackson's passionate nationalism, his idealisation of all things African and mistrust

of every move made by the colonial authorities, which corres-
ponded with the mood of West African intellectuals at the time.
This was a period when colonial administrator and missionary
alike assumed the virtues of their Christian civilisation to be
absolute, in relation to African savagery and darkness. These
high moral convictions were an inspiration to the pursuit of
imperialism—but devastating to the self-respect of young
Africans who were being taught to reject their own background
and all that it represented. Jackson attacked white prejudice,
white hypocrisy, white arrogance, when he saw it, and so
perhaps helped to soothe the wounded pride of his compatriots,
and give them courage to fight back.

So the nineteenth century ended after seeing the establishment of a lively, outspoken political Press in all four territories
of West Africa. The changes in the twentieth were to be first of
all changes of technique.

The great achievement of the nineteenth century Press in
West Africa was in fact that it gave a voice to a subject people,
through its literate élite, and established a tradition of political
criticism and debate which served both to keep the colonial
administration alive to public opinion, and to make public
opinion aware of itself. In 1918 *The Gold Coast Independent*
(revived in 1909 by Dr. F. V. Nanka-Bruce and Dr. C. E.
Reindorf) boasted of this awareness: "It may be crude, rough
hewn," it wrote, "but it is growing and developing vigorously.
If it is estimated that there are over 100,000 persons in all West
Africa who are carefully following developments on Western
lines, there is no telling to what extent these figures may grow
in the next 50 years."

It is worth noting that at this period the *Independent* talks of
West Africa as a whole, rather than of the Gold Coast only, and
this sense of identification with all the peoples of the coast
seems to have been present in most of the early newspapers,
which indeed often circulated far beyond the borders of their
own colony. *The Vox Populi* (originally *The Voice of the People*,
which appeared for the first time in 1917) claimed to be "the
most influential paper in West Africa backed by important
kings and chiefs, and reaching not only the literate classes but
all illiterate masses whose cause it necessarily advocates
throughout the Gold Coast, Ashanti, Nigeria and generally
British and French West Africa." What, incidentally, the

illiterate masses made of a serial that started "Jean Carstey had the sort of red hair that laughed in every twist," is unfortunately not recorded.

The turn of the century, however, brought horizons far wider than those of the West African coast, when the first cabled news service was introduced in 1910 by *The Nigerian Times*. The "Telegraphic Intelligence from Reuters Agency" was nearly a fortnight old, and the brief items seem to have been selected, whether in London or Lagos, with a gleeful inconsequence: a speech by Kier Hardie, a statement by President Theodore Roosevelt, the result of the Oxford and Cambridge Boat Race.[1] But they brought to the Lagos newspapers a new dignity as dealers in international news.

To Lagos too belongs the distinction of producing the first successful daily newspaper in West Africa, although *The Gold Coast Daily Express* had appeared for four months in Accra as long ago as 1895. Herbert Macaulay founded *The Lagos Daily News* in 1925. It appears, strangely enough, to have had no Reuters service, and the rolling cadences of Macaulay's editorials, quoting liberally from Addison, Greek mythology, Roman history and Dr. Johnson, put one in mind of the nineteenth century, rather than the twentieth.[2] The front page of the issue of 3rd January, 1933, for instance, yields, under the heading "General News," a quaint miscellany of extracts from Dickens, Shakespeare and the Bible, followed by the announcements that Dr. Adeniyi-Jones has opened a dispensary at Ebute-Metta; that the King (of England) is encouraging the Household Cavalry to wear moustaches; and that Mrs. Eugene Coker from Jos, who has been staying with her sister in Lagos, has left for Ibadan to visit her sister-in-law.

What was new about the *Daily News* was neither its technique nor its content, but the fact that it had been founded as an organ for Macaulay's National Democratic Party. It was the first party paper.

But it survived no later than 1936, and was outlived by a

---

[1] This news, according to Reuters, would have been received by multi-addressed cables sent out simultaneously to subscribers in various parts of the world. Since cable costs were then very high, as many short items as possible were packed into a single cable.

[2] In this it would nothave been untypical of the 1920's in West Africa, which the Nigerian editor Increase Coker has described as the period of the "black Victorians".

second daily, first published in 1926, *The Nigerian Daily Times*, forerunner of the largest daily in Nigeria today. The *Daily Times*' first editor was another outstanding figure of West African journalism, Ernest Ikoli, a former Master of King's College, Lagos, who had received his journalistic training under John Payne Jackson on the *Weekly Record*. As a journalist who had worked his way up from a reporter, if so specific a title can be given to Jackson's assistant, he was the first true professional in the business, which had previously been dominated by men who had no training, and to whom journalism was generally an occupation secondary to business, politics, or the law. From the *Weekly Record*, Ikoli went to the *Nigerian Messenger*, and then to the *Daily Times*, later becoming editor of *The Daily Telegraph* and *The Daily Service*.

All these papers helped to make the 1930's an exceptionally fertile period for the Press both in Nigeria and the Gold Coast. In 1931 Dr. J. B. Danquah started his *West African Times* in Accra, the first West African daily paper to provide a regular service of international news (again, through Reuters). In its first week, a foreign story, on a railcrash in London, made the main front page headline. And a 'Ladies' Corner' by Marjorie Mensah introduced one of the first African ventures into woman's journalism: "Of course, it is my fault," she writes breezily, "there are some of us who may not know what a mannequin is—Well, look here, girls, a mannequin is simply a person—a beautiful one preferably—that a firm usually engages to dress in all the latest in fashion, make a little detour in a special place and for the benefit of feminine society and also to serve as a means for the firm advertising the articles worn . . . More chat tomorrow."

Accra enjoyed two daily newspapers at this time, the second being *The Spectator Daily*, which had been founded in 1927 as *The Gold Coast Spectator*. The *Spectator* was not only remarkable for its internationalism, but it actually had its own correspondent in Moscow, Chatwood Hall, who contributed stories headlined "Soviets Raise Nobility of Toil by Medals," and "People Work for self, not Capitalist." Another special contributor was the West Indian George Padmore, later a colleague of Nkrumah in the struggle for Ghana independence.

In Sierra Leone, *The Sierra Leone Daily Mail* (since 1952 the *Daily Mail*) was already appearing by 1933, and *The Sierra*

Leone Guardian and Foreign Mails, founded before the First World War, had become *The Daily Guardian* the same year. And it was in 1933 also that in Lagos *The Daily News* and *The Daily Times* were joined by *The Daily Service,* started as an organ of the new Nigerian Youth Movement, a rival to Macaulay's National Democratic Party. The *Service* had a descendant in Nigeria, the *Daily Express,* up to December 1965.

The 'thirties perhaps represented the end of the hey-day of the one-man editor-printer who had been for long a feature of West African journalism. One such was Duse Mohamed Ali, an Egyptian graduate of the University of London who settled in Lagos and founded *The Comet,* an independent nationalist weekly. And another was William Coulson Labor, who published a series of small papers in East Nigerian towns. Labor came from Sierra Leone, where his father had been an editor-printer before him. "He covered local news stories in shorthand himself," writes Increase Coker, later editor of the Lagos *Morning Post,* "typed out the manuscripts, edited and set them into types; he check-read the proofs, paged the assembled material on the 'stone,' and supervised the printing. He did almost everything, short of actually operating the machines. In this way he produced about 2,000 copies of his newspapers every week." A pioneer of the Press in East Nigeria, Labor started at Aba, whence he moved to Enugu and Port Harcourt.

It was thus into a scene of flourishing newspaper enterprise all along the coast that burst in 1934 the most dynamic figure in modern West African journalism—Dr. Nnamdi Azikiwe, one of the most compelling personalities of the African national-ist struggle.

Azikiwe went to the United States to study in 1925, at the age of 21, and stayed there nine years. James Coleman, in *Nigeria: a Background to Nationalism* has described how, as a poor student at segregated negro colleges in the South, Azikiwe was com-pelled to work as a dishwasher, a steward, a coalminer, and even as a boxer. He was thus open to the full impact of dis-crimination and economic insecurity that affected all but a very few black Americans. But at the same time he was able to see in the 'thirties the growth of a militant negro Press, and of a new political consciousness which showed itself in the rise of Garveyism and the rediscovery of Africa, in Communist Party and trade union activity, in race riots and political demonstration. Coleman makes what he calls two "suggestive connections" between Azikiwe's American experience and his subsequent career: the first, in his internationalism, his readiness to treat "lynchings in America, pass laws in South Africa, or boycotts in the Gold Coast" as seriously in his newspapers as the struggle for independence in Nigeria; and the second, in the influence of sensational, race-conscious American negro journalism on the style and tone of his own papers.

Azikiwe once wrote, in his booklet 'Renascent Africa,' that "there is no better means to arouse African peoples than that of the power of the pen and of the tongue." And it is in this light that he consistently saw his journalistic career. In 1934, he wrote from New York to the *Spectator* on the Gold Coast, asking for a job. He was given more than this, a paper to himself, the new *African Morning Post*. Here he tried out his new ideas in collaboration with a Sierra Leonean, I. T. A. Wallace-Johnson, a trade union organiser and a Marxist, who had formerly edited *The Negro Worker* in Paris, and *The Daily Telegraph* in Lagos. The *Morning Post* was vivid, emotional and odd. It described itself as "Independent in all things and neutral in nothing affecting the destiny of Africa." Obituaries were recorded "with trembling hands." Complaints were voiced because a "nude madman" was "stalking the streets." An article on the social difficulties arising from marriage with a white wife was vehemently attacked in an editorial the following day for 'race prejudice.' And an editorial on war preparations in Europe in 1937 headed 'Stop that Madness' was full of characteristic passion, and irony at the expense of Africa's imperial masters: "The world in general is mad, but Europe is especially so. Is it the beginning of the end of the white race, or is it a temporary fit which will soon subside?" In 1937, however, an article by Wallace-Johnson entitled 'Has the African a God?' landed both of them in a criminal libel suit, and when he was acquitted on appeal, Zik left for Nigeria to found the *West African Pilot*.

As an innovator of popular journalistic techniques, he had arrived in West Africa at the right time. The number of children in primary school in the Gold Coast had risen from 15,000 in 1902 to 65,000 in 1935, and in Nigeria the number of primary schools had risen from 127 in 1906 to 4,069 in 1937.

For the first time, the reading public was not merely a privileged coastal intelligentsia, but a relatively wide cross-section of the population. The 1930's also saw the emergence both in the Gold Coast and Nigeria of the first political parties, and the beginnings of that mass political awareness that in the post-war period was to lead to the achievement of political independence. Zik's *Pilot* was to be one of the principle formers of this new consciousness.

From the first, he spread banner headlines across his pages, introduced photographs, and simplified his text *Daily-Mirror*-style with one sentence per paragraph. A Woman's Page was started, a Gossip Column, book reviews and short stories. Within three years, the paper was selling 12,000 copies daily, an unheard of circulation on the West Coast.

Though the *Pilot* strove for national distribution, lack of transport and communications facilities made the task nearly hopeless. In any case, Zik was very well aware of the importance of local issues to a popular newspaper, and Zik's Press Ltd. therefore embarked on the creation of a chain of newspapers, the first in West Africa, embracing the main centres of all the three regions of Nigeria. In 1940, he established the *Eastern Nigerian Guardian* at Port Harcourt; in 1943, the *Nigerian Spokesman* at Onitsha, also in the East, and the *Southern Nigeria Defender* at Warri, in what is now the Western Region. In 1944 he acquired *The Comet* on Ali's death, converted it into a daily, and in 1949 transferred it to Kano as the first daily paper in Northern Nigeria. In the same year he founded a second northern daily at Jos, but this had later to revert to weekly publication. At one time there were six daily newspapers in the chain, covering all the main centres of the largest, most sprawling and socially disunited country in Africa.

The *Pilot* became in 1945 the first post-war African subscriber to a special West African Coastal Service of Reuters news which had been developed during the war for the benefit of troops en route round the coast. It comprised 800 or 1,000 words a day, which Zik's Press picked up in morse by radio. Transmission was converted soon after the war to 'hellschreiber,' the precursor of the modern teleprinter. Azikiwe was also himself for a time Reuters correspondent in West Africa.

The modernity and professionalism of these enterprises, however, should be set in the very amateurish perspective of their time, when the most elementary facilities were not available to the Press. Abiodun Aloba, a journalist who worked for some years on the *Daily Times*, has written an entertaining account of the working conditions of the period which deserves quotation at some length.[1]

"When I joined the Nigerian Press fourteen years ago," he says, "not a single newspaper had a photo process department. The teleprinter was unknown. The telephone a luxury. Correspondents covering the Convention (of a political party), often the party secretary himself, would have gotten the stories ready a couple of days after it was all over. Sent them by post to reach the Lagos editor a week later.

"If pictures had to be taken and for political purposes the editor wanted them published he sent them to the United Kingdom (two weeks by sea) for processing. And when they were published six weeks later, the caption read, 'Photographs do not lie. This picture, showing mammoth crowds, was taken at the Convention of the N.C.N.C. held in Kano last June.'

"And when the newspaper reached some remotest part of the hinterland another month later, it was read to eager clusters of villagers as a gospel, or passed from hand to hand, and from one mission house to another (only teachers really read newspapers) with wild enthusiasm.

"The newspaper office was tucked away in some street corner, the desk of the editor adorned with a telephone—the only telephone for all—which sometimes did not work for days. Nor was it needed for more than the social activities of the editor. A distant call was expensive. A local call, reporting a fatal accident, produced little or no result; the news reporter arrived at the scene when life had returned to normal, and returned to the office to do his story when time hardly permitted more than a lucid paragraph.

"If the newspaper went to bed in the early hours of the morning, that was about the best that could be expected; for then, provided the machine did not break down, newspapers were on the streets at 9.0 a.m., and circulation went up—to nine or ten thousand.

"The editor, a disgruntled teacher or a dismissed clerk was nevertheless the respected gentleman with the bowler and the walking stick. No one knew exactly what his salary was; but

[1] From an article in *Gazette*, Leiden, vol. V, no. 2, 1959.

everybody knew he drank free whiskey, ate with the greats, and lived on the patronage of his social and political clients.

"Indeed, when once an assistant editor, Mr. Ernest Ikoli, now recognised veteran of Nigerian journalism and correspondent of the London *Times*, asked for his salary, he was confronted with the disdainful eyes of an irate editor: 'Salary? Don't you know you are working for the nation?' "

Change, however, in this post-war period, was on its way, and it was not long before West African newspapers found themselves working not only for the nation, but also for profit.

CHAPTER 3

SOUTHERN AFRICA: THE PAST

THE PRESS IN South Africa has had a turbulent career from the beginning. *The Cape Town Gazette*, published for the first time in 1800, was the first newspaper on the continent,[1] beating *The Royal Gazette* in Sierra Leone by a year. And less than a quarter of a century later, the conflict started.

In 1823 two applications to publish were made to the Governor. One applicant was Thomas Pringle, a British immigrant, suspected, in his own words, of those "most disgusting principles of Republicanism." His collaborator was to be the Rev. Abraham Faure, a missionary associate of the liberal Dr. John Philip, much detested in the colony on account of his complaints to London about the brutality of the 'Boers' towards their slaves. Pringle and Faure asked permission to publish a monthly journal "to enlighten South Africa." The second applicant was George Greig, a British-born printer, who sought to publish a periodical which, he assured the Governor in his prospectus, would exclude "all discussion of . . . the policy or administration of the Colonial Government." The Governor at the time was Lord Charles Somerset, long remembered in the Cape for his corrupt and petty tyranny, and both applications were summarily rejected.

But Greig discovered that the law prohibiting publication without prior authority applied in fact only to periodicals and not to newspapers, so in January 1824, with Thomas Pringle and James Fairbairn as editors, he produced the first issue of *The South African Commercial Advertiser*, as "the first attempt to establish a medium of general communication at the Cape of Good Hope." It was printed on an old wooden press borrowed from Dr. Philip.

Soon afterwards, the Colonial Secretary sanctioned the publication of a non-political magazine, and Pringle started

---

[1] With the possible exception of the broadsheets published in Egypt during the Napoleonic occupation.

his *Journal*. But his 'disgusting principles' soon got the better of him, when he criticised too freely the conditions of the 1820 British settlers brought out to the Eastern Cape, and the paper was suppressed. (Faure, who had started a periodical in Dutch, *De Zuid Afrikaansche Tijdschrift*, was more cautious, so his paper managed to survive.) Somerset was determined to put an end to the new Press, which already threatened to throw a great deal of unwelcome light into the darker corners of his administration. In particular, the *Advertiser* was causing the Governor considerable embarrassment by publishing accounts of the court proceedings in libel actions brought by him against those who accused him of various corrupt practices in his administration of the colony. He instructed Greig to stop publishing the libel proceedings, and to keep to the limits of his original prospectus. Greig refused, and was given a month to leave the country, but before leaving he published the 'facts' of the dispute in a broadsheet of May 5th, 1824. "His Majesty's Fiscal having assumed the censorship of *The South African Commercial Advertiser*," he wrote defiantly, "by an official order, sent to the Printing Office, by a Messenger late in the evening before publication, demanding proof sheets of the paper for the next day (this day), and prohibiting its being struck off 'till we had received his further directions thereon,' we find it our duty, as BRITISH SUBJECTS, under these circumstances to discontinue the publication of the said paper *for the present* in this colony, until we have applied for redress and direction to his Excellency the Governor and the British Government."

For a full year, Greig campaigned for redress in London, supported by some of the most distinguished editors of the day, including Thomas Barnes, editor of *The Times*, and by the London Missionary Society to which Dr. Philip belonged. By August 1825 he was back publishing the *Advertiser* again, though still limited by the terms of his prospectus. Somerset had it suppressed once more in 1827, and this time leading Cape citizens paid Fairbairn's fare to London so that he could take the matter up afresh with the Government in Whitehall. Fairbairn promptly rushed into print with a public account of the wrongs suffered by His Majesty's loyal subjects at the Cape. "From the first moment," he complained, "that public attention began to be drawn by its (the Press') means to the long arrear of wrong, outrage and cruelty inflicted on the defenceless inhabitants of that Colony, scarcely a month has elapsed in which some attempt has not been made to baffle or crush it . . .

"Are such a people to be for ever trampled under foot? Is there no moderation, no sympathy, no pride in England, that, for its own honour, will put an end to the abominable scene of oppression, insolence, and bad faith practised so long in this settlement? What gain has England in our loss? By what have we merited such treatment? We have cost her neither blood nor treasure. We never wronged her. How, then, is it, that while she boasts of her high principles, we receive only contempt, or irreparable injury at her hands?"

He eventually gained his victory on April 30th, 1828, when a new Colonial Secretary sanctioned a Press Law for the Cape based on the law of England. Publishers were to deposit £300, plus £300 in guarantees, with the authorities, after which they were free to publish, subject only to the law of libel. So the principle of Press freedom was established.

The colonists were not slow to take advantage of this new-won liberty. The *Advertiser* was soon a focus for the growing demand for representative institutions of government; *De Zuid Afrikaan* spoke for the supporters of slavery; and *The Grahamstown Journal*, a new weekly, rooted itself firmly in the settler community of the Eastern Cape. Correspondents wrote accounts to the *Journal* of cattle raids by the 'Caffres,' of violent clashes along the disputed border with the Xhosa, and the unwillingness of the administration to give them adequate protection. Court reports told of how Hendrik Nieuveld, a Hottentot, had been sentenced to twenty-four lashes and a week's imprisonment for stealing an iron wagon chain; or Marthinus Johannes Scheepers, a Boer, had been fined £11 for compelling a sick slave to work. Many disappointed immigrants aired their grievances in a vigorous correspondence column: "But alas," wrote one melodramatically on March 13th, 1832, "instead of the heaven-born terms of 'Liberty, Freedom and Unanimity,' we were constrained to hear nothing but a jargon on the subject of sordit [*sic*] profits and more sordit views!"

It is a feature of these early years that Press enterprise flourished not only in the capital, but in small and remote towns throughout the colony. *The Friend of the Sovereignty*, founded in Grahamstown in 1850 "to further the march of civilisation north . . . and boom real estate," moved to Bloemfontein two years later, where, as *The Friend*, it is still published. Tiny Kingwilliamstown in the Eastern Cape had its *Kingwilliamstown Gazette*; and Kimberley *The Diamond Fields Advertiser*. The first newspaper to use Afrikaans, as distinct from Dutch, was *Di Patriot*, founded in 1875 as the organ of Di Genootskap van Regte Afrikaners, or Society of True Afrikaners, "to stand up for our language, our nation and our people."

But by far the most important publications were the Cape Town papers. *The Cape Argus* was established in 1857, and *The Cape Times* in 1876. These were to generate in time the great newspaper empires of modern South Africa, and from the beginning they were businesslike, professional papers, looking to London for their example, and for a long time for their editors and senior staff. The Cape, with its comparatively large and prosperous white community of farmers, merchants, skilled and professional men, could after all afford what no other corner of Africa then could afford—a commercially viable Press, that would be able to find the capital to expand, and to introduce the new techniques of newspaper production being developed in Europe.

One of the major shareholders in the *Argus* in its early days, for instance, was a Member of the Cape Parliament, Saul Solomon, whose printing firm printed the paper, and who had learnt his trade as an apprentice in the works of George Greig. But it was not long before another power in the land was taking an interest in the growing newspaper. This was Cecil John Rhodes, who had made his fortune in the new Kimberley diamond fields, and was casting about for means to fulfil his already grandiose political ambitions. Investment in a newspaper, especially in view of the fact that he planned to stand for Parliament, could be expected to pay off handsomely, and accordingly in 1881 Rhodes provided the finance to enable the then editor of the *Argus*, Francis Dormer, to buy control of the paper from the so-called 'negrophilist' Solomon. *Argus* policy was now to be one of 'prudence' in racial matters, in the interest of the great mining industry with which it became progressively more closely involved.

By 1880, following the advent of the daily *Cape Times*, the

Argus had changed from twice weekly to daily publication. It received a cabled service of foreign news from Reuters over the recently laid cable link with Europe. Already, the characteristic which has distinguished the career of the Argus Press— astute and imaginative business management—was giving the paper an advantage over its competitors, and when in 1886 it launched a public company, leading businessmen took shares, among them directors of the Union (now Union-Castle) Steamship Line, Imperial Cold Storage, and Syfret's (now a large accounting, insurance and financing concern). Rhodes apparently bought shares through a nominee. Thus the *Argus* established itself as the paper of developing South African commercial enterprise.

In 1886, gold was discovered on the Rand, in the then South African Republic ruled by Paul Kruger. Within months, the Argus had sent a representative to open a branch of the company there, and by 1889 it had acquired a Johannesburg newspaper, *The Star*. *The Star* had been founded in Grahamstown by two brothers, Thomas and George Sheffield, who had transported it by ox-wagon, press and all, to Johannesburg in 1887. They had launched it on the three or four thousand inhabitants of the dusty, mushrooming mining settlement with brave words: "*The Star* will be loyal to the institutions of the land which gives it shelter and the protection of its laws. But loyalty to the institutions of a country does not mean subservience to those who are in power for the time being. True loyalty to the State consists in doing for it that which is best calculated to preserve its Constitution intact, at the same time endeavouring to bring about such reforms as will give to all who submit to its laws a voice in the government of it." Such a manifesto might not be irrelevant in the context of South Africa today; but the voices demanding a share in government in 1887 were not those of the black workers already being recruited for the mines, but of the 'uitlanders,' 'the aliens' (that is, all who were not Afrikaners and citizens of the Republic) who had poured into the Rand in the gold rush. These, and the interests they represented, were anxious to gain control over policy towards the mines; while Kruger was just as determined to protect his ideal State, his Republic under God where the Afrikaner was free to live out his ideology in peace, and to keep the black man forever in his rightful place as a servant without rights under the law. And the English-language South African Press was to prove the spokesman of the 'uitlanders,' and not of the black workers.

When Dormer bought the controlling interest in *The Star*, a new company was set up, the Argus Printing and Publishing Company, which is still the principal of the group. By 1891, most of the great names in gold mining were shareholders, including Barney Barnato and Solly Joel. Rhodes retained his shares. Plant and editorial expansion followed, *The Star* became a daily, and in 1893 introduced rotary printing and linotype setting.

But its policy of support for the 'uitlanders' was bringing it into increasing conflict with Kruger, who tried to counter the hostility of the English-language Press with a State subsidy for two sympathetic papers, *The Press* in Pretoria and *The Standard and Diggers' News* in Johannesburg. Then came the Jameson Raid. Dr. Jameson, close associate of Rhodes, marched on the Rand in an attempt to wrest the goldfields from the Boers by force. The Raid came to grief—and *The Star* was found to have been deeply implicated in the plot. The Republic Government retaliated with a stringent Press law requiring the registration of names of all printers and publishers, and empowering the President to prohibit the circulation of "matter the contents of which, in his opinion, might be in conflict with good morals or dangerous to the order of the Republic." Little time was lost in banning *The Star*, which however came out the next day as *The Comet*, and successfully contested the ban in the courts. The following year the Boer War broke out, which was to put an end to the Kruger Republic, and to postpone for another fifty years the crisis of relations between the 'English Press' and Afrikanerdom.

Rhodes' adventures meanwhile had led him away to the north, looking for gold in what was later Southern Rhodesia. There he and his 'Chartered', the British South AfricaCompany for which he had obtained not only land and mining concessions, but a Charter from Queen Victoria to administer the territory, once again felt the need for Press support, and once again the Argus followed. It bought a duplicated weekly grandly entitled *The Mashonaland Herald*, produced at Fort Salisbury by an enterprising young South African named Fairbridge, bought printing machinery, and launched *The*

Rhodesia Herald in 1892. *The Chronicle* followed in Bulawayo two years later, only a year after King Lobengula had been defeated in battle in his last desperate attempt to win back the land and mineral rights of which he had been defrauded.

Loyal to the connection with Rhodes, the Argus papers consistently campaigned for continued Company rule, as opposed either to direct rule from Whitehall, or settler self-government. Indeed, it continued to do so well after self-government had actually been achieved in 1923, and might well have lost its readership in Rhodesia altogether had it not reversed its policy in 1926, the year in which a separate company, the Rhodesian Printing and Publishing Company, was formed to publish the two Rhodesian papers. This was neither the first time nor the last that the Argus found itself out of consonance with its readers, in carrying out the behests of the mining magnates.

Indeed, this special connection with the mining industry still represents the main, and only important, distinction between the policies of the Argus group, and the other English-language 'white' newspapers in South Africa. All of them white owned and controlled, have traditionally agreed on certain fundamental aims: the perpetuation of white rule, the provision of cheap labour for farms and industry, control of the black population through pass laws. The Cape papers in the 19th century did adopt a relatively liberal policy towards the African franchise—a limited franchise for Africans operated, and *The Cape Times* lent its active support to its extension. The *Argus* was more reserved, especially when Rhodes replaced Solomon as chief patron. But for actual examples of how the Argus tends to back the mining companies in a crisis, one must look to Johannesburg. Thus when in 1913 white strikers clashed with the police, and General Smuts, as Minister of Defence, sent in troops to put down the 'unrest', it was *The Star* that most vigorously defended the Minister's decision. As a result, the *Star* building was attacked and burnt down by angry miners. And in 1922, when troops were again sent in to suppress a strike, and Smuts' aeroplanes bombarded miners' homes, both the *Argus* and *The Star* again distinguished themselves by discovering Russian gold behind the strikers, and even 'Bolshevik Robes in the Trades Hall.' *The Star* in fact came out with a special Sunday edition on March 12th, 1922, at General

Smuts' own request, to calm the population after the 'siege' of the city was over, and the strike defeated.

By then, a rival daily had taken root in Johannesburg, the *Rand Daily Mail*, established just after the Boer War in 1902, with Edgar Wallace as its first editor. The *Mail*, together with the *Sunday Times*, founded in 1906, was the pioneer of modern popular journalism in South Africa, bringing improvements in lay-out, more illustrations and cartoons, and more venturesome feature journalism. The *Sunday Times* has today the largest circulation of any South African newspaper, and the Argus group has never been able to outsell it in the Sunday field, although as a national force it was already, by the 1920's, ahead of all its competitors. In 1903 it had taken shares in the Central News Agency, which in due course established a virtual monopoly over newspaper distribution in South Africa, and through its subsidiary Kingston's, in the Rhodesias. In 1917 it obtained a share in *The Friend*, Bloemfontein, and in 1918 bought *The Natal Advertiser*, later the *Natal Daily News*. By 1922, *The Diamond Fields Advertiser*, Kimberley, had been added to the group, and in 1930 the *Pretoria News* was to come under Argus control. There was even for a time a plan to enter into the publishing field in Portuguese Moçambique (which supplies some 100,000 African workers annually to South Africa's mines).

The Argus had thus the advantage over its rivals not only of large capital resources, but of pooled journalistic and technical facilities. In order more effectively to compete, the morning newspapers decided eventually to co-operate by sharing news and feature material, correspondents abroad and certain technical services. *The Cape Times*, the *Rand Daily News* and the *Natal Mercury* (founded about 1850), together with the *Sunday Times* first embarked on a programme of exchange of material, and they were joined by the two main Eastern Province (Cape) papers, the *Eastern Province Herald* and the *Evening Post*, Port Elizabeth. Only the *Mail*, *Sunday Times*, and after the beginning of the Second World War the new *Sunday Express* (founded by the theatre and cinema magnate I. W. Schlesinger in 1934) belonged to a single financial group, however, South African Associated Newspapers, though the Eastern Province papers were to join it after the war.

Meanwhile, the Afrikaans Press too had been growing. And

if the English-language papers presented a degree of unanimity on basic questions, the Afrikaans papers can be even more closely identified, for all, with a few short-lived exceptions, remain the organs of Afrikaner nationalism, closely associated with the Nationalist Party and its allies. Newspapers in Dutch had existed since the earliest days—*De Zuid Afrikaansche Tijdschrift* founded in 1824, *De Natalier* of Pietermaritzburg in 1844, *De Staats Courant* in the Transvaal Republic in 1857. In 1873 *De Volkstem* was started in an attempt to counteract the growing influence of the English Press, to be followed by *Het Vaderland* (now *Die Vaderland*) in Pretoria. But the first Afrikaans paper was *Di Patriot* (1875) and the first Afrikaans daily, *Die Burger*, Cape Town, was not established until 1915, under the editorship of Dr. D. F. Malan, who was to become Prime Minister in the Nationalist Government of 1948.

These papers had poor financial backing. The Afrikaners had not accumulated capital, they were largely an agricultural people, and the Boer War had ruined thousands of farmers. In addition, Afrikaans readers were scattered in farms and villages, not concentrated in towns and cities like the English-speaking population. It thus became deliberate Afrikaner Nationalist policy on the one hand to stimulate the accumulation of Afrikaner capital through a series of banking and financing ventures started in the 1920's and 1930's, and on the other to develop an Afrikaans-language Press, as essential prerequisites to gaining political power. Accordingly, it was Dr. Malan who raised £100,000 to launch a party organ just before the last war, *Die Transvaler*, whose first editor was another future Prime Minister, Dr. H. F. Verwoerd. Dr. Verwoerd, in the words of a High Court judge in 1943, turned *Die Transvaler* into a "tool of the Nazis," and to this day it is seen as spokesman for the most extreme wing of the party.

Since the Afrikaans Press has always been relatively weak next to the rich and powerful English newspapers, Nationalist politicians have attempted on several occasions to redress the balance by legislation. Their attitude to the Press can best be understood if set in the background of their ideology, as expressed in a Draft Constitution for the Republic of South Africa, published in *Die Burger* and *Die Transvaler* on 22nd and 23rd January, 1942, and since quietly buried by Nationalist leaders as embarrassing, but never repudiated in principle.

Article 2 (ii) reads: "The Republic is grounded on a Christian-National Foundation and therefore acknowledges, as the standard of the government of the State, in the first place the principles of justice of the Holy Scriptures; secondly, the clearest direction of the development of the national history; and thirdly, the necessary reformation of the modern government of states, especially with an eye to the circumstances of South Africa." It goes on to say that the State will have the power to make sure that "individual citizens, as well as the organs of public opinion, such as the existence of parties, the radio, the Press and the cinema, whilst their rightful freedom of expression, including criticism of government policy, will be protected, shall not be allowed, by their actions, to undermine the public order or good morals of the Republic internally or externally."

In 1937, the Nationalist Hertzog, then Prime Minister, called the editors of the daily papers together to threaten that if they did not cease their attacks on the Nazi and Fascist Governments in Europe, he would introduce a Press Bill to bring them under control. He had in fact a bill ready, but when war was declared he fell from power for opposing the Union's entry into the war against Germany. When the Nationalist Party came to power in 1948, however, one of its first acts was to appoint a Commission to enquire into the Press.

The 'Non-White' Press

Parallel with the development of the white Press, there had also grown up in South Africa a non-white Press, unread by whites, not distributed by the Central News Agency nor benefiting from the news and technical services being developed by the big dailies, poor and limited in circulation, but rich in political excitement. The beginning was in the mission papers, often in vernacular languages, such as *Isigidimi SamaXosa* (the *Xhosa Express*) published by the Lovedale Mission in the Transkei, and edited by John Tengu Jabavu, until he was dismissed for using the paper to attack members of the Cape Parliament. In 1884, Jabavu started his own paper, *Imvo zaba Ntsundu* (*Native Opinion*), with financial backing from a group of white liberals. In English and Xhosa, it had four pages, sold at threepence, and campaigned for African political and educational advance. Jabavu's style was clear, concise and urbane. His campaign against the Cape Franchise Bill of 1887, which, while recognising no overt colour bar, set the voting qualifications so high as to exclude all but a very few Africans, led the Prime Minister, a Mr. Sprigg, to abuse him in Parliament as "a highly educated native who publishes a newspaper in which he sets forth seditious articles . . . I am not sufficiently acquainted with the Kafir tongue to read the articles, but I am informed they are most libellous and seditious." *Imvo* replied indignantly that "Loyalty to the Queen is one of the talismanic words engraven on the tablets of our heart."

Jabavu's weapon was rather sarcastic understatement than sedition. He attacked the British Colonial Secretary for justifying the Franchise Bill to the House of Commons—"And this after the express announcement in the Assembly here that the object of the Bill was to disfranchise Native voters?" And he attacked the white Press, for condoning the Bill, notably the *Cape Argus*, "which acquiesces in the shameful conversion of might into right . . . on the ground that, in its view, the grievance is not great." But he gave up the fight for the franchise in the end, on finding that his white supporters had betrayed him, and after that *Imvo* lost most of its élan. Jabavu was eventually one of those who opposed the formation in 1912 of the Native National Congress (or African National Congress as it was called later), the first nation-wide African political organisation; and he thus exiled himself, and his paper, from the mainstream of African politics.

Imvo still survives, sadly changed, a white man's tool. *Indian Opinion*, on the other hand, founded in Natal by Mahatma Gandhi in 1906, has maintained a measure of independence. Gandhi pioneered his passive resistance techniques in South Africa in the early years of this century, in defence of the rights of Indian traders, and after he returned to India his paper, in English and Gujerati, was edited by his son Manilal. On Manilal's death in 1958, it was published by his wife, and edited for a while by an African, Jordan Ngubane, a leader of the South African Liberal Party. Its general tone has been conservative, however, as was that of *Indian Views*, founded in 1914, also in English and Gujerati, mainly to keep Indian immigrants in Natal in touch with events in India.

By 1914, there were already five major African newspapers: *Imvo*; *Izwi la Bantu*, founded by the Rev. Walter Rubusana, a

founder member of the African National Congress, in opposition
to *Imvo*; *Ilanga Lase Natal* (the Natal Sun) started in 1906 by a
Methodist Minister, later first President of the A.N.C., Dr.
John L. Dube; *Ikwezi le Afrika*, founded in 1902 by the Church
of England, though it was later taken over by a European
publisher; and *Abantu Batho*, organ of the A.N.C. *Abantu Batho's*
first editor was Dr. Pixley Isaka ka Seme, under whom it
played a leading role in Congress' first political campaigns:
against the Land Acts of 1913 depriving Africans of land rights
outside the 'reserves', and against a proposal to extend the pass
system to women. This latter campaign Congress won, post-
poning the imposition of women's passes until the time of the
present Government, which introduced them against massive
opposition in 1959. The paper lived until 1932, after which the
A.N.C. never again published an official newspaper. Of the
five African papers publishing in 1914, only *Imvo* and *Ilange*
survived into the 1960's.

Meanwhile, a second stream of the non-white Press was
forming out of the various socialist movements that grew up in
the period of the First World War. The first, and one of the
most significant, of these movements was the African Peoples'
Organisation (A.P.O.), based on the Coloured people of the
Cape, and founded in 1909 by a socialist, Dr. Abdurahman.
Its organ was *APO*, a militant campaigning sheet that advocated general strike and economic boycott as weapons against
white domination, nearly fifty years before they were used on a
mass scale in South Africa. "Our political destiny is in our own
hands," exhorted *APO* in 1909, "and we must be prepared to
face the fight with grim determination to succeed . . . How are
we to set about it? In our opinion there is but one way and that
is the economic method. Undoubtedly the Coloured and
Native races of South Africa hold the strongest weapon ever
placed in the hands of any class. The very stability, the prosperity, even the continuance for but a few days of the economic
existence of South Africa depends on the labour market; and
we are the labour market."

White socialists had been organising themselves since 1904,
torn between a growing awareness of the black proletariat, and
the undoubted prejudices of their supporters. The Socialist
Democratic Federation published *The Cape Socialist* in 1904,
The War on War Gazette followed in 1914, and *The International*,

organ of the International Socialist League, a breakaway from the new Labour Party, in 1915. An editorial in *The International* in 1915 admirably expresses the principles of race solidarity, though this was unfortunately not the consistent line of the paper: "An internationalism which does not conceive the fullest rights which the native working class is capable of claiming," it says, "will be a sham. One of the justifications of withdrawal from the Labour Party is that it gives us untrammelled freedom to deal, regardless of political fortunes, with the great and fascinating problem of the native. If the League deals resolutely in consonance with Socialist principles with the native question, it will succeed in shaking South African capitalism to its foundations. Then and not till then, shall we be able to talk about the South African proletariat in our international relations. Not till we free the native can we hope to free the white." The following year, however, another *International* article spoke of "an ethnological tendency . . . which makes for the natural apartness of white and black," and claimed that one of the virtues of socialism was that, by destroying capitalism, it would allow this natural apartness to reassert itself!

Imprisoned by their whiteness, then, the early socialists could not assume leadership of the black proletariat, and this role was filled by the Industrial and Commercial Workers' Union, the I.C.U. led by the Nyasa-born Clements Kadalie, one of the giants of South African working class history. The I.C.U. published *The Workers' Herald* until 1929. From 1928, the South African Communist Party entered the field with *The South African Worker*, and later its vernacular counterpart *Umsebenzi*, followed in the 1940's by *Inkululeku* (Freedom), which ceased publication with the disbanding of the party in 1950, when the Suppression of Communism Act became law.

This complex of popular, polemical and radical newspapers, springing most of them from political organisations and dedicated to the political advance of the oppressed communities, was recognised in due course by the white establishment as potentially too powerful for comfort. It was, significantly, the Native Recruiting Corporation of the Chamber of Mines that first decided to embark on its own publishing venture directed at an African public, in an attempt to divert popular discontent into safer channels. It published *Umteteli wa Bantu* (Voice of the People) from 1921, opposing the colour bar on the one hand, but attacking organised resistance to it on the other. Particularly, *Umteteli* campaigned against the project to form an African Mineworkers' Union before the war, and against the African Mineworkers' strike of 1946.

Similarly inspired with the desire to guide the African into paths of co-operation with the white economy was the Bantu Press, born in 1931, white owned and managed. A prime mover in the venture was B. F. G. Paver, subsequently Chairman of the Rhodesian Broadcasting Corporation, and the plan was to amalgamate several existing newspapers for Africans under a single management. A memorandum drawn up at the time promised that "Amalgamation will prevent irresponsible exploitation and will benefit individual papers by supplying an organisation capable of maintaining a guiding policy in both political and commercial development." Several commercial interests were persuaded to invest, including the Argus Printing and Publishing Company, which held a minority share (16 per cent in 1946). The Argus was to be deferred to in matters of editorial policy, and the secretary of the Argus company was given a seat on the board of directors. Another shareholder in the 1950's was the Anglo-American Corporation, the main company in the Oppenheimer goldmining empire.

The slogan of the Bantu Press was "A Bantu Paper in every Province from the Cape to the Congo." Its first project was to amalgamate *Mochochonono*, a Sotho paper started in Maseru, Basutoland, in 1911, *Imvo*, and *Ilange Lase Natal*, all of which were bought by 1934; and to start a new newspaper, with a national circulation, *The Bantu World*, to be published in English, Xhosa, Zulu, Sotho and Tswana. The *World* made its first appearance in 1932. Next came expansion northward, and the establishment just before the war of *The Bantu Mirror* in Salisbury, in English, Ndebele and Lozi, followed in 1944 by *The African Weekly* in English, Shona and Chinyanja. These two papers were sold not only in Southern Rhodesia, but in Northern Rhodesia and Nyasaland as well. By 1946, of a total of thirteen weeklies published for Africans in South Africa and Rhodesia, the Bantu Press controlled eleven, as well as three other monthlies. Twelve years later, it had newspapers in all three of the British High Commission Territories as well: *Lentsoe la Basotho* in Basutoland, *Iswi Lamaswazi* in Swaziland,

and *Naledi ya Becsuanas* in Bechuanaland. According to the South
African editor, Brian Bunting, in a 1958 pamphlet 'The Story
behind the Non-White Press,' the British administration gave
"material and moral support" to the establishment of these
newspapers, especially in Basutoland where a radical African
monthly, *Mohlabani* (The Warrior), was giving strident voice
to the growing demand for self-government. The Administration actually agreed to underwrite the costs of the new paper to
the extent of £2,000 a year for two years, and sent a minute
round to District Commissioners and Heads of Department
asking them to co-operate. B. M. Khaketla, then editor of
Mohlabani, was offered the editorship, which he indignantly
turned down, as he related later. "The paper is called *Voice of
the Basotho*," he wrote. "We call it 'The Voice of Government,
of Europeans, of Capitalists, of Exploiters, whose only interest
is to squeeze the last penny out of the already empty purses of
the Basotho." An African was eventually appointed 'editor',
but real editorial control continued to rest in Johannesburg.

African leaders in South Africa held views on the Bantu
Press no less contemptuous than Khaketla's. Though editors
and staff of most of the South African papers were Africans, all
worked under white supervision, and final editorial control.
The open hostility of the *World*, main paper of the group, to
the African National Congress actually led to the exclusion of
the *World's* correspondent from an A.N.C. Congress in 1955.

No independent African paper was for long able to withstand
Bantu Press competition; but the 300,000 South African
Indians in Natal, on the other hand, seem to have had a genius
for seeing that their community was continuously served by a
variety of small, and apparently always struggling, newspapers.
Like their counterparts in East Africa, Indian businessmen
have been ready to put their money into publishing as a public
service, rather than with much hope of profit, and so *Opinion*
and *Views* survived, and in the years just before and after the
war, at least nine other papers made their appearance. Some of
these were communal papers, dealing largely in news of India
and Pakistan, but *The Leader* and *The Graphic* campaigned
against the colour bar, and a series of militant broadsheets—
The Passive Resister, organ of the South African Indian Congress' passive resistance campaign of 1946, *The Searchlight*
published at the same period, and *The Spark*, started in 1953—

all had short but spectacular careers that are remembered in the South African liberation movement. *The Spark*, though inspired by the Transvaal Indian Youth Congress, was far from communal in its appeal, and became the organ of the Consultative Committee of the Congresses, which formed a liaison between the African National Congress, the South African Indian Congress, the Congress of Democrats, the Coloured People's Congress, and the South African Congress of Trade Unions. Its last editor was Nelson Mandela, the A.N.C. leader now serving a life sentence for 'sabotage'.

No newspaper seems ever to have been directed exclusively at Coloured readers. Far more numerous than the Indians, the Coloured community of the Cape has always been less cohesive, encouraged by whites to regard itself as an appendage of white society. A few newspapers in the past have been directed primarily at Coloured readers—among them *The Sun*, established in the Cape in 1931, to support the ruling United Party; and the more rebellious *Cape Standard*, established in 1935, which gave some support to the Communist Party. *The Torch*, founded in 1946, was the only one to survive into the 1950's —it was suppressed in 1963. It was a vituperative, bitter weekly, supporting the Non-European Unity Movement, a movement of Coloured and African intellectuals, advocating total withdrawal from white society through boycott.

By far the most important of the Cape Town 'non-white' papers, however, was the *Guardian*. It was not properly a Cape Town paper at all, since it had a national circulation; nor was it specifically non-white in its orientation, particularly in the early days after its foundation in 1937. It was first a socialist weekly, supporting the anti-fascist struggle of the white working class and white trade unions, for South Africa had its share of greyshirts and brownshirts and bloody battles on the steps of the Johannesburg City Hall. It generally supported the policies of the South African Communist Party, and was run by communists, but with the war the paper's anti-fascist policies won it a much broader respect, and the 25th Birthday issue of its successor, *New Age*, (March 22nd, 1962) boasts that the *Guardian's* circulation grew so fast that it was the only South African newspaper to be granted an increase in newsprint allocation during the war. After the war, with the coming to power of the Nationalists and suppression of the Communist

Party, the *Guardian* found itself rudely cut off, just as it was
finding a new strength. This was not among the white workers
who, fearful of the end of the protective colour bar, had helped
to vote the Nationalists into power, but in the new alliance of
African nationalism and Indian radicalism, realised in the 1946
pact of co-operation between the A.N.C. and the S.A.I.C.[1] In
spite of its earlier involvement with the white working class,
the *Guardian* had always attacked the colour bar at its roots—
the economic exploitation of the non-white masses—and it was
this theme that was now to dominate its few remaining years,
and those of its successors in the 1950's.

The picture at the beginning of Nationalist rule, then,
was of an overwhelmingly white-owned and controlled Press,
dominated by one extremely powerful group with close
connections with the mining industry. Afrikaans papers were
technically and financially weak; and non-white opinion had
only a very few independent outlets. The most influential
papers—the English-language dailies—had been happy enough
under United Party rule, and all of them had supported
General Smuts' government. But the 1950's were to change all
this, and to see a new struggle around the issue of Press
freedom.

---

[1] South African Indian Congress.

CHAPTER 4

POST-WAR WEST AFRICA

THE POPULARISATION OF the West African Press that had started in the 1930's was to be carried further in the post-war period. Now, as Increase Coker commented, "the smiling face of a third class clerk in the Government or commercial houses appeared side by side with that of a lawyer or politician. Gone, clearly, was the day when newspaper publicity was the prerogative of only those at the top of society." Gone too was the day of the amateurs, the lawyers and politicians who ran a newspaper on the side; and going, the era of the editor-printers whose extravagances had enlivened political and social life for over 50 years.

For the years after the war saw the rise of the newspaper chains, the first indigenously owned and run groups on the continent. Zik's group was joined in the mid-1940's by the Government-sponsored Gaskiya Corporation in Northern Nigeria. This was an outgrowth of the Northern Literature Bureau, dedicated to the encouragement of Northern regional vernacular languages and literature, which had been publishing a Hausa weekly, *Gaskiya ta fi Kwabo*, since 1939. The Corporation was backed with Government money, a new press, and block-making facilities. It launched an English-language weekly (now published twice weekly), the *Nigerian Citizen* at Zaria in 1948, and was soon publishing periodicals in the Fulani, Tiv and Kanuri languages as well.

The Daily Service at this time was still appearing in Lagos. With the formation in 1951 of the Action Group, the *Service* became its mouthpiece, as the Zik papers already were for the Eastern-based National Council of Nigeria and the Cameroons (the N.C.N.C., since its foundation in 1944 the leading Nigerian nationalist organisation). The Zik newspaper chain, publishing in all three regions, gave the N.C.N.C. a voice on a national scale, and the *Service* soon took steps to provide its party with similar advantages. Together with *The Nigerian Tribune*, Ibadan, it formed the Amalgamated Press of Nigeria.

More capital was found, rotary presses and a photogravure plant were bought. By 1958 the Amalgamated Press had obtained control of a company—Allied Press Ltd.—publishing a string of small provincial dailies, so that it now grouped a whole network of papers covering all regions. Among the group's publications were *The Midwest Echo*, Benin, in the West, *The Middle Belt Herald*, Jos, and *The Northern Star*, Kano, in the North, and *The Eastern Observer*, Onitsha, and *Cor Advocate*, Uyo, in the East. The following year it launched a Sunday paper, the *Sunday Express*.

Nigeria had thus developed three major newspaper chains, one Government-run, the others financed by local private capital, at a time when most countries in Africa, beside Egypt in the north and the white-ruled territories in the south, could afford little more than a party broadsheet. One reason for the development was the personality of Azikiwe himself. Another was perhaps the very difficulty of communicating in so vast and divided a territory as Nigeria: to this day, road and rail transport are at the mercy of geography and the weather. Any political force with national ambitions had to find a way of making itself heard in all regions simultaneously, not merely in one area, or among the people of one language group. But almost certainly the most important reason was the fact that in Nigeria an African middle class had developed to the point of being able to set up African-controlled banks. Newspapers could thus draw on the resources of a bank for capitalisation and development loans—and this was true of no other colony in black Africa.

The very existence of these already established newspaper chains, that had introduced the habit of newspaper reading into every region of Nigeria, may have attracted foreign Press enterprise, when it did at last come to West Africa in 1947. In that year, the giant British *Daily Mirror* bought *The Nigerian Daily Times*, Lagos, and the move was greeted in Nigeria with very mixed feelings. "It is not fair to say categorically," wrote Abiodun Aloba twelve years later, "as many in West Africa would want it believed, that it was part of the British plan to stem nationalism in the territories. It is not quite true to say that it was the desire of the British to invade the only economic field dominated by native people. Although it would appear to be more correct to admit that the coming of the group was essentially based on the economic vigilance of its Chairman, Mr. Cecil King himself. Mr. King at least realised that there was no harm in exporting abroad profit otherwise taxed at home" (this was the period after the war when taxation in Britain was abnormally high, and many British companies were diversifying their interests by investing overseas: R.A.), "and that, in any case, some good could be done to the native people, so obviously in need of a good Press, by giving them newspapers such as varied their interests without doing damage to their native aspirations."[1]

Whatever its motives may have been, the group brought with it technical improvements as yet unheard of in West African journalism, and to its credit it pursued from the start a deliberate policy of Africanisation, training journalists and printers and machine-operators whose skills have subsequently enriched not only the group's own papers, but the whole of West African journalism.

The Mirror changed the name of *The Nigerian Daily Times* to the *Daily Times*; and its format to tabloid. It brought the first privately owned rotary printing-machine to Nigeria, and photo-engraving, typesetting and typecasting plants. It brought in skilled foreign journalists, and a full-time training officer. From 25,000 in 1951, the circulation of the *Daily Times* rose to 55,000 in 1955 and 96,000 in 1959. By 1965 it stood at over 120,000, the highest in West Africa.

For more than ten years, the *Mirror* papers were unquestionably the most potent force in West African journalism. In 1950, the group set up the *Daily Graphic* in Accra, and in 1952 the *Daily Mail* in Freetown, Sierra Leone. For the first time, West African papers could afford correspondents in all main towns, and the London office of West African Newspapers Ltd. (later Overseas Newspapers Ltd., as *Mirror* interests expanded in the West Indies too) provided 'own correspondent' foreign news and feature coverage. Modern tabloid page make-up, imaginative use of type, liberal illustrations and stress on short paragraphs, simple language and 'human interest' stories, soon took the *Mirror* papers well ahead of their competitors in all three countries. This was a challenge the indigenous Press was ill-equipped to meet.

---

[1] *Gazette*, Leiden, vol. V, no. 4, 1959.

Ghana, the first of the three countries to become independent, was the first to take up the challenge. As early as 1947, Nkrumah and his colleagues in the Convention Peoples' Party (C.P.P.) had started their own daily paper, *The Accra Evening News*, which proved an invaluable ally in the fight for independence. It was a ramshackle affair, produced with much enthusiasm and little of anything else. "It was set by hand," remembers Douglas Rodgers, a British journalist who worked with Nkrumah on the paper, "and printed on an old flat-bed machine. There was even a shortage of type. We printed all night, and next morning as one edition was rushed off the presses, the machines had to be stopped while people were still clamouring for copies, so that the type could be used again for the next day's paper!" Paper and printing were poor, the text rich in slogans and totally inadequate in news coverage (correspondents were simply C.P.P. activists who might or might not send in a report). In common with many other similar broadsheets produced at different times all over Africa, it was a campaigning organ rather than a medium of information. But it was some indication of the seriousness with which the Ghana leadership has always viewed its Press, that it was a daily.[1]

But the *Evening News* was poor competition for the *Graphic*. So as soon as independence was in sight, the C.P.P. leaders laid plans for a vast expansion of their publishing activities. The Guinea Press was set up, financed by the Industrial Development Corporation with help from local businessmen, to publish a new and improved *Ghana Evening News*, a more ambitious and 'serious' morning newspaper, to be called *The Ghanaian Times*, and, in due course, a new Sunday paper.

Today, the morning paper is the bigger daily of the two, and the more informative. It usually has twelve pages, tabloid size (the format of all three papers). Main front page news is treated at some length, and may be foreign or domestic. Page two is headed 'Spotlight on Africa,' a number of brief items covering French- as well as English-speaking Africa. Ghanaian news fills pages three and five, ranging from policy statements

[1] Part of this profound respect for news media stems from the preoccupation of Nkrumah himself. Virtually every important newspaper venture, including *The Evening News* (of which he was editor), the Ghana News Agency and *The Spark*, has had the President's hand in it, and he is fond of reminding young journalists that he, too, has had printer's ink on his fingers.

to news of agricultural, educational and social development programmes, and occasional human interest stories. Page four is reserved for international affairs, which stress the 'third world' and the American civil rights movement, and include a fair proportion of news from the communist countries; while the feature on the centre pages may be a full-page analysis of Portuguese policy in Africa, or a picture story on the working of the blood-transfusion service. There is a sports page, and a total of perhaps two and a quarter pages of advertising, about half of it Government advertising.

The *News*, on the other hand, retains some of the exhortatory style of its past. It uses a little 'spot' colour (including a red and green masthead), though make-up is scrappy, printing poor and spelling unpredictable, in comparison with the more professional-looking *Times*. But the range of material dealt with is much the same. Sub-editing aims to make the reader feel that the paper is speaking directly to him: "Ideological Orientation is Vital," it tells him, or "It's cheaper to build your house with burnt bricks," or simply, "The New Tax System and You."

There are now plans for a new daily, the *Gazette*, to start publishing in 1966, as a quality paper dealing with serious news, features, political and cultural affairs, in more depth than in any of the established dailies. The new venture will be stretching Ghana's resources, both financial and journalistic— but the fact that it is to be undertaken indicates a demand for a higher journalistic standard, stimulated no doubt by the vast expansion of secondary education since independence. Indeed, the steady expansion of Ghana's Press shows what *can* be done by a country determined to build its own news media.

Including the *Graphic*, then, there are now four daily papers in Ghana. But until 1961 there was another, *The Ashanti Pioneer* of Kumasi. The *Pioneer* was a private paper, established in 1939, which reflected in the 1950's the views of the Ashanti-based opposition to the C.P.P., the National Liberation Movement. It is now internationally famous, not so much for what it was, as for its brief struggle for the right to continue publishing in face of a censorship order, in September 1961, when it was required to submit its contents to the Minister of Information before publication. It was suppressed some months later, but it went down fighting, supported by such

international bodies concerned with Press freedom as the
Commonwealth Press Union and the International Press
Institute. Partly as a result of this incident, Ghana is now one
of the very few Commonwealth countries with representation
in neither of these organisations; and President Nkrumah has
earned a reputation in the West as an enemy of democratic
liberties. Journalists who had watched the efforts of the paper
to survive against apparently impossible odds—lack of any real
capital and equipment—since 1939, regretted its passing as
journalists regret the death of any paper. Others attacked the
censorship on ideological grounds. The Government argued
the necessity for law and order in a situation, during the first
Presidential election, where Ashanti elements had resorted to
violence, and when ugly tribal hostilities were in danger of
destroying the country's four-year-old independence.

Ghanaians complain that too much has been made of the
Pioneer affair, and there is no doubt that many of the critics had
ulterior motives in attempting to discredit the Nkrumah
Government at a time when it was embarking on new and
radical policies. Reaction to the *Pioneer* was in any case bound
up with Western mistrust of the whole concept of a one-party
State, which Ghana formally became in 1961, and this tended
to blind critics to those efforts made in Ghana to encourage the
Press as an educational and progressive force. But the fact
remains that political opposition makes for more exciting
journalism than exposition, and that political conflict is an
irreplaceable stimulant to a lively Press. The *Pioneer* only
symbolises a deeper dilemma of one-party Government: how
to retain the dialectic of political conflict, without impeding
the revolutionary momentum of the State? Many African
Governments are having to face this dilemma, and we shall
return to it in a later chapter.

Meanwhile, the *Graphic*, though it supported Nkrumah's
campaign for self-government, had also given some support to
the Opposition in the period just before independence. After
independence, in 1957, it never openly attacked the Government, and tension, though it existed, never led to a show-down.
Instead, the *Mirror* itself approached the Government in 1962
to suggest that it buy the *Graphic*, and arrangements were made
accordingly for it to be published by an independent trust set
up for the purpose. David Williams, the 'Mirror' man most

closely involved with the African papers from the beginning, explains that, although the *Graphic* was, and still is, making a profit, "there remained an anomaly in the fact that it was still owned from London", when management was already entirely in Ghanaian hands. No similar anomaly, however, seems to be felt over the position of the Nigerian and Sierra Leone papers owned by the group, which are also now African-run.

The *Graphic's* staff has not changed since its change of ownership, nor has its 'personality.' It is still represented abroad by Overseas Newspapers. And so its presence remains something of a curiosity in Ghana, where the official conception of the role of the Press is a 'revolutionary' one, and journalists on the Guinea Press papers see themselves as political activists committed to the building of a new society. The *Graphic* looks dutiful rather than committed: one difference is in the 'Fleet Street'-type training of its journalists, with its stress on 'professionalism', compared with the mainly political background of those on the other Accra dailies.

Perhaps surprisingly, the *Graphic* does not compare well with the others as far as news coverage is concerned. It carries main news on the front and back pages, and foreign news on page two. One page is usually devoted to a serious political feature, either written locally or sent from the London office. But it retains its preference, in common with the *Daily Times* and the *Daily Mail*, for court drama and scandal as the main source of popular appeal: "Drug Probe Starts", or "Accused: I fell down Unconscious." The beauty queen, too, is still in her customary place on the front page. There are women's features, and a regular Junior Graphic section.

Another independent paper, *The New Ashanti Times* of Obuasi, a weekly started by the Ashanti Gold Fields Corporation as a local information sheet for its employees, is still publishing. Helen Kitchen, in her study of 'The Press in Africa' in 1956, rated it technically as second only to the *Graphic*, but she added that although its contents appeared to be largely non-political, African nationalists suspected it of being "a tool of commercial imperialism." Today, it is published by an independent company, the Ashanti Times Press.

Ghana has in addition five vernacular fortnightlies, covering all the main languages, and nearly a dozen specialist monthlies, among them *The Co-operator*, *The Party*, *Modern Woman*, *The*

Farmer, *Ghana Labour*, several Christian mission publications, and *The Spark*.

The Spark was started in 1962, as an organ of the Bureau of African Affairs (a department of the President's Office), which also publishes the more strident *Voice of Africa*. *The Spark* was to be a serious Marxist analytical journal on African questions, and it has a French counterpart, *l'Etincelle*, which duplicates some but not all of *Spark's* material. Africa has not produced many discussion journals with a continental perspective: *Africa South* (Cape Town, 1956-61) was one, *Spearhead* (Dar-es-Salaam, 1962-63) very briefly was another. The Algerian *Révolution Africaine* for a while attempted an English edition, with the idea that both papers would be distributed on a continental basis, but the project failed. In French, *Jeune Afrique* of Tunisia is the only paper that has succeeded in acquiring a continental status; while the only African publication in English comparable with *The Spark* is probably South Africa's *The African Communist*, which is distributed fairly widely in Africa, though it seems to be printed in London.

Nkrumah, in a message to *The Spark* on its hundredth issue in November 1964, explains that the idea for the new theoretical newspaper was his own. "The new African needs a new ideology," he wrote, "socialist in content and continental in outlook. The propagation of such an ideology demands an ideological journal or journals serving all Africa.

"In the second half of 1962, having convinced myself of the imperative necessity for such a journal, I invited two of my associates in the Bureau of African Affairs to work out the details of a newspaper that would specialise in ideological work and thought and provide the intellectual revolution which could dispel the doubts and confusion concerning the ideology of the African Revolution . . . I named the new journal '*The Spark*.'"

The paper contains detailed and often long analyses on theoretical and topical African questions: it has run a series on 'The Socialist Revolution in Africa', and another on 'Studies in Consciencism' (the name Nkrumah has given to his particular interpretation of Marxism); articles on the results of the British General Election of 1964; exposures on the composition and activities of the mercenary force in the Congo, on 'Who Robs Zambia', and on 'The Mechanics of Counter-revolution' (an attack on the dismissed Minister of Finance, Komla Gbedemah); and an appreciation of the achievements of the Russian Revolution. Contributors are mostly Ghanaian, but have included British, South African and other African writers.

Editorials are serious, passionate and sometimes flamboyant in the best traditions of rich-phrased West African journalism. "How long", demands an editorial on 'Stanleyville', on 27th November, 1964, "is the world prepared to tolerate the naked open aggression of American, Belgian and British imperialism in the heart of the African continent? How long will the world stand by while Congolese women are shot before the eyes of their little children? How long do we contemplate, passive and inactive, while Congolese patriots are tortured and murdered by hired assassins of imperialism? How is it possible in the present day and age for a man to be hauled head first, stretched like a beast, up the gangway of a plane by two soldiers while men photograph the scene and airport personnel look on? Why does not the conscience of the world shriek aloud at such horrors being perpetrated?"

The Spark expects to find a considerable proportion of its readership abroad, and derives much of its élan from the fact that it operates within the context of international ideological conflict. But within Ghana there is no voice of opposition against which the party papers could pit themselves, and to this fact have often been attributed the many weaknesses of the modern Press in Ghana, the substitution of abuse for comment, and pictures of Osagyefo for news. At their worst, Ghana papers have been known to publish six pictures of the President in a single issue! To regard these crudities as an inevitable degeneration once 'opposition' has been stifled, however, is to fail to appreciate the positive role which Ghanaians see for their mass media. The period since 1962 has been a revolutionary period for Ghana, in that it has been a period of concentrated national effort, which required the mobilisation of the people to support a programme of development and change. The Press was to be a principal means of effecting this mobilisation, and the attitudes that it was to foster were the simplest: loyalty and national pride, commitment to the ideas of national and continental unity, of liberation for the oppressed peoples of Africa, and socialism for Ghana. The figure of the President as symbol of these ideals, the propagandist tone of the articles, were seen as instruments in fostering the attitudes that national policy required. But there does seem lately to have been a change, not in policy, but in tactic, and in skill. The main newspapers reflect a desire to educate and to convince as much as to exhort, and the considerable expansion of news coverage already makes of the *Times* and the *News* more informative and lively papers. The news coverage is a direct consequence of the development of the Ghana News Agency, which has grown into the biggest in black Africa. A remaining weakness springs from the still inadequate professional training of journalistic staff: stories are insufficiently followed up, news items are inadequately related to what has gone before, and each day's issue gives the impression of having been made up in a vacuum, and not within a continuing plan to examine the questions of the day in depth. But notwithstanding all these failures, a study of the Ghana newspapers today impresses on two counts: first, on the extent of news coverage (which is balanced to include all parts of the world), and second, on the thoroughly indigenous nature of the product. There are no syndicated features from abroad, no Paris fashions, 'pop' charts or Christmas turkeys, such as figure incongruously in too many African papers. The penalty of this policy is that foreign background and interpretive material is thin, for no Ghana publication can afford staff correspondents abroad. Such international material as the G.N.A. is able to obtain is itself remarkable, for the expenditure involved is crippling. To this extent, foreign-owned papers, with links with an international Press empire such as Thomson's or the I.P.C. (Daily Mirror), have an enormous advantage, and the *Graphic*, through its continuing link with Overseas Newspapers, is even now able to command a range of foreign feature material that the other papers lack.

One problem, however, remains, even once the crudities have all been eliminated. It is the problem that arises out of the very nature of a one-party Press, and it confronts 'official' papers anywhere: if public ideological conflict must, for reasons of State, be excluded, how is that dialogue to come about between paper and reader, that makes of a newspaper not merely an organ of information from above, but a vehicle of comment from below? The relationship between a newspaper and its public is a peculiarly intimate one, that needs room to grow, and a party paper that hopes to develop this relationship fully needs to be able to show that it is not only the voice of the people as expressed through the party, but also a voice for individuals inside and outside the party. Neither the *Times* nor the *News* runs a regular letter column, the normal outlet for individual dissent. But the *Sunday Spectator and Vanguard*, the Guinea Press Sunday, runs a column 'Things as I see Them', by Scrutator, that indicates that the problem is not un-recognised. Scrutator takes up grievances, and makes public complaint, to the Police, Government Departments, or the Trade Union Congress: "Ministry of the Interior: Who is to take action about this fare fleecing by some drivers? They are heartless profiteers, they are. Step on their necks, you should," he grumbles, or "T.U.C. Accra: You are doing a lot of sackings. Profits down you say. I am not in a position to question this profit question, but I should like the T.U.C. to look into this side of the matter. So, look out there."

The *Sunday Spectator* is predominantly a feature paper, with very little hard news. It publishes short stories, a pen-pal column for young people, a Women's Corner, not on fashion but, for example, the campaign on infant feeding run by the National Food and Nutrition Board, and a page in vernacular languages. There is a short international commentary, but the strength of the paper is in its intimacy of tone, and, on occasion, its vigour of language, that combine to make it the most 'popular' in character of the Ghana nationals.

If the Ghana Press tends abroad to be derided as monolithic, the Press in Nigeria is admired for its variety. But this too is something of a myth, for the comparative profusion of titles in Nigeria is far less encouraging to any real conflict of ideas than might be expected. With the possible exception of the *Pilot*, which continues to print a high proportion of foreign news, the Nigerian papers are inward-looking, preoccupied with local issues—but the confusion of Nigerian political life, where party divisions do not often clearly reflect differences of principle so much as regional and tribal loyalties, or conflicts of personality, tends to produce a journalism of personal and party abuse rather than of political debate. Even when, for the General Election of December 1964, certain opposition parties and trade unions united to demand the release of political prisoners,

the liberalisation of internal policies and a foreign policy closer
to that of the Organisation of African Unity, and the campaign
was reflected in the papers that supported them, the front split
up again after the election, when its major element, the
N.C.N.C., once more joined a coalition Government.

Political polemic is also inhibited by a Press Law passed in
1964, which compels newspapers to register the names of their
publishers and editors, and provides for fines and imprisonment
for the publication of 'false' reports; and by the old sedition
laws, passed during the colonial period, which have been used
on a number of occasions against newspaper editors. In May
1965 Peter Enahoro, editor of the *Daily Times*, could still tell
the assembly of the International Press Institute that he saw
Nigeria's Press as a free Press, and express confidence that as
long as newspapers were prepared to defend their freedom, it
would remain so, but other Nigerian journalists interviewed
since have expressed more misgivings, claiming that the 1964
law particularly had already had the effect of stifling both
news and comment among opposition newspapers.

Rather than politics, in fact, the stock-in-trade of Nigerian
journalism is the human interest story, culled from the criminal
courts or the latest scandal involving a public figure. Interpretation of the law of libel, as opposed to that of the sedition
laws, seems to be liberal enough to permit personal attacks of a
kind rarely met with in the British Press, or even in that of
East Africa. And headlines are not designed to spare delicate
sensibilities. Thus the *Daily Sketch*, the West Regional Government newspaper, is rich in headings such as: "Death for Akure
Farmer—he laughs as judge shows him the way to the gallows.'
Its world news is largely confined to 'briefs', where 'U.S. Jet
Shot Down' and 'India Joins Space Race' receive equal
attention with a story on the breaking of a prostitution ring in
St. Louis, U.S.A. Political and general interest features are
usually syndicated stories from British or American agencies.
But regular signed articles, sometimes from an outside contributor, do deal with major matters of national policy. Not
long before the 1964 election, for instance, the *Sketch* published
a scathing attack on the then Foreign Minister, Dr. Jaja
Wachuku, for his policy over the Congo. And the paper regularly
devotes a whole page to 'Our Readers' Views.'

East Nigeria too has its regional Government paper, th

Nigerian Outlook, and the North *The Northern Nigerian*, established in 1965, with mainly ex-patriate staff. The Federal Government has since 1961 had its *Morning Post* and *Sunday Post*, set up to meet the challenge of the powerful independent groups, two of which, since Thomson International of Canada had bought a half share in the Amalgamated Press in 1960, were already in foreign hands. The two papers are published by the Nigerian National Press Ltd., and owned entirely by the Federation Government. The N.N.P. has first-class modern plant and machinery, and, in the context of West Africa, a handsome establishment of some 700 employees, spread over the whole country, including sixty-five members of the editorial department. All were by 1965 Nigerians, with the sole exception of an expatriate Press Engineer.

The *Morning Post* is a dignified publication, as befits the voice of Government, but it is neither ponderous nor dull. It publishes an admirably wide range of foreign news and features: a random issue contains a double-page picture story, 'New Strides taken in Tanzania', a feature, 'United Front against Apartheid', a profile of the President of the United States (syndicated), and another on the National Youth Theatre in the German Democratic Republic. It also includes book and film reviews, and sporting features. But its circulation, claimed at about 50,000, has at no time looked like rivalling the 120,000 daily sales of the *Daily Times*.

Increase Coker, editor of the *Morning Post* and the *Sunday Post*, believes that the financing of a newspaper is ideally the business of private rather than Government capital, and his attitude to editing a Government newspaper is very different from that of Mr. T. D. Baffoe, of *The Ghanaian Times*, for instance. Whereas the *Times* sees its function as essentially an extension of the function of government, the *Post* sees it as essentially separate, and undertaken by Government only as a compromise, and preferably a temporary one. Coker endeavours to make his paper a vehicle for news, information and entertainment, and he strives for that independence in the treatment of his material that he would expect as an independent editor. For example, during the attempted General Strike of October 1964, he continued to report the statements of the strikers' Joint Action Council, in spite of Government appeals to the information media to refrain from doing so. This attitude was shared by most of the national newspapers. On another occasion, however, the *Post's* policy seems to have differed from that of the *Times* and the *Express*. Reporting of the politically explosive trial for sedition of Dr. Victor Allen, the British university lecturer accused of helping to plan the strike, was kept to discreet minimum in the *Post*, although its rivals made it front page news.

The only non-Governmental indigenous group is now the Zik group. Its papers remain radical, and outward-looking, and the *Pilot* indulges still in the vituperative editorials that made it famous. "A national Government comprising the N.P.C. octopus and a sprinkling of Southern renegades and vagabonds will solve nothing," it spat during the constitutional crisis of 1964-65. It is said that some of these editorials are still written by Dr. Azikiwe himself, and if this is true, the Government is likely to hesitate before taking any decisive action against the paper in direct defiance of the President. But the editor, Herbert Unegbu, was arrested on a charge of sedition as recently as 1964, though he was later found not guilty and released. He had published a poem during the election, urging his readers to vote for U.P.G.A. (the opposition alliance) and for the release of Chief Awolowo, former leader of the banned Action Group, who was then in prison convicted of treason.

Type-faces are mixed up, letters get printed upside down, paper is poor, photographs dull and static, and advertisements few. The *Pilot* is now the only national newspaper without a good modern press. But its pan-Africanism, its occasional political exposures, and contributions from outside, from old comrades in the independence struggle (Fenner Brockway writing on British Guiana, for instance), help to retain readers' loyalty, and something of the element of excitement that it has been able to generate for nearly thirty years.

Of the two foreign groups, the Daily Times is by far the bigger, the more powerful and the surer of touch. The Daily Times of Nigeria Ltd. publishes two newspapers, the *Daily Times* and the *Sunday Times*, both of them technically excellent, format and design being rather reminiscent of the *Mirror* itself. Not only is the circulation of the daily the highest in West Africa, but so are the profits of the company, which amounted in 1961-62 to £134,109 before tax. In these papers, the tendency already observed to ignore foreign news in favour of crime stories is carried furthest, news from the law courts frequently providing the lead story: 'Village Fight Ends in Death, Wrestler Sent to Assizes', 'Three Women in Ikeja pay haul charge', and so on. In one issue of the *Daily Times* in early 1965, the only items of non-Nigerian news were about a Bristol mother who gave birth prematurely after laughing too hard at a variety show, and about a South African 'pop' singer who calls himself Beau Brummel! But news of Nigerian politics is usually fairly full, there are regular correspondence columns in which dissenting views are freely expressed, two or three pages of sporting news, women's features (fashion and cosmetics), gossip columns, and cartoons.

The second foreign group, the Amalgamated Press of Nigeria Ltd., was wholly financed by Thomson's. After buying a half share in the company in 1960, Thomson was apparently compelled subsequently (in 1962) to take over full responsibility, the Nigerian shareholders being unable to continue to shoulder the heavy losses involved. And even Lord Thomson's considerable resources have not been able to drag the company off the rocks. Amalgamated Press published three main papers—the *Daily Express* (formerly the *Daily Service*, the *Service* surviving only as a monthly magazine), the *Sunday Express*, and a Yoruba weekly, *Ihorin Yoruba*—all of them excellently produced and liberally illustrated. There was a page or more of picture journalism, called 'Photo-Express', in every issue of the daily, and there were good action photographs on every page, some of them bought in London, but many taken on the spot by Express staff. In fact, the paper was remarkably similar, in appearance, to its namesake in London, even down to the lettering of the masthead, and anyone seeing it on the day following the death of Sir Winston Churchill might have been forgiven for wondering whether he had not laid his hands on the London paper by mistake! For the *Express* was the most Western-orientated of all the Nigerian papers, using plentiful foreign syndicated material and giving wide coverage to events in Europe and America. The death of Sir Winston filled three whole pages, including page one—more space than in any other African paper I have seen. Its weakness was its African news, which was sparse, and its domestic coverage, like that of the *Times*, stressed crime and court reports—'Mother Accused of Killing her Son' merited a full page headline in one issue—

and the exposure of scandals, the speciality of 'Mickey Mouse' who adopted a fine moral tone worthy of William Hickey[1] himself.

Unhappily, however, heavy financial losses forced both the *Daily Express* and the *Sunday Express* to cease publication in November 1965. Their demise was also almost certainly hastened by political conflict with the central Government, since they had supported the West-Region-based political opposition.

A few newspapers remain independent of either groups or Governments. The *Daily Telegraph* in Lagos is one, owned by Dr. Mbadiwe, a somewhat recalcitrant member of the cabinet. It has received some capital from West Germany, without which it would certainly not have survived. There are also a number of specialist publications, aimed at women, farmers, trade unionists, including what is a unique venture on the continent, *The Children's Newspaper*, published by the Ministry of Information. But it may be that increasing investment in the nationals will eventually have the effect of destroying the local and specialist ventures in which Nigeria has been so rich in the past. The *Daily Times* and *Morning Post* are distributed in all three regions (and so until its death was the *Express*), running their own fleets of lorries for the purpose, and with their incomparably greater resources, better techniques and wider news coverage it would be surprising if they could not rapidly put their weaker competitors out of business. There is no doubt, on the one hand, that wider distribution for a national Press could strengthen national unity immeasurably; but on the other, the passing of local Press enterprise, as outlets for local opinion in a country where one of the major political problems is to develop communication with those out of easy reach of the capital, would leave a gap not readily filled.

Both the remaining countries of English-speaking West Africa, Sierra Leone and Liberia (The Gambia has no Press to speak of, and Freetown papers circulate there), have a rich Press tradition from the past which is but ill reflected in the newspapers of today. Sierra Leone has two dailies, *Shekpendeh*, organ of the opposition, and the *Daily Mail*, which belongs to the Mirror group. *The African Vanguard* is published twice

[1] The gossip columnist of the London *Daily Express*.

weekly, and there are four weeklies, one of which is published at Bo, in the former inland Protectorate. The *Daily Mail* was founded, as *The Sierra Leone Daily Mail*, in 1933, and bought by the Mirror in 1952. Of all the papers in West Africa, this is the one with a news sense closest to that of Fleet Street, and the only one through which main events in Britain and the Commonwealth could be continuously followed. It does have some preference for African news, which usually occupies most of the back page, the front page being normally devoted to home news. The proportion of political material is high, compared with the other Mirror papers in West Africa, and apart from news will include features on foreign affairs supplied by Overseas Newspapers in London. But the paper is a small one, often only eight pages, so there is no room for daily women's or children's features. Advertising accounts for about three and a half pages in the eight.

The Liberian Age, The Daily Listener and the *Liberian Star* of Monrovia are no bigger than the *Mail*, and infinitely less well produced. Post war Press history in Liberia is a dreary tale, of the failure of one attempt after another to establish an independent voice in Monrovia. The weekly *African Nationalist* came to a sudden end in 1947, after its editor, a West Indian immigrant named Charles Frederick Taylor, was imprisoned for libelling the President. *The Friend*, founded in 1953 as an opposition bi-weekly, collapsed for financial reasons after political opponents broke into the works and smashed equipment. *The Independent Weekly*, started in 1954, closed down after its editor, Mrs. Bertha Corbin, was imprisoned for contempt of the Legislature. The two sole survivors, *The Daily Listener*, founded in 1946 by Charles C. Dennis as Liberia's first daily, and *The Liberian Age*, now a bi-weekly, support the Government, and have received Government subsidies and gifts of machinery. But their standard of production remains no higher than that in Nigeria twenty years ago—pictures are wooden, printing poor, full of typesetting and spelling mistakes. Local news is limited to the activities of Government officials and statements by the President, and foreign coverage mainly disposed of in 'briefs' on an inner page. In contrast to the Press in the former British colonies, the Liberian papers have in the past been Atlantic- rather than Europe-orientated, main news items involving the United States. "Africa in the U.S. Press" is a regular half-page feature in *The Liberian Age*, United Nations news occupies about a third of a page, and features often cover topics such as "Students in the U.S." Pan-African themes are scarce, and so is any serious consideration of subjects of international controversy. A happy taste for expression in verse, however, lightens the rather ponderous effect—this is a tradition of West African journalism dating from the last century, and it is pleasant to see it survive, even if only in praise-poems to the President or memorials to someone loved.

"It was a day in Senegal," wrote the poet of an official visit in 1962,

> "When Tubman went ashore
> All along the streets
> Up to the Palace door
> Thousands had gathered
> To greet Africa's doyen
>
> * * *
>
> As if their hearts afire
> With joy for Africa's hero
> Ah it was a day in Senegal
> Grand and stately, royal and regal,
> When Tubman went ashore."

A new paper, however, was started in 1964, the *Liberian Star*, managed under contract by the Thomson Organisation, and edited by Liberia's senior journalist, Henry B. Cole. Though a modest affair, making little use of the techniques of modern newspaper design, large pictures or striking type-faces, it is a clean-looking job, that makes an effort to cover the main items of local and international news, with occasional feature coverage in depth—a whole centre page spread, for instance, was devoted to the findings of the Warren Report, on the death of President Kennedy. But perhaps the best way to communicate the paper's total inadequacy as a national voice, is to say that it contains no political comment. Such editorials as there are, seem to deal with non-controversial subjects such as an increase in the export of rubber.

To English-speaking West Africa as a whole, then, the post-war period has brought political independence—but, ironically, this has not, except in Ghana, meant independence, in the sense of indigenous control, for the Press. In fact, it has diminished the number of African-controlled newspapers, and introduced two major foreign Press groups, with whose professional and technical expertise the indigenous papers are finding it progressively more difficult to compete. Though in every case edited by an African, the foreign-owned papers must all follow a policy acceptable to their owners, whose interests are separate from those of the people whom their papers are to address. At the very least, this means that the foreign groups will retain a bias towards private economic enterprise and the Western view on international affairs. In other words, they cannot help being a political force.

The Governments are therefore faced with the dilemma either of excluding foreign Press enterprise altogether, and investing vast sums of Government money in mass media development, as Ghana has done, or reconciling themselves to the inevitable processes of commercial Press development, whereby rich papers gradually devour poor ones, and the small papers are eventually forced out altogether. This process has already taken place in most of the highly developed countries of the West. In Africa, it is complicated by the fact that the rich papers are foreign, and the poor ones are indigenous.

CHAPTER 5

POST-WAR SOUTHERN AFRICA

SOUTH OF THE Zambesi the prospect is different: the spectacle there is not of a popular Press struggling for room to grow, but of a popular Press almost totally suppressed. Here a 'white' Press financed mainly locally but in part from abroad, rules the roost, and makes the minimum concession to the needs of a black majority.

The centre of Press power in Southern Africa is not government, nor Fleet Street. It is the Chamber of Mines. Mining capital plays a part in financing most of the biggest English-language newspapers of South Africa and, in particular, it is the power behind the Argus Group. Argus has from early days been connected financially and through cross-directorships with Central Mining, and Rand Mines[1]; and three of the outstanding figures in South African mining history have been credited with the role of *éminence grise* behind the policies of the group. The first of these giants was Cecil John Rhodes, the second was John Martin, and the third is Harry Oppenheimer.

John Martin was a Scottish immigrant who joined the Argus Company in Johannesburg in 1905. By 1915 he was general manager of the Argus Printing and Publishing Company, and from 1926 to 1949 its chairman. In 1926 he was appointed a director of Central Mining Investment Corporation Ltd. By 1946 he was a director of the Bank of England, and of Cable and Wireless Ltd., Managing Director of the Central Mining Investment Corporation, Rand Mines Ltd., and Crown Mines Ltd., and director of thirteen other mining or associated companies, including the Native Recruiting Corporation, and the Witwatersrand Native Labour Association (the two companies that are in charge of labour recruitment for the Chamber of Mines).

At that time, according to H. Lindsay Smith, a South African journalist who wrote a study of the South African

[1] Two of the biggest mining groups on the Rand.

Press in 1946, called *Behind the Press in South Africa*, the largest shareholders in Argus Printing and Publishing were Johannesburg Consolidated Investment, Central Mining, and Rand Mines, who between them held 117,516 of a total of 245,000 issued £1 shares.

In 1963, of eight directors of the company, four were also directors of major mining companies. W. N. Frames was Chairman of one and director of five such companies, including Rand Mines and Rand Selection Corporation. T. Reekie was director of some fifty companies, mainly gold and coal mining and finance companies, and including Rand Mines (Managing Director), Rand Mines Exploration Co. and Rand Mines (South West Africa). K. Richardson was a director of seventeen companies, several of them on the Northern Rhodesian copperbelt, and including Rhodesian Anglo-Americans. D. A. B. Watson was a director of Rhodesian Anglo-American, of De Beers Consolidated Mines, the Diamond Corporation, Rand Selection Corporation, and the Witwatersrand Native Labour Association.

The appearance for the first time of Anglo-American and De Beers on the list of cross-directorships brings up the question of Mr. Oppenheimer. Rumours have for long been circulating that he was endeavouring to gain control of the Argus; and Nationalist politicians have credited many of the policies of Argus papers to his inspiration, and used the idea to attack the "English monopoly press" for bowing to the whims of their cartoonist's favourite butt, "Hoggenheimer." Oppenheimer has never been a director of the Argus, nor is he known to have held shares directly. But in early 1965 a merger between one of the Anglo-American companies and Central Mining Selection has given him a direct interest at last.[1]

Mr. Oppenheimer is South Africa's biggest mining tycoon, Chairman of the giant Anglo-American Corporation (the biggest group on the Rand and one of the two groups on the Zambia copper-belt); and of De Beers Consolidated Mines, which dominates diamond mining in South Africa and South West Africa, and has a 49 per cent interest in the Williamson diamond mines of Tanzania. He is also Chairman of the Diamond Corporation, a virtual monopoly of diamond selling throughout the world. His political policies have inspired pages

[1] See chapter 17, page 240.

of speculation and analysis from journalists and commentators
who have seen contradictions, for instance, in his simultaneous
support in 1959 for the formation of the (white-led) Progressive
Party, which advocates extension of participation in Government to non-whites; and of the South Africa Foundation,
formed to encourage trade and other economic relationships
abroad, and therefore, in the opinion of its critics, to "white-
wash apartheid." A satirist in the quarterly *Africa South*
suggested in 1959 that these contradictions could be resolved
only by the proposition that "what is good for Anglo-Americans
is good for South Africa!" But there is perhaps no real mystery
in a policy that advocates the lifting of the industrial colour bar
on the one hand, and opposes international pressures against
South Africa that might damage her economy, on the other.
Here Mr. Oppenheimer, Anglo-Americans and the English-
language Press have long agreed.

Argus controlled, in 1965, six daily newspapers and two
Sundays (one of them in Afrikaans) in South Africa, and a
constantly expanding periodical press; through its subsidiary,
the Rhodesian Printing and Publishing Company, it controlled,
before 1963, every daily newspaper in the Federation of
Rhodesia and Nyasaland, and since the break-up of the
Federation, the two dailies in Southern Rhodesia (though the
Thomson organisation, through African Newspapers Ltd.,
published a rival, the *Daily News*, in Salisbury until it was
banned in August 1964). Rhodesian Printing and Publishing
was also a major shareholder in Rhodesian Television until
the Rhodesian Government bought its shares in 1965. The
South African dailies are the *Cape Argus* (Cape Town), *The
Star* (Johannesburg), the *Daily News* (Durban), *The Friend*
(Bloemfontein), *The Diamond Fields Advertiser* (Kimberley) and
the *Pretoria News*. Argus also publishes the *Sunday Tribune* and
Sondagnuus (Johannesburg), and shared control with South
African Associated Newspapers (which publishes the *Rand
Daily Mail*, *Sunday Times* and other papers) of the *Sunday
Chronicle* (established in Johannesburg in 1964 only to disappear
again in 1965.) In Rhodesia, the group runs *The Rhodesia
Herald* (Salisbury), *The Chronicle* (Bulawayo), and two Sundays,
the *Sunday Mail* and the *Sunday News*. Until 1963, it had also
owned *The Northern News*, which it bought from Sir Roy
Welensky in 1951. With the approach of independence for

Zambia, however, the *News* was sold to the Heinrich Printing and Publishing Company (Heinrich's primary interest had been in beer), who in turn sold it, in 1964, to the London and Rhodesian Mining Company (Lonrho).

Argus also has significant links with the Central News Agency, which monopolises newspaper distribution in the Republic, and through its subsidiary, Kingstons, in the Rhodesias; and with the South African Press Association, the national news agency. S.A.P.A. is co-operatively owned by all the main newspaper companies, but Argus' share was calculated by H. Lindsay Smith in 1946 to be a third of the shares issued, and it has grown since then. Up to 1964, S.A.P.A. acted as the collector of domestic news and channel of foreign news both in South Africa and the Rhodesias, but since the break-up of the Federation, a new company, the Inter-African News Agency, I.A.N.A., has taken over the business in Southern Rhodesia and Zambia. I.A.N.A.'s main share holders are the Argus papers in Rhodesia, and *The Northern News* in Zambia, but since its manager, Mr. Ralph Wilson, is also manager of S.A.P.A., and it has no foreign correspondents of its own and no separate agreement with Reuters (which provides S.A.P.A.'s foreign news), its status seems to be little more than that of a non-South African label for Rhodesian newspaper stories.

A bad second to the Argus group, among the English-language newspapers, is South African Associated Newspapers Ltd., which publishes the *Rand Daily Mail*, the *Sunday Times* and *Sunday Express* in Johannesburg, and the *Eastern Province Herald* and the *Evening Post*, Port Elizabeth. Together with the other main English-language morning newspapers in the Republic—*The Cape Times*, and the *Natal Mercury*—these are grouped in a loose association, for purposes of journalistic co-operation, as South African Morning Newspapers. They share 'own correspondent' news stories, and an office in London to deal with foreign coverage. (The *Sunday Express*, since it competes with the *Times*, is not in fact covered by this co-operation). But Morning Newspaper facilities are still small, when compared with the much larger Argus London office (which has a separate establishment for the Rhodesian papers) and the Argus' unique, and highly competent, 'Africa News Service', which sends correspondents all over Central and East, and sometimes West, Africa.

The 'Morning' papers however do include some of the most courageous of the big newspapers at present publishing in South Africa. One is the *Rand Daily Mail* of Johannesburg, which under the editorship of Lawrence Gandar (awarded the International Award of the British Institute of Journalists in 1964) has been in the forefront of attacks on the 90-day no-trial law, on conditions in South African prisons, and on proposed Government measures to restrict the freedom of the Press. Gandar's policy has been questioned even by relatively sympathetic colleagues, on the ground that he is provoking head-on collision with a Government that is only too ready to install a censorship; and that in any case he is in danger of losing popularity with his readers, and advertisers, and so endangering the future of his paper.

The point is that the English-speaking 'United Party' Press has always suffered from a form of schizophrenia, contracted not so much from the party itself, which has been moribund for too long to have much effect on anyone, but from the mining industry. On the one hand, the Press is anxious to defend 'liberal' values by opposing the most extreme of the Nationalist's anti-popular legislation; on the other, it is committed to defend South African capitalism, and in particular, the mining industry, which is irretrievably bound up with the colour bar. While protesting at Nationalist injustice, the Press dare not encourage the revolutionary force that would put an end to the injustice, for fear that it would put an end to white profits at the same time.

Thus, even the *Rand Daily Mail*, which in August 1965 risked prosecution under the Prisons Act by publishing an exposure of South African jails[1], has never launched a campaign on the inadequacy of African miners' wages (which have risen by only a few shillings to approximately £4 per month in seventy years).

The English-language dailies had a joint circulation in 1962 of 702,000. The Afrikaans-language dailies sold a mere 166,000. Of the Sundays and weeklies, the English-language papers sold 1,154,000 and the Afrikaans-language 592,000. In fact approximately 60 per cent of the white population of the

---

[1] The exposure did however cost Gandar his control of the paper. In December 1965 he was 'kicked upstairs' by his company, and redesignated 'Editor-in-Chief'.

Republic is Afrikaans-speaking, and if South Africans were to read newspapers as they vote, 60 per cent of the population would be reading Afrikaner Nationalist newspapers, and only 40 per cent English-language opposition papers. There are a small number of non-whites, who generally read English papers, to account for; and the language division does not strictly accord with party lines (there were in 1963 three Afrikaans-language weeklies that were not Nationalist publications, and at present there is one English-language weekly that is Nationalist) but these adjustments only underline the total of non-Nationalist papers sold (1,431,000 as against 315,000, on the 1962 figures). This discrepancy has been the source of great bitterness among Nationalist politicians and newspapermen, and has in part inspired the long Press war between the Nationalists and the 'English' Press, that originated before the last war, and has yet to reach its climax.

Most of the Nationalist papers are much more recent in origin than their competitors. They were all started as political organs, more or less closely attached to the Nationalist party, and all of them have had leading Nationalists (now Cabinet Ministers) on their Boards. They were campaigners, and news coverage has never been their strength, though many of them have lately tried to remedy this weakness. Many Nationalists clearly buy English newspapers for news.

There are at present four Nationalist dailies: *Die Burger*, Cape Town, established in 1915; *Die Transvaler*, Johannesburg, a morning paper started in 1937; *Die Vaderland*, the Johannesburg evening in Afrikaans; and *Die Volksblad*, Bloemfontein. Since 1964, a weekly in English, the *Financial Gazette*, has been published in Johannesburg in an attempt to break into the 'English' market, which has been greatly expanded over the last few years through the Government's immigration policy. *Die Burger* and *Die Volksblad* are published by the Nasionale Pers; *Die Transvaler* and the *Financial Gazette* by the Voortrekkerpers, whose chairman is Dr. Verwoerd, the Prime Minister; and *Die Vaderland* by the Afrikaanse Pers, which also publishes the Sunday *Dagbreek en Sondagnuus*. Afrikaanse Pers was merged in 1963 with the Voortrekkerpers, making Dr. Verwoerd for the first time a major force in the Republic's printing and publishing industry. The move also helped to define a political division said to exist between the 'Cape' Nationalists and their

Transvaal colleagues. The Nasionale Pers broadly reflects the policies of the 'old' Cape Nationalism, and the Voortrekkerpers papers the more blindly extreme attitudes of the Transvaalers. Too much should not be made of the distinction —there are no signs of any serious split—but *Die Burger* has on occasion counselled caution while *Die Transvaler* has been ready to plunge ahead (their divergent advice in October 1965 to Rhodesia over a U.D.I., is an example); and enough rivalry is evidently felt between them for *Die Burger* to have decided in 1965 to launch an Afrikaans Sunday paper, *Die Beeld*, as a rival for Dr. Verwoerd's *Dagbreek en Sondagnuus*, in spite of strenuous efforts by Afrikaanse Pers to prevent it.

Dr. Verwoerd need not fear for the security of his Press empire, however. According to the *Sunday Chronicle* in January 1965, the companies now under Dr. Verwoerd's chairmanship had received Government contracts worth "at least £3million" during the past four years, and nearly half the Cabinet members serve as their directors (on Afrikaanse Pers Beleggings Beperk sit the Minister of Posts and Telegraphs, Dr. Albert Hertzog, a member of the Broederbond, the Nationalist 'secret society', Mr. Jan de Klerk, Minister of Labour, Mr. Schoeman, Minister of Transport, and Mr. F. H. Odendaal, author of the Odendaal report on South West Africa). These companies have also been entering seriously into the field of publications for Africans; apart from Government periodicals such as *Bantu* the Afrikaanse Pers publishes *Bona*, an "educational magazine for Africans", of which the Department of Education buys some 250,000 annually for free distribution to African schools, and *Imvo*, bought from the Bantu Press; and the Voortrekkerpers publishes *Our Own Mirror*, formerly *Elethu*, independently published in Natal. *Elethu* was a weekly for urban Africans, featuring sport, crime, love-problems and anti-colour-bar but non-rebellious politics; but the words 'colour-bar' and 'apartheid' have dropped entirely out of the *Mirror's* vocabulary, and the main political story is usually not on South Africa at all, but aimed at discrediting one or another of the independent African states ("Bright African Star fades—Ghana faces Economic Ruin.") It is likely that it will gradually be adapted, like Dr. Verwoerd's other publications for Africans, as a thoroughgoing propagandist for Bantustans and apartheid.

The post-war period has been a boom-time for publications aimed at the African market. The Bantu Press has expanded, and became a subsidiary of Argus. As well as *Imvo*, it eventually sold *Zonk*, a non-political picture magazine, to the Afrikaanse Pers, and now concentrates on developing *The World*, which has become a daily. *Umthunywa*, a Transkei paper in the Bantu Press group, is a probable priority for development now that it has been taken directly under Argus management, for so far the 'self-governing' Transkei has no newspaper of its own but the *Government Gazette*, and it seems unlikely that African capital will be available to finance one.

Most of the publishing ventures by Africans had petered out after the war. One of the last to die was the militant *Inkundla ya Bantu*, published in Verulam, Natal. Govan Mbeki, one of the African leaders sentenced to life imprisonment at the Rivonia trial, was a former editor. *Inkundla* was founded in 1937, and ceased publication in 1952 for financial reasons. None of the wealthy African families who at the turn of the century had been able to send their sons abroad for education, and to assist in providing the capital for those newspapers that flourished at the time, was wealthy any longer. Government policy since Union, in limiting African rights to own land, to work in certain professions or to gain industrial skills, had ruined them, and made it impossible for a new middle class to arise.

By far the most celebrated of the publishing ventures "for Africans" was *Drum*. It was started in 1951 as *African Drum* with a well-known South African cricketer as its editor, and a nostalgia for the old tribal ways. It was not a success, and when Jim Bailey, son of the legendary mining millionaire Sir Abe, took it over, he decided to turn it into a magazine for Johannesburg, for the urbanised Africans who were the real reading public. Under its two English-born editors, Anthony Sampson and Tom Hopkinson (former editor of *Picture Post*), *Drum* was soon bursting with vitality, covering anything from boxing to shebeens (illegal African drinking houses), from witchcraft to prison conditions. It expanded into colour, and a West African and East African edition. But in April 1965 the South African *Drum* followed its East African edition into oblivion, and became a mere colour supplement to Bailey's other publication, the Sunday *Post*—a newspaper, intended originally for Coloured readers, and now selling both in the Cape and on the Rand as a rather miserably uncommitted paper for non-whites.

Though *Drum* gave a chance to a few highly talented African journalists, however, it could do little to break down apartheid in the profession. Few of the South African dailies have yet had an African on their reporting staff, and even when a non-white journalist is employed, the obstacles in his way are enormous. An African is always subject to arbitrary arrest, on a pass, or other technical offence; he has no freedom of movement, and will be refused access to official functions, to 'whites only' premises, even to libraries. Officials will seldom give information to a non-white journalist, and vetting of Parliamentary Correspondents has become so strict that more than one white journalist has been excluded for writing reports displeasing to Government. A non-white correspondent would have no chance.

The colour bar also works in reverse to inhibit the Press, for white journalists need special permission to enter African townships, and are thus hampered in the collection of news about African life and African activities.

A few newspapers, however, have existed, employing a multi-racial staff and accepting the difficulties that this entails. These are the political papers, the tiny fringe of radical publications that have provided some outlet for popular aspirations, and some voice for the non-white political movements. The most important of these was, for twenty-five years, the *Guardian* series of weeklies: for when the *Guardian* was banned in 1950 it was succeeded by another paper, which settled down for a while with the name of *Advance*; when it too was banned, *New Age* took its place, and finally, for a few months before its final decease in 1963, *The Spark*. These weeklies were the sole consistent voice in support of the big political campaigns against apartheid in the 1950's, the Defiance of Unjust Laws Campaign of 1952-53, the Congress of the People in 1955, the mass demonstrations of the women against the pass laws, the strikes and the protests. It ran exposure stories on farm-prisons and labour conditions, on police brutality, on the kidnapping of Anderson Ganyile from Basutoland in 1961, on the first of the torture reports from political prisoners in 1962 and 1963.

New Age was financed by donations from sympathisers all

over the country. Since the C.N.A. refused to handle it, it was
distributed through its own newspaper sellers, many of them
Africans whose commission on sales was their only livelihood.
Tattered copies were handed round in the townships, and read
aloud to those who could not read. To read *New Age*, let alone
sell it, was a political act, and the sellers were subjected to
harrassment and intimidation from the authorities. So were
the journalists, who were banned under the Suppression of
Communism Act from public gatherings, confined to a single
magisterial district, some placed under house arrest, and
eventually so confined as to make any participation in the
affairs of a newspaper impossible. All leading members of the
staff were banned from speaking to other banned persons (that
is, to each other), from preparing anything for publication,
from writing for publication, and from entering any building
where the business of publishing was conducted. Not even the
resilient *New Age* could recover from the blow, and the series
came to an end. With the death of the paper which Chief
Luthuli had called "the fighting mouthpiece of African
aspirations", the African political movement was left without
a voice. (The English dailies had by then begun to cover
African politics to some extent, but it was not until 1960 that
they had even got so far as to drop the patronising word 'native'
in favour of 'African' in their columns.)

Fighting Talk, a monthly founded by the ex-servicemen's
Springbok Legion after the war, and published later as a
political discussion magazine with emphasis on African affairs,
died at the same time as *New Age*. *Workers' Unity*, though
technically not defunct, has not appeared since mass arrests
decimated the staff of the South African Congress of Trade
Unions in 1963; and numerous other publications, organs of
the Transvaal Indian Youth League, the South African
Congress of Democrats, the Defence and Aid Fund (which
published a *Treason Trial Bulletin* throughout the treason trial
of 1956-61) have struggled for a while, but not survived. In
1958 there appeared the short-lived *Africanist*, edited by Robert
Sobukwe, the vehicle of the Africanists who broke with the
African National Congress in 1959. And in 1962, *Forward*, once
a Labour Party paper, was revived by a former Labour member of Parliament and trade unionist, Alex Hepple. Primarily
a trade union paper, *Forward* conducted two major political

campaigns before it too ceased publication at the beginning of
1965: one of them on increasing press control, and the other
on the mass political arrests of 1963 and 1964.

In 1965, of all the anti-apartheid publications that were
flourishing five years previously, only *Contact*, a small fortnightly
founded by the Liberal Patrick Duncan in 1958, was still
appearing. Duncan blazoned on his masthead that *Contact* was
"against all forms of totalitarianism, such as fascism, communism and apartheid", but after he was banned, in 1961, and
left the country to live first in Basutoland and then abroad,
new editors concentrated their energies more exclusively on
apartheid. What is most remarkable about *Contact* is the
courage and resource with which it has managed to keep going.
Four of its editors have been banned and one held in 90-day
detention. Through lack of funds, it resorted for a while to
duplicated reproduction, and when no printer was prepared to
print it, managed to buy its own small press, only to have to
relapse again in 1965 into duplicated format and irregular
appearance. Besides *Contact*, a few clandestine broadsheets
circulate—one called *Focus* appeared in Cape Town for a time;
there are bulletins of the women's Black Sash, an organisation
of liberal women, and the Civil Rights League; and the
illegal *African Communist* is published by the underground South
African Communist Party. The Government has all but
silenced the non-conformist press.

Its next step will be further pressure, and possibly legislation,
against the English-language newspaper groups. One of the
first acts of the present Government was to set up a Press
Commission in 1950 to enquire, among other things, into
"accuracy in the presentation of news in the press in South
Africa, as well as beyond the borders of South Africa, by
correspondents in the Union, having particular regard to (*a*)
the selection of news (*b*) the mixing of fact and comment (*c*) use
of unverified facts or rumours as news, or as a basis for comment; and (*d*) reckless statements, distortions of fact, or
fabrication, and the use of any of these as news, and as basis
for comment"; and into "the adequacy or otherwise of existing
means of self-control and discipline by the Press over (*a*)
editors, journalists and correspondents serving local newspapers
and periodicals (*b*) correspondents of overseas newspapers and

periodicals, and (c) free-lance journalists serving the local or overseas Press."

The Commission laboured for nearly twelve years before the first section of its report, covering tendencies towards monopoly in the control of the Press, in the collection of news, and distribution of newspapers, was published in 1961. It found, in summary, that the English-language Press dominated the South African Press Association, to the extent that it could control 87.4 per cent of the votes at a general meeting; that Reuters agreement with S.A.P.A. placed it in such a position that other world agencies could not compete for news distribution in South Africa; that the Argus Group, South African Associated Newspapers and Nasionale Pers dominated the Press; that both Afrikaans and English-language dailies were biased in the reporting of political affairs, so that no one reading newspapers in one language only could obtain a full picture of events; and that the C.N.A. enjoyed a monopoly of newspaper distribution. The Commission recommended that S.A.P.A. should curb its monopoly of newspaper distribution and cease its bias in favour of Reuters, under threat of losing its licence; that it should alter its voting system so that Afrikaans language should have an equal say with English-langauge papers; and that a full investigation be made into the question of the C.N.A. monopoly by the Board of Trade.

No steps have been taken in connection with the first recommendations, partly because among the earliest voices to spring to the defence of S.A.P.A. were those of the Afrikaans newspapers themselves, particularly *Die Burger*. It is the opinion of most South African journalists that the Nationalist Press itself fears censorship, and will resist Government steps to control the opposition Press for this reason. The investigation into the C.N.A. however, has taken place, and a report was published in May 1965. The C.N.A. and the newspapers involved had agreed, said the report, that the agreement whereby the C.N.A. undertakes distribution of a new newspaper only with the agreement of certain newspapers owners, was a monopolistic restriction, and so was the requirement that unlimited additional guarantees should be paid to the C.N.A. on request.

The Government already has the power to prohibit the circulation of any newspaper which is not a member of the

Newspaper Press Union (the association of proprietors of the main dailies and Sundays), under the Publications and Entertainments Act of 1963. The N.P.U. managed to buy exclusion from the Act's provisions only by adopting a 'code of conduct', to be administered by a Board of Reference consisting of a former Judge, and two representatives from among the owners of the English and the Afrikaans newspapers, one from each group. The South African Society of Journalists has denounced this code as a form of self-censorship, and instructed its members to ignore it.

That the code is having the effect of self-censorship was clear from one of the first cases referred to the Board, when two statements in a signed article appearing in the *Sunday Express* were complained against. The article alleged that the government employed the political police to restrain and silence almost every form of outspoken protest; and that this feeling was not expressed with more vigour because men were afraid of the personal consequences to themselves, or their businesses or jobs. The Board found "that the article complained of contains both overstatement and unfair comment and that the newspaper failed in its duty to avoid these violations of the code of conduct." As Brian Bunting remarks in his book *The Rise of the South African Reich*, "It is doubtful if the Publications Board could have served the government better in the way of recommending Press censorship."

However, no one believes that the Government will be prepared to stop here. Attacks against the 'English' press have not relaxed. Several journalists were held under the '90-day' law in 1963 and 1964, including Ruth First, formerly Johannesburg editor of *New Age*, Margaret Smith of the *Sunday Times*, Paul Trewhela of the *Rand Daily Mail* (since imprisoned as a member of the illegal Communist Party), Hugh Lewin and Raymond Eisenstein (also sentenced to jail terms for 'sabotage'). In the case of the first two at least, the main purpose in holding them was to obtain information, and to intimidate other journalists who might be tempted to report anti-government activities with some degree of sympathy.

There is no doubt in the minds of most journalists that further restrictions on the Press are being planned. One Bill already passed extends the provisions of the Official Secrets Act to cover "police activities in the preservation of internal security and the maintenance of law and order." True to their record in framing the Code of Conduct, some newspaper proprietors have 'accepted' the Act, but others, including the Port Elizabeth *Evening Post*, and the *Rand Daily Mail*, dissociate themselves from such a stand. The *Mail* argued in an editorial in May 1965 that "when this Bill is passed the Minister will be free to run a real Gestapo, with his security men operating in the dark and the newspapers trying to guess how much they can report. The onus of guessing right will be on the Press and the penalty for guessing wrong will be heavy. And meanwhile the public may have no knowledge of what is being done in their name."

In Rhodesia, the Law and Order (Maintenance) Act of 1962 has already proved a more effective Press gag than all the maze of legislation in South Africa. The Press there had in any case never developed as an opposition: a few duplicated newsheets published by successive African Nationalist parties, and a remarkable publication entitled *Dissent* produced by a group of lecturers at the University College of Salisbury in 1958 and 1959 have been the sum of the radical Press in Rhodesia, apart from those few papers—such as the *Central African Mail*—that have circulated there from across the Zambesi. The *Mail* has in any case been banned in Rhodesia. There have been some papers independent of the all-powerful Argus: the African Newspaper Publications, former associates of the South African Bantu Press, which produced white-controlled papers for Africans, and was bought by Thomsons in 1961, and the *Central African Examiner*. This weekly, which has survived many vicissitudes both of ownership and policy, first supported the project for Federation, then questioned Federation and was severely rebuked, then settled for a modest role as sympathetic critic. It is now (1965) edited by the liberal Mrs. Eileen Haddon, who has earned Government disapproval for the interest she has taken in political prisoners, and her attempts to obtain them legal defence and assistance for their families. She has been restricted to the Salisbury area under the Law and Order (Maintenance) Act.

Thomson's *Daily News*, started as the first daily newspaper directed to an African readership, in 1962, had a short life, since it was banned in August 1964 under the Law and Order

(Maintenance) Act, apparently for reporting violent clashes between African nationalists, and for publishing a 'false' report. These at least were the charges later brought against the company, which was fined in December 1964 for falsely reporting that supporters of the People's Caretaker Council had attacked a gang of Zimbabwe African National Union 'thugs' in retaliation for a Z.A.N.U. attack on a school. The evidence showed that the P.C.C. attack came first. The paper was also found guilty of falsely reporting that the country's chiefs had lost the support of the majority of the African people; and that in a Court trial the Crown had conceded that the police had tortured witnesses!

In the light of these hazards, the Argus papers pursue a policy of extreme caution. They simply do not report African politics, violent acts, nationalist statements or stories of political arrests, unless they are the subject of court cases, or of Government announcements. But, by early 1965, even these papers expressed alarm at the prospect of a "takeover of the free Press in Rhodesia by Government", as the President of the Rhodesian Guild of Journalists put it to a meeting in Salisbury on 14th May. As early as May 1964, rumours were circulating that the Government had a Press Bill drafted, possibly containing provisions for the registration of journalists and some control over overseas correspondents. Mr. Pieter van der Byl, Parliamentary Secretary responsible for Information, set up a new Information Department at that time, and appointed a former propagandist of the South African Broadcasting Corporation, Mr. Ivor Benson, to head the new bureau. Mr. van der Byl explained that the freedom of the Press was not the freedom of newspapers to do as they liked. It was the freedom of the public to have access to an unbiased and unslanted Press. Southern Rhodesia was "at war" with propaganda against the country. "One has to get back to the primitive thing 'my country right or wrong'," he said, echoing his Prime Minister who had insisted on another occasion that "Ideally the Press should be loyal to the country." The Bishop of Matabeleland commented appositely that this was "getting near the policies of Dr. Goebbels."

The State of Emergency following the illegal declaration of independence in November 1965 in any case put an end to what liberty of the Press remained. The Rhodesian papers had no record of struggle to defend themselves, such as the South African papers have. But it would be a mistake to suppose that they sympathised with the project to declare independence unilaterally. One of the few stands the *Herald* ever took against the Government was to publish, against the Government's instructions, the findings of the tobacco growers' investigation into the probable economic effects of a U.D.I. As spokesman for Rhodesia—and indeed for South African—capital, the *Herald* opposed a unilateral declaration, and continued to warn against it. Since full-scale censorship was introduced, the *Herald* has appeared defiantly with its editorial columns blank, and white spaces in the news reports.

Thus the trend is towards conformity, in both Rhodesia and the Republic, though there may be battles to come before this is finally accomplished. Meanwhile, the voices stifled within these countries are making themselves heard. Clandestine publications are appearing in South Africa, and in Rhodesia *Gonakudzingwa News*[1] was produced for a while by detainees in the camp, until it was banned at the beginning of 1965.

But usually the voices of opposition come from exile groups abroad—offices of the African National Congress of South Africa producing *Spotlight on South Africa* and *South Africa Freedom News*, offices of the Zimbabwe African People's Union producing *Zimbabwe News*. These duplicated news and propaganda sheets, produced with inadequate funds but considerable resourcefulness, may well prove training-grounds for future journalists, and help to form a base even for the future Press of independent countries, just as in Algeria the propaganda department of the F.L.N. (National Liberation Front) later became responsible for the establishment of a new Press in independent Algeria to replace the Press of the 'colons.' In South Africa at least, the established Press has not disgraced itself to the extent that the 'colon' Press did in Algeria, and perhaps it never will. But it has failed to align itself with the popular struggle for freedom, and been content to remain the creature of white interests. The mantle of Fairbairn, Greig and Pringle, the courageous fighters for freedom 150 years ago, has fallen instead upon the journalists who work underground, smuggling news and information to the outside world.

[1] Gonakudzingwa is the name of the detention camp where Joshua Nkomo and other African leaders were imprisoned.

One last area of Southern Africa, where the Press has not been without political significance, is the Portuguese-ruled territory of Moçambique. There, newspapers have been appearing since the turn of the century. The oldest of the current dailies, *Diarió*, was established in 1905. And in spite of strict Government censorship since 1933, there are today five daily papers in the country.

Diarió was founded as *The Lourenço Marques Guardian*, organ of the large English-speaking community, and it was only in 1956 that it began publishing in Portuguese, after it had been bought by the Catholic Diocese of Lourenço-Marques. The Lourenço-Marques Bishopric is regarded as representing the most reactionary wing of the Church in Moçambique, and *Diarió* has accordingly proved the Government's most reliable Press ally. More interesting are *Nõticias* (the biggest Moçambique paper, founded in 1926), its companion evening *Nõticias da Tarde*, and *Tribuná*, the newest of the dailies, founded in 1962. All these were until recently independent papers, *Nõticias* owned by a local businessman with extensive financial interests in the territory; and *Tribuná* by a company in which the major shareholder was himself a journalist, Joao Reis. *Tribuná* was unique among the dailies, in that it employed African journalists, and concerned itself seriously with race relations, a preoccupation which led it to take a courageous stand on various occasions in defence of human rights for Africans, and thus into direct conflict with the authorities.

The fifth daily is the *Diarió de Moçambique*, established in 1950 by the Bishop of Beira, as a voice for 'liberal', 'progressive' Catholicism. *Diarió de Moçambique* has become a focus not only for thinking churchmen, but also for the lay white opposition, and to some extent for the black 'assimilado' minority. Its journalistic standards are the highest among the Moçambique dailies. But its attempt to follow an independent political policy has involved it in constant skirmishes with Government—it has been censored, suspended more than once, and survives only at the cost of a day-to-day struggle with the local administration.

The degree of criticism these papers allowed themselves was in fact very modest. None was in any sense a radical paper, except in the context of the extraordinary intolerance of the Portuguese regime. None would have risked the outspoken editorials that English-language newspapers can still indulge in, in the Republic, though in the case of *Nõticias* and *Tribuná* they had a roughly similar relationship with the regime, in that they represented large independent commercial interests that found the rigidities of dictatorship irksome. But the fact that they stood out at all—and that *Diarió de Moçambique* still, at the end of 1965, stands out—has had a totally disproportionate effect in encouraging the democratic forces that have never yet been totally suppressed. It is for that reason that in 1964 Government took steps to bring them under yet stricter control.

In August of that year *Nõticias*, and in September *Tribuná*, were taken over by the Banco Naçional Ultramarino (the Portuguese National Bank) since when both have been run as mouthpieces for the administration. Joao Reis was arrested, together with numbers of other Moçambique intellectuals, black and white, and the senior editorial staff of *Tribuná* were dismissed.

Similar steps were taken at the same time against the few papers addressed to African readers. These were all weeklies, of which there were at least three of some importance. *O Brãdo Africano* had been established as long ago as 1918, by the Associacao Africano de Lourenço Marques, and before the imposition of Press censorship had made a name among white and black alike as an organ of popular opinion. The names of the African journalists whose talents created it are still remembered in Moçambique. But after 1933 it was compelled to limit itself to non-political subjects, though it retained a readership among the Africans and 'mesticas' (Coloured people) of the capital, amounting to some 35,000 readers weekly. When in 1964 a new editor, an African named Dr. Domingos Arouca, seemed likely to forge the paper anew into an organ of public opinion, the Government acted again, and in April 1965 Dr. Arouca was arrested for allegedly 'pro-nationalist' activities.

Another weekly, *A Voz Africana*, was founded in 1932 by the Centro Africano de Manica e Sofala, in the north. It is believed to have had some backing from the remarkable Bishop of Beira, and the staff, including the editor, was African. But in December 1964 the editor, Luis Bernardo Honwana, was among those intellectuals imprisoned in the wave of arrests that followed the takeover of *Nóticias* and *Tribuná,* and the third weekly, *A Voz de Moçambique.*

A Voz de Moçambique, also published by an African cultural association, the Associacao os Naturais de Moçambique, was founded only in 1959, and dealt from the beginning with political, social and economic problems. Though its policies were always moderate, they brought it into conflict with the local censor, and in 1964 *A Voz* was bought over by the Banco Naçional Ultramarino.

So came to an end Portugal's brief experiment in allowing some degree of self-expression to a carefully selected group of African intellectuals—for it does seem to have been deliberate administrative policy for a while to encourage an intelligentsia which would be a show-piece for Portuguese colonialism, a demonstration to answer the rising international condemnation of Portugal's regime in Africa. Once the lid was lifted only a little, it had to be jammed down tight again, lest the pot boil over. Censorship is now so rigid that even the fate of most of the journalists mentioned in this chapter, is unknown.

So by the end of 1965, practically every authentic popular voice in Southern Africa had been silenced. The censor's scissors were making ugly holes not only in the papers of Moçambique and Angola, but in those of Rhodesia, after its illegal declaration of 'independence', as well; and they dangled threateningly over the newspapers of the Republic. Only in the British High Commission Territories, soon to become independent, did there seem any chance for an African Press to develop; but even there, no independent paper yet existed. *The Swaziland Times* was owned by the South African Argus group; and the Basutoland Government's *Lesotho Times,* in Sotho and English, was no more than a popularised government gazette. The mass of the people of Southern Africa, amongst the most articulate on the continent, were voiceless.

CHAPTER 6

ZAMBIA

ZAMBIA'S HISTORY BELONGS with Southern Africa, for its Press until independence was little more than an appendage to that of Southern Rhodesia, which in turn was controlled from South Africa. But its problems today are no longer those of the settler-run south, for as an independent State Zambia looks to closer co-operation with East Africa. Saddled with an economic structure heavily dependent for trade and transport on South Africa and Rhodesia, yet urged by domestic and Pan-African pressures to align itself against the white minority regimes, the Zambia Government finds itself daily confronted with dilemmas that only revolution in South Africa will resolve. And it inherited in the country's one daily newspaper, a Press that underlined the dilemma.

Though the *Livingstone Mail*, a venerable local paper with no pretensions to national status, dates back to 1906, 1944 seems to mark the beginning of national newspaper enterprise in Northern Rhodesia. It was the year in which the Bantu Press' Southern Rhodesian subsidiary, African Newspapers, launched the *Bantu Mirror*, which was intended to circulate partly in Northern Rhodesia. And it was also the year in which Roy Welensky, the future Prime Minister of the Federation of the Rhodesias and Nyasaland, started a twice weekly paper at Ndola, in the copperbelt, called *The Northern News*. It was an amateurish affair. Welensky is reputed to have written much of it himself (although it was his partner who was editor), including 'Aunt Sally' letters under pseudonyms, to which he would reply crushingly in the next issue under his own name! It sold about 2,000 copies. As leader of the 'unofficials' in the Legislative Council, Welensky was already ambitious, and shrewd enough to appreciate the power of a newspaper as a political instrument. He used *The Northern News* primarily to further his campaign for amalgamation with Southern Rhodesia, as a first step towards white independence in Central Africa.

In 1948, a new settler organ appeared, the first newspaper to be published in Lusaka the capital. This was the *Central African Post*, owned by Dr. Alexander Scott. Scott had just retired from medical practice, and, as his widow put it in a radio broadcast some years later, "because the best way of ensuring continued expression of one's views in print is to be one's own newspaper proprietor, the idea of starting a paper of his own in Lusaka appealed to Dr. Scott as the most exciting way of spending his retirement." He was, in short, an 'amateur' in the ancient British tradition of amateurs, who have meddled to good effect and ill in their own and other people's affairs for a long time past. He was an amateur politician, and an amateur newspaperman, apparently totally ignorant of the technical side of newspaper production. But he founded a series of newspapers that were to play a unique part in the making of modern Zambia—not least because they provided the only real counter to *The Northern News*.

The first issue of the *Post*, it seems, had to be set letter by letter, by hand, since the linotype operator had not yet arrived from England. "It was little more than a broadsheet", his widow remembered, "and apart from three long editorials and two fulsome articles on health by the 'Newspaper Doctor' whose identity was not difficult to guess, it contained nothing but a few items of world news lifted from the B.B.C., and gossip notes from such out of the way places as Abercorn, Mongu and Fort Jameson. As a Lusaka paper, it surely deserves distinction for not containing a single item of Lusaka news, although the back page was solid with local advertisements, all invented by the works manager to fill up space, and inserted free of charge."

The *Post* at first supported the idea of Federation with Southern Rhodesia, but Scott disliked Welensky, and this rivalry on the one hand, and the rising tide of African opposition to federation on the other, led him more and more to oppose Welensky's ideas, and in the end federation itself. So while the *Post* had started as a lively but coventional voice for settler views, its successor was to be regarded by the African nationalist leaders as a friend and valuable ally.

Meanwhile, the Argus empire had come to Northern Rhodesia. In 1951 it had bought *The Northern News* from Welensky, and within two years turned it into a daily. Within five, it was selling 20,000 copies a day. As Harry Franklin, one-time chief of the Northern Rhodesia Broadcasting Company, remarked some years later, "its subsequent professional editors did more for Roy Welensky than he himself could have done." And in 1957, the Argus bought the *Post* as well.

This had run into financial difficulties, and Scott had been forced into a partnership with Kachalola Ltd., owned by B. F. G. Paver, formerly of the Bantu Press, in 1952. Since Kachalola already had links with the Argus, direct control meant only one more step. But Scott was deeply disappointed when the transfer took place, regarding it as a breach of faith by African Newspapers, as he foresaw that Argus control would mean the death of his paper. This indeed is what followed. The Argus closed it down, leaving the field free for *The Northern News*.

The very next year, 1958, Dr. Scott started a new paper, the *African Times*. This time, he intended to reach an African readership as well as those liberal whites already disenchanted with the five-year-old Federation, which had placed them at the mercy of the reactionary south. Unlike the *Post*, the *Times* was a campaigner, with a clear and popular cause. And the mere fact of its existence helped to shed some light in dark corners. One of its more celebrated scoops was the right-wing settler leader Sir John Gaunt's boast to a political meeting that he would rather share government "with a black mamba" than with a black African. Since *The Northern News* reporters left the phrase discreetly out of their reports, it was left to the *African Times* to pass it down to posterity, and on to the African leaders, who belaboured Sir John with it for years afterwards.

But the *African Times* died too, and though Dr. Scott hankered after a new paper, he could not finance it alone. It was finally David Astor, editor of the London *Observer*, who agreed to put up half the capital for a new venture, the *African Mail*, which started publication in 1960. In 1962 it changed its name to the *Central African Mail*.

The *Mail* was the most professional and the most militant of the three Scott papers, campaigning courageously against Federation, for independence, and for 'one man, one vote', the slogan of Kenneth Kaunda's United National Indpendence Party. It had become in fact a frankly African-orientated paper, edited by an African, Titus Mukupo, later Minister of Information in independent Zambia. But it was never an *African* paper, in the sense of being fully African controlled, and continued to bear the clear stamp of liberal British values bestowed on it by its fairy godmother, the *Observer*. The *Observer* also helped it to wider foreign news coverage than most African weeklies can afford.

As a weekly, though, it remained but a puny rival for the daily *Northern News*, the champion of Welensky and the Federation, and of white rule in Southern Africa. In 1961, the *News* was there to promote the cause of Katanga against the United Nations; in 1962, to attack the Afro-Asian move to impose economic sanctions against South Africa. But in 1963 a gradual shift of policy took place, to accommodate the independence that was by then inevitable. By October 1964, the retiring editor had managed to earn for himself an honoured place at the independence celebrations!

Soon after independence, rumours began to circulate that the Argus was considering selling the newspaper to the Heinrich Syndicate, which had started two papers of its own, the Sunday *Zambia News* and the daily *Zambia Times*. Heinrich's major interest was in beer, but he launched, not very successfully, into newspaper publishing, and appointed as his editor Titus Mukupo, who since leaving the *Mail* had been running a small news service, the Central African News Agency, to keep sympathisers abroad in touch with the independence struggle. Why the Argus should have wanted to sell at all is something of a mystery, for *The Northern News* was flourishing and in no danger of competition from Heinrich, and one can only surmise that it foresaw some possible political embarrassment, as a South African-based concern, in continuing to publish a paper in an independent African country. Whatever its reasons, however, this particular deal was overtaken by another event.

This was the surprise entry towards the end of 1964 of a new force into the Zambia Press scene. On 12th November, Lonrho, formerly the London and Rhodesia Mining and Land Company, which has long had land, mining, ranching and other interests in the three countries of the Central African Federation, announced to its shareholders that it had bought control of Heinrich's, and with it, of the *Zambia Times* and the *Zambia News*. On 24th December, Argus confirmed that it had sold *The Northern News* to Lonrho, and the group found itself in control of the only two dailies, and the only Sunday newspaper, in Zambia.

Lonrho has been remarkably reticent about its motives in

acquiring these newspapers. Enquiries addressed to the group's head office in London have been abortive; and the Company Report for 1964 (published in March 1965) makes only the briefest reference to "the subsidiary publishing interests of Heinrich's Syndicate Ltd.," and no reference at all to the purchase of *The Northern News*. The Chairman's report, made in April 1965, refers to none of the newspapers. But speculation that the motive must in fact be fundamentally political is borne out by the fact that Lonrho also made some attempt, early in 1965, to gain control of the only remaining Zambia paper of any consequence, the *Central African Mail*, which was once more in need of a backer when David Astor found himself forced for financial reasons to withdraw his capital.

Whatever the ultimate significance of the change of owner-ship, however, changes have taken place in the *News*. The *Zambia Times* predictably was closed down, and the *News* emerged in July 1965 as the *Times of Zambia*, once more the only daily in the country. It had a new editor, Richard Hall, formerly Managing Editor of the *Mail*, who set about tuning it to a pitch to attract African, and not solely European, readers.

Under Lonrho, *The Northern News* continued—and at the end of 1965 was still continuing—to use the news services of the Inter-African News Agency (I.A.N.A.), the Rhodesian agent of the South African Press Association, and this fact tended to colour its foreign reporting. The story on the Security Council debate on economic sanctions on South Africa in February 1965, for instance, was told from a strongly 'Western' angle. Coverage of European and American news was generous, in proportion to news of Africa. But domestic reports were generally sympathetic to Government, and editorials scrupul-ously respectful. Even when, true to the traditions of the white-controlled Southern African Press, it lectured striking railway workers nearly every day for a week in April, it was careful to quote President Kaunda's own strictures on the men as a text. When it did step out of line, in May, and complained of the President's threat to retaliate should Southern Rhodesia take economic action against Zambia following a Unilateral Declaration of Independence, it was again speaking with the voice of its cousins in the newspaper family to the south. Only with the appointment of Hall as editor, did the tone of the editorials begin to reflect real popular preoccupations—they

4

attacked apartheid and the imprisonment of its opponents in the Republic, the Smith government in Rhodesia, with a new conviction; and dealt with domestic problems with a greater insight.

But the evidence of divided loyalties in the *News* had already convinced the Zambia Government that it needed a Press of its own; so when the *Central African Mail* found itself in financial difficulties, it decided to step in to save the paper which had given the struggle for independence so much loyal support. Negotiations were completed for the purchase of the paper, which was announced on July 30th. The official statement explained that Government intended the *Mail* to become in due course "a truly national newspaper", and that it should "reflect public opinion of all shades in Zambia, suppressing no comment or criticism or view point which is sincere and constructive, since conflict and controversy are the lifeblood of a newspaper, and the main basis of its influence on its reading public. The Government will endeavour to expand the circulation so that full and accurate information and explanation of its own policies and plans, its actions and achievements, can be presented to as much of Zambia's population as possible."

Kelvin Mlenga, editor of the *Central African Mail* at the time of the takeover, has remained editor of the renamed *Zambia Mail*. Indeed, the wording of the official statement is so close to Mlenga's own phrases in defining the role of the Press in Africa, that one is entitled to guess that he had a hand in drafting it. Mlenga will certainly want to retain as much independence as possible in the policy of the paper, and certainly in the first few months under Government ownership very little has changed either in tone or content. But he himself would probably be ready to admit that since Independence, the paper had found itself in something of a political vacuum, which the closer identification with government might well help to fill. The *Mail's* raison d'être had virtually been the struggle for political freedom, and this objective gained, it had no positive ideology to continue to drive it forward. Government's very need to project itself, and to advance its own campaigns, should be a source of energy in the future, as well as a potential source of conflict, so that this unique experiment of taking over an existing private newspaper, with a marked liberal personality, will be worth watching with some attention.

CHAPTER 7

EAST AFRICA

As in South and Central Africa, the Press in British-ruled East Africa was largely a European creation; and this fact has left its mark on the newspapers of Kenya, Uganda and Tanzania today. The centre of gravity of the white settler papers, which are still the dominating force in the Press throughout the area, remained in Britain. Their editors prided themselves on their place in the British Empire, and felt involved with events in Europe rather than in the rest of Africa. And because they also prided themselves on carrying the traditions of Fleet Street out into the colonies, they saw as their major function the transmission of news. The point is worth making, because the African Press tradition as developed in West Africa, tended to be first of all a tradition of political lobbying and campaigning. Whereas in West Africa, newspapers developed as a voice to express the protests of the ruled, in East Africa they were from the beginning vehicles for the culture and concepts of the rulers, with the considerable resources of white capital at their command.

Newspaper history in Kenya dates back to the turn of the century, soon after the Uganda railway had 'opened up the country' for European trade and commerce, and incidentally introduced a vigorous Asian community into East Africa, which was destined to play a considerable part in building its Press. It was in fact a Parsee, A. M. Jeevanjee, who, having made his fortune as contractor for supplies for the railway, started the weekly *African Standard* in Mombasa in 1902, with the help of an English editor-reporter named W. H. Tiller. This was the modest beginning of the most powerful Press group in East Africa today, the *East African Standard*.

Even in those days, an "attenuated Reuters service" of news found its way into the paper. Jeevanjee soon sold out to an English partnership, Anderson and Mayer, and Anderson's son was still in 1965 Chairman and Managing Director of the company. In 1910 the renamed *East African Standard* moved up country to the new commercial centre, Nairobi, and the *Mombasa Times* was set up in Mombasa to take its place. Several small newspapers had already come and gone in the new capital. The weekly *Leader of British East Africa*, founded in 1908, was the only one that survived, but the *Standard* was soon able to eclipse it by producing a daily edition from May 24th—Empire Day—1910. The *Leader* stopped publication in 1923.

The *Standard* was, and remained consistently for nearly sixty years, the voice of settler demands for more independence from Whitehall, for funds and soldiers to deal with 'the natives', for aid in developing the land. But relations with the Colonial Administration were not so strained as to prevent the Governor of Tanganyika from inviting the *Standard* to set up a newspaper in Dar-es-Salaam in 1930, and so the *Tanganyika Standard* was born, to be followed much later, in 1953, by the *Uganda Argus* in Kampala. Uganda already had a weekly newspaper in English, the rather staid *Uganda Herald*, but this too could not survive competition from a more adventurous and better produced daily, with the resources of an inter-territorial group behind it.

After the 1939-45 war, the directors of the *East African Standard* decided that the 'image' of their newspaper needed some refurbishing if they were to adapt themselves to a changing future. The 60th Anniversary Issue of the East African on 16th November, 1962, describes the reasoning behind the shifts of policy in the 1940's and 1950's in the following terms: "The growing discontent in India with the status of a subject people began to set in motion the stirrings of new thought in Africa as well. A constant and careful appraisal of the policies of the many famous English language newspapers of India showed that these newspapers were out of sympathy with the national aspirations of the Indian people and that in consequence the nationalists had to establish their own newspapers in the interests of their movement. When subsequently independence had been attained, these famous newspapers had long ceased to exert any influence upon public affairs and a new set of newspapers had earned the respect of their people. This lesson from India was to influence the policy of the *East African Standard*."

It might perhaps have been more morally creditable had

these changes been introduced for reasons of principle rather than expediency: but instructions were given to the three English-language dailies and the Swahili weekly (*Baraza*, founded in 1939) to take care in "airing the needs of all communities", to pay attention to the "dignity of the individual irrespective of race." Designations by tribe or by race began to disappear from news reports, and African and Asian names to appear occasionally in the letter columns. However, despite the new and admirable intention to 'lead' (presumably white) public opinion, anyone who saw the *East African Standard* during the years of the Mau Mau rebellion (1952-54) might have been forgiven for seeing it as an extremist settler mouthpiece. It expressed all the white hysteria, all the angry settler demands for more and more repressive action by the Colonial Office, that made this the ugliest period in Kenya's history. And even afterwards, in the period of progressive constitutional reform preceding independence, Tom Mboya, Minister of Justice and later of Economic Development, remembers that "the Kenya Press consistently stated we were moved not by nationalism but by emotionalism, and thus led Europeans into doubting whether there was such a thing as African nationalism—until in 1960, when Mr. Macleod said Kenya must eventually be an African State, they were shocked into realising their Press had never told them the truth. They made—or tried to make— African leaders into objects of scorn, and encouraged their European readers to regard them as 'irresponsible agitators.' As for Kenyatta, the Press led the Kenya Europeans to believe that he would never return . . . What sort of service to the future of their readers was this?"

Mboya refers only to "the Kenya Press." But the Press then was the *Standard*, and his strictures must be taken as applying first of all to it. The most lurid of the settler publications of those days, however, was *Kenya Comment*, mouthpiece of a right-wing settler group led by Sir Ferdinand Cavendish-Bentinck. Sir Ferdinand was the Speaker of the Legislative Council, who resigned in 1960 in protest at the promise of an eventual African majority in the House. His paper has passed away with the ancient order; but it had a talent for sheer bigotry that deserves to be recorded as a reminder of what white-owned newspapers were capable of inflicting on their readers. In 1958 Mr. Ernest Vasey, then Kenya Minister of Finance, later Sir

Ernest, was reported as saying on television while in London, that "to anybody who believes in democratic principles, an African majority (in the Government) is inevitable." *Comment* the following week produced a string of insulting insinuations that managed to accuse him, without actually using the phrases, of being an upstart Jew suffering from an inferiority complex because he was not as good as a Kenya gentleman!

"For some while the writer has been suspicious of Mr. Vasey's intentions," began an editorial headed 'Can we afford Mr. Vasey?' on March 28th, 1958. "It has seemed that the apparent refusal of the Minister of Finance to support European enterprises such as tourism, settlement and various commercial developments, has been because of some obscure doctrinaire political policy. It has been said that Mr. Vasey has some very left-wing friends, and is bent on pursuing a course which will end us up in the arms of Russia. This is hard to believe when one knows Mr. Vasey, it is even harder to believe when one reads of anti-semitism in Poland, Rumania and Russia which would make the machinations of Streicher pale into insignificance. No, the accusation of a strong left-wing influence and bias does not hold water when examined.

"It is of course known that the Minister and his wife are very friendly with Tom Mboya, it is also known that Mr. Vasey has been Mboya's adviser and mentor, but the advice can just as easily have been good as bad.

"To try and see something dark and sinister in the Minister's behaviour is to give him credit for more depth than he in fact possesses. Mr. Vasey is an ordinary, nice, little man, who by virtue of his background has possibly not been able to grow with the responsibilities and honours which have been thrust upon him."

Those were swashbuckling days. Today, the *Kenya Weekly News*, published in the agricultural centre of Nakuru, is no longer what the *Observer* once described as "the white settlers' social and political register", but is striving for a reputation as a 'responsible' paper. The *Standard* has apparently already earned it. Asked when this transformation actually took place, one young Kenya journalist replied promptly, "13th December, 1963"—the date of independence! To put the change on so cynically precise a date may be a little unfair. But Lord Delamere, for long believed to be a major power behind the

Standard, was nearly as abrupt in his change of attitude to Kenyatta, who from being despised as the evil genius behind Mau Mau, became in a few short months the man whom "we have to thank" for the peaceful transition to independence. Lord Delamere publicly thanked the new Prime Minister in a television interview on Independence Day.

Ownership of the paper has not changed, since the *East African Standard* decided on a policy of 'responsible' support for an independent African Government, and nor has the interest—that of the European minority—that it represents. With due caution, it may be expected to support those among the conflicting political forces in the country that it sees as most likely to advance these interests. But it tries now to speak to, if not for, a wider section of the population, and that excessive provincialism that characterised the paper in the past has given way to a broader concern with local and domestic affairs. African news, and not an account of Lady X's garden party, occupies the bulk of news space. Government statements get main headlines, photographs of the President figure regularly on the front page. Former links with the South African Press Association, whose Reuter beam used to be received in Nairobi as the main source of international news, have been broken, and news comes through the Kenya News Agency, though the paper also subscribes to Reuters general service direct. The letter column flourishes, and African and Asian letter-writers now predominate over Europeans. If 'white' institutions—ranging from Winston Churchill to Christmas turkeys—still occupy an appreciable number of column inches, they no longer do so at the expense of all else.

Until 1965, however, staff remained almost entirely white, and the paper boasted that all its journalists are British-trained. *Baraza,* the Swahili weekly, on the other hand, has had an entirely African staff since an African editor was appointed for the first time in 1961. He is Francis Khamisi, a former member of the Legislative Council. Khamisi says that he has full editorial freedom, and feels at present no conflict in working for a white-owned paper in independent Kenya. The main problems, he finds, spring from difficulties of communication—*Baraza* has already part-time correspondents in the main towns, but he would like to be able to expand coverage outside the urban areas. Here, lack of sufficient telecommunication facilities, and even transport, are in the way of any newspaper that seeks to achieve genuine nation-wide coverage and distribution. And this is where the Standard's rivals, the 'Nation Group' papers, score over their competitors.

East African Newspapers Ltd. was first registered in 1959 in Nairobi, by Michael Curtis, former editor of the London *News Chronicle*, and a white Kenyan, Charles Hayes, who ran a Swahili weekly called *Taifa Kenya*. Its main financial backing, however, has come from the Aga Khan, many of whose Ismaili followers have settled in East Africa. Ever since he bought 50,000 shares in January 1960, the Aga has bought regularly, and at the beginning of 1965 he held 737,250 of some 800,000 shares issued. The Thomson Organisation supervised the setting up of the papers, and the buying and installation of plant. It also had originally some money in the venture, which has subsequently been withdrawn, although rumours have persisted that Thomson was somehow "involved in the Nation." These seem to have gained circulation mainly because of Thomson's known interest in gaining a foothold in East Africa, an interest deeply resented by the nationalist Press. When in December 1964 *The Nationalist*, Dar-es-Salaam, accused the Press Lord of being the real power behind the Nation, it received prompt denials both from Michael Curtis, Chairman of East African Newspapers, and James Coltart, Managing Director of the Thomson Organisation.

The *Daily Nation* and the *Sunday Nation* both started publication in Nairobi in 1960, followed by a Swahili daily, *Taifa Leo* (formerly *Taifa Kenya*). An attempt was made in 1962 to establish a separate *Uganda Nation* in Kampala, with the idea that a separate Tanganyika edition would also be brought out in Dar-es-Salaam, for the group intended from the beginning to function on an inter-territorial basis. But the Uganda experiment proved too costly, and lasted only a year, so the Tanganyika plan too was dropped. Instead, the *Daily* and *Sunday Nation* are distributed in all three countries, with special outer pages for each edition of the Sunday paper. Ventures into 'vernacular' publishing in Uganda and Tanganyika, however, proved more successful. In 1960 the Nation bought control of a former Katwe (Kampala) newspaper *Uganda Empya*, run by E. M. K. Mulira (now a member of Parliament), and brought it out as a daily, *Taifa Empya*, first in English, and from 1961 in Luganda. And in 1962 it bought a half share in *Mwafrika*, run by Robert Makange, in Dar-es-Salaam. Until it finally stopped publication early in 1965, *Mwafrika*, with a circulation of nearly 14,000, seemed to be the most successful of the Tanganyika weeklies.

The Nation papers were an entirely new experience for East Africa. If the character of the *Standard* had always been essentially provincial, the Nation tried to bring a new professionalism and sophistication to local journalism. Technically, the papers were first-class, printed on web-offset machinery that at the time of its installation was not only the most up-to-date in Africa, but a proto-type unique in the world. And the tabloid format, liberal use of pictures and jazzy sub-editing and lay-out brought for the first time in East Africa the concept of the newspaper as entertainer. The Nation papers go for glamour.

The group has also the most extensive news staff in all East Africa, having full-time correspondents in every region. Advertisements excluded, up to 75 per cent of the *Daily Nation* is taken up with news—though sport and 'human interest' stories tend to push political items into corners, and coverage of the world outside Africa is sparse. There is a women's page, complete with fashion pictures from London and Paris; a "tell your fortune by the Stars" column; and a week-end supplement including film reviews, pictures of film and 'pop' stars, television stories, cartoons and social gossip. The letter page is on the whole more trivial than that of the *Standard*, dealing mainly with such matters as pen-friends, or complaints about the manners of the young.

Yet despite efforts to gain a popular image as a voice of Africa, the Nation papers are regarded still as foreign papers, rather than indigenous products. African politicians have been bitterly suspicious of them, accusing them of building up one leader against another; and in January 1964 both the English newspapers were banned from Tanganyika altogether, for a period, for "distortion of news about Tanganyika" at the time of the army mutiny in Dar-es-Salaam. Since it is common knowledge that the papers are steadily losing money, it is difficult for Africans to avoid the conclusion that their backers have political, as much as financial, ambitions.

Part of the difficulty clearly arises from the fact that, in spite

4*

of the Nation's declared intention to train African journalists, the staff on the English papers for a long while was all white, except for an Asian journalist, Chota Karadia, and an African reporter, George Githii. Karadia tells a story that illustrates the paper's inhibitions at the time. In June 1963 he wrote a warmly appreciative review of Josiah Mwangi Kariuki's book, *Mau-Mau Detainee*, which was published in the *Daily Nation*. Practically the entire white staff threatened to resign in protest, and a second review, more reserved, written by someone else, was published in the Sunday paper. Until an African editor, Hilary Ngweno, was appointed, it is even alleged that discriminatory rates of pay were offered as between ex-patriates, local whites and local non-whites.

By 1965 new efforts had been made both to introduce more African staff, and to adjust editorial policy to reflect African preoccupations. The English papers have remained cautious, in that they have been careful to align themselves firmly behind the President; but *Taifa*, rather interestingly, since its readership is the highest of the three (nearly 40,000 daily) and almost entirely African, has tended to support the ebullient and left-wing Vice-President, Oginga Odinga.

Some negotiations have been reported in the past between Government and the *Nation*, which led to speculation that the paper might be taken over officially. As long as no serious conflict between Press and official policy occurs, however, it is generally felt that it is highly unlikely that Government will wish to incur the tremendous burden of running its own daily paper. The appointment of a new editor in mid-1965, however, may possibly bring the group closer to the present African political leadership, for the new man is George Githii, who since working as a reporter on the *Nation* in earlier days, has been Private Secretary to the Prime Minister and then Personal Assistant to the President.

Thus the most powerful and liberally financed newspapers in East Africa are still white- or foreign-owned and controlled. But as long as the Press in East Africa has existed, there have also been smaller, popular papers, many of them run by Asians. Unlike Africans, Asians have been able to accumulate some capital to enable them to finance newspapers, most of them published in English and Gujerati, for their own community: at the same time as Jeevanjee was launching his

African Standard in Mombasa, *Samachar* was appearing in Zanzibar, and as a weekly in Gujerati and English it was still publishing in 1965. *Zanzibar Voice* was founded in 1922, and it too survived into 1965. While Kenya has produced not only a series of Asian-owned weeklies, but three dailies: the *Kenya Daily Mail* of Mombasa, founded in 1926 and still publishing; the *National Guardian* and the *Daily Chronicle*, both in Nairobi. The *Daily Chronicle* especially deserves a place in Kenya's Press history, together with its companion weekly, the *Colonial Times*.

The *Chronicle* was edited before the 1952 Emergency by Pio Pinto, the courageous journalist who after seven years detention under Emergency Regulations, edited the Pan-African Press newspapers until his assassination in February 1965. Pinto turned his paper into far more than a communal organ, for he voiced the demands of Africans as well as Asians for social justice and a share in government. He was an associate of the African leadership, and lent his support to Kenyatta's Kenya African Union; and though the *Daily Chronicle* was unable to survive the Emergency, the *Colonial Times* did, supported by a small number of Asian businessmen who struggled to keep alive one liberal voice in an otherwise rather barren scene.

But the vast majority of the peoples of East Africa are African; and they have been the worst served by the Press. Low literacy rates, political repression (particularly in Kenya) and above all the lack of any strong middle class (such as has existed in South Africa, for instance) able to accumulate the capital needed to invest in a newspaper, have hampered the growth of popular African papers. Most of those newspapers that during the colonial period were directed at an African readership, were either sponsored by Missions, or by Government, as a safety valve to divert political energies from the developing militant nationalist organisations. Among the mission papers, the most successful is probably *Munno* in Uganda, which was founded by the Catholic White Fathers in 1911. After the upsurge of political feeling caused by the banishment of the Kabaka of Buganda in 1953, *Munno* became a political as well as a religious organ, and later a voice for the Democratic Party defeated in the 1963 election. *Munno* is now one of the three Luganda dailies in Kampala. But there have been for fifty years numbers of small, often localised, mission papers throughout the region—the Catholic *Rafiki Yetu*, dating back to 1925, and the more recent Anglican *Rock* in Kenya, among them.

The Colonial Office on the other hand seems to have turned its attention to the question of newspapers for Africans only in the 1950's, when it was beginning to feel the pressures of mounting demands for political progress. In Uganda, the only area where an African Press did already exist, it was decided not to start new newspapers, but to establish a Government Information Service, which would supply general news as well as official information to local newspapers. But in Tanganyika, a series of more than 20 local papers, run by district councils, native authorities and growers' co-operatives, were established with Government support, apparently to encourage interest in local affairs; and three Swahili papers in the capital, which were handed over to a "trust" in 1958. *Mwangaza*, a daily, died at the end of a year, for financial reasons; *Baragumu* was taken over by the Nation group in 1960; and *Mambo Leo*, which achieved a circulation of 30,000 weekly, continued publishing for a further couple of years. Of the local papers, one weekly, one fortnightly, and six monthlies were still appearing in 1965, when of all the similar ventures in Kenya, only one, a Swahili weekly called *Sikio*, survived. The Tanganyika papers had, for all their Government sponsorship and even supervision, at least been African-run. But in Kenya, the Kenya Vernacular Press, set up in 1952 just before the outbreak of the Mau Mau rebellion, was quite frankly intended as a counter to nationalist ideas, and editors were European, instructed to "encourage" the expression of African opinion—provided that it supported the general objectives of Government! A Government subsidy was even provided for *Tazama*, a Swahili weekly published by the Standard group and therefore an instrument of the settlers. Since African public opinion had by 1952 already crystallised in passionate opposition to Government, and the foundation of the Vernacular Press was in any case accompanied by the systematic repression of those independent African publications that did exist, the experiment was bound in the long run to fail; though there is no sure way of telling now what impact consistent anti-nationalist propaganda in what were practically the only papers available to Africans, had at the time.

Yet, in spite of all the difficulties, an African-owned and controlled Press has existed in East Africa, throughout the years of colonial rule. In Uganda, where missionary activity was in early days most successful and most intense, the spread of mission education provided an African readership, by the beginning of the century, that was totally lacking in Tanganyika (under German rule until the 1914–18 war) and Kenya (set aside for settler occupation, and not the encouragement of an African educated class). Thus the earliest African papers emerged in Buganda, the ancient kingdom in Uganda, where a prosperous ruling class did exist, and the literacy rate was significantly higher than anywhere else in East Africa. In Katwe, a tin-roofed African village just outside Kampala that is laughingly referred to as Kampala's Fleet Street, ill-printed, frequently libellous newspapers have been springing up and dying out at a rate to defeat the historian, since the early years of this century. *Ebifa mu Uganda* was established in 1907, *Gambuze* in 1927, *Dobozi Iya Buganda* in 1928. *Uganda Eyogera* and *Uganda Empya* (now *Taifa Empya*) were both founded after the war, in 1953, *Uganda Eyogera* becoming the campaigning voice of the Uganda National Congress, ancestor of the present ruling Uganda People's Congress. Under the veteran U.N.C. leader Joseph Kiwanuka (now a Member of Parliament, but in the 1950's practically as often in jail as out of it, whether for 'seditious' publication or political activity), it led, together with Mulira's *Uganda Empya*, the fight to bring the Kabaka back from exile. The two papers led the campaign to boycott the Royal Visit to Uganda in 1954, and it is a measure of the power of the Luganda Press at the time that the boycott was an outstanding success.

Kenya too had a political African Press, established well before the Second World War. Helen Kitchen, in her study of the African Press published in 1956;[1] estimated that there were forty or fifty papers for Africans before 1952, ranging from those sponsored by missions or by Government, to what she calls 'extremist news sheets'. Jomo Kenyatta was editing *Muigwithania* in 1925; and the Kenya Central Association of the 1920's and 1930's, and the later Kenya African Union, of which Kenyatta was President, sponsored local and national publications, mostly in Kikuyu. After the war, what seem to have been

[1] *The Press in Africa*, editor Helen Kitchen, Washington, 1956.

dozens of one-man political broadsheets were appearing, edited by the political leaders of the time; Achieng Oneko, later Minister of Information, ran *Ramogi*, Francis Khamisi, in 1965 editor of *Baraza*, had his *Mwalimu*, and Oginga Odinga, in 1965 Vice-President of the Republic, was helping to run the *Nyanza Times* at Kisumu. The *Times* was set on a comparatively sound financial footing when Odinga was able, through his recently started Luo Thrift and Trading Corporation, to buy a printing press from the *Daily Chronicle* in Nairobi; Oneko brought *Ramogi* to Kisumu in the wake of the new press, and soon the Luo Thrift Press was printing half a dozen publications in Kikuyu, Luo, Kikamba, Swahili, and Maragoli. But all these except only the *Nyanza Times*, were suppressed with the Emergency of 1952, and those African publications that remained were instructed to publish in Swahili, to facilitate censoring!

When political life returned to 'normal' in the post-Mau-Mau period, some African publications revived. They still laboured under special disabilities, however, because the State of Emergency was not repealed in the Kikuyu areas of the country (including Nairobi) until 1959, and among other restrictions this prohibited the formation of a national political party. No newspaper, then, could draw on the financial or distribution resources of a national organisation. Those papers that did establish themselves were duplicated, and local. One such was *Uhuru*, organ of the People's Convention Party in Nairobi, which supported Tom Mboya's candidature for the Legislative Council. An old copy dated 1958 has a leading article in English, the rest being in Swahili. The editorial is a vehement attack on the Emergency Regulations, and quotes Nkrumah and Lenin (who is not mentioned by name, the quotation being the well-known one beginning "Man's dearest possession is life.") Inside are news items on the progress of the campaign for more seats in Legco; a profile of a party member and trade union leader; notices of meetings, and letters to the editor.

The only African-controlled printed paper to survive from freer days before the emergency, was the *Nyanza Times*, which within the strict limits of censorship had somehow managed to retain its reputation as the champion of Jomo Kenyatta even when to advocate Kenyatta's release was a legal offence.

In the much freer atmosphere of Tanganyika, formerly a Mandated Territory under the League of Nations and after the Second World War a United Nations Trust Territory, several private publishing ventures were started in the early 1950's. *Zuhra*, a weekly in English and Swahili, was started by Robert Makange, later editor of *Mwafrika*; the conservative *Bukya na Gandi* was set up in Bukoba in Northern Tanganyika, boasting of its dedication to "truth, tact and tolerance"; and *Tanganyika Mpya*, also in Bukoba.

But the real ancestors of Tanganyika's modern political Press were the early duplicated organs of the Tanganyika African National Union (TANU). *Sauti ya Tanu* comprised in 1957 one or two duplicated sheets of party news in English and Swahili, and statements on policy by the party leader, Julius Nyerere. The usually reasoned and moderate tone of *Sauti* contrasts sharply with the indignation of Kenya's *Uhuru*, reflecting the more leisurely pace of Tanganyika's independence struggle and the absence of a strong white settler community to obstruct African advance. But the battle did grow in intensity and the TANU leadership were soon convinced of the need for a strong party Press as an organising force among the people—Tanganyika is an enormous country, with very little urban concentration of population even today—and a voice for party policy that would be necessary not only during the freedom struggle, but after independence. The Tanganyika leaders had two advantages over their colleagues in Kenya and Uganda—they had a single relatively well organised national party (no rival to TANU was ever of very real consequence, and the party had support among whites and Asians as well as Africans); and in Swahili a lingua franca spoken almost everywhere in the territory. So the ambitious venture of the National Times Press, launched in 1959 by TANU leaders, with Nyerere as Chairman, to publish an English daily, a Swahili daily and a Gujerati weekly, was the first of several attempts to challenge 'foreign' monopoly of daily newspaper competition. The National Times was under-capitalised, however, its equipment was out of date, and though for a time an English newspaper was published, called *The National Times*, under Nyerere's own editorship, the dream of a daily remained unrealised.

Thus it is that when independence was won between 1961
and 1963 by each of the East African territories in turn—by
Tanganyika in December 1961, Uganda in October 1962 and
by Kenya and Zanzibar in December 1963—such African
newspapers as existed were still in no position to compete with
either the Standard or the Nation. TANU, in 1961, ran one
printed weekly in Swahili, *Uhuru*, but the only other independent African weekly, Makange's *Mwafrika*, was soon to be
forced for financial reasons into partnership with the Nation.
In Uganda, though *Uganda Eyogera* survived, *Uganda Empya*
had already been taken over by the Nation before independence;
and in Kenya, the *Nyanza Times* still stood alone. Brave
attempts at independent publication had been made in
Zanzibar, where both main political parties—the Afro-
Shirazis and the Zanzibar National Party—published duplicated news-sheets, but *The Worker*, a trade union periodical, had
been confiscated twice in 1962 alone, and ZANEWS, a small
information service run by Mohamed Rahman Babu (now a
Cabinet Minister in the United Republic of Tanzania), was
seized no less than five times in the same year. Since both the
Standard and Nation papers were distributed there, Zanzibar's
situation was no different from that of the countries on the
mainland.

The African leaders recognised clearly enough that sheer
lack of competition was helping the two big groups to continue
blundering along, with a political ineptitude that on occasion
amounted to sheer contempt for African opinion. One example
of this ineptitude was the incident on the *Daily Nation* in June
1963 over the review of 'Mau-Mau Detainee.' Another was the
failure of the *Tanganyika Standard* to give any but cursory
recognition to what, to every African, was a great political
victory—the achievement of Self-Government on April 30th,
1961. On April 29th, the day the new cabinet was announced,
which would lead the country to Independence, the *Standard's*
main headline, stretching across the full width of the front page,
dealt with the fate of British colonial servants whose contracts
would come to an end with independence: "Compensation on
'Instalment Plan': Scheme for Ex-patriates Announced." And
it repeated its mistake two days later, when the new Government took office, when only two stories in the entire paper
dealt with the country's new constitutional status: a 23-line

blocked-in piece on the front page announcing that the Bishop of Central Tanganyika had called for prayers for the new rulers; and a double column at the bottom of the page "Uganda Africans will celebrate May 1st." Among the reports that were considered more important than self-government were one on the annual conference of the British Conservative Party's Commonwealth Council, and another on a delay suffered by the Queen on a Mediterranean cruise! Significantly, it was the *Uganda Argus*, which had never been entirely without competition from an African Press, that was consistently the most sympathetic of the Standard papers to African aspirations.

But the task of developing effective competition was a daunting one. Constitutional advance had in none of the four territories brought the economic advance that would make African-owned private capital available to establish newspapers on a commercial basis. Even in Katwe, the time had already passed when it was possible to buy an ancient flat-bed and produce a moderately successful weekly. Since the advent of the Nation, production standards have risen, but the numbers of newspapers have dwindled, leaving by 1965 only two dailies, *Munno* and *Taifa Empya*, neither of them African-owned—though the definition is arguable in the case of *Munno*, since the Catholic Church is now headed by an African Archbishop! E. M. K. Mulira estimates that it is no longer possible to start a new newspaper in Uganda with a capital of less than £10,000, so much have salaries increased on the one hand, and the demands of the readers grown on the other.

Any new attempt at newspaper publishing, then, had to be seen as a heavy financial responsibility, to be undertaken for political and not for commercial reasons. It would have to be financed by Government, by a political party or a political grouping, or—as has happened in one case at least—with foreign support, given on a political and not a commercial basis.

It was the Tanganyika Government that first confronted the problem. In April 1962, just after independence, TANU decided to turn *Uhuru* into a daily, and provide it with a companion English-language daily, to be called *The Nationalist*. Already the Tanganyika leaders were finding that the demands of nation-building, and of the strongly anti-colonial policy to which they were increasingly committed, imposed on them policy decisions that led them into conflict with interests in the territory, and with many of their former 'friends' abroad. Nyerere's warm support for Kenyatta (only recently released from detention) alarmed many of those who had looked upon him as a reliable friend of "the West;" and so did his Government's active support for the African liberation movements in Southern Africa. It was clear that these policies should be presented to the public by Government itself.

But the difficulties in implementing this resolution turned out to be unexpectedly great. At the end of 1965, *Uhuru* was still a weekly; and *The Nationalist*—established first because of its greater international impact as an English paper—did not appear for the first time until April 17th, 1964. Its immense cost to the party makes *Uhuru's* advent as a daily unlikely for some time.

The Nationalist is published by the Mwananchi Printing and Publishing Company, on whose Board sit senior TANU officials and Government Ministers. The editor-in-chief is Joel Mgogo, a leading TANU member, who was also at one time Chairman of the Tanganyika Broadcasting Corporation. James Markham, an experienced Ghanaian journalist who worked with Nkrumah in the days of the *Accra Evening News*, was brought in as Managing Editor, and staff were recruited in Tanganyika and abroad. Several of those who were accepted turned out, ironically enough, to be former ex-patriate staff members of the *Tanganyika Standard*! The dearth of trained African journalists was indeed so great, that the only recruitment could be among those already working on other papers, at least until such time as those students sent abroad for training should return.

The Nationalist is the best edited and presented of all the African-controlled papers in East Africa. A little larger than tabloid size, it is printed on a modern rotary press from the German Democratic Republic, and usually runs to eight pages. Although sub-editing is still weak—and, in common with other African papers it relied too often at the beginning on trivial 'filler' material from feature agencies—the professional standard and news coverage have improved enormously. The paper now provides excellent coverage of African news, stressing liberation struggles in Southern Africa, and news of Zambia, Kenya, Congo, and Algeria. There are cartoons and photographs to lighten a rather heavy text, which may run to full-page coverage of a political speech, an economic analysis, or the background to Zanzibar's 1964 revolution.

By basing itself firmly on news, including extensive foreign coverage, *The Nationalist* has avoided the parochialism that afflicts many Government papers elsewhere; and by retaining a policy of free comment in its correspondence column, it has managed to retain the impetus of conflict. Indeed, conflict has at times invaded the editorials themselves: for instance, an attack on West Germany in 1965 followed an equally vehement attack on East Germany in 1964. In this, the paper reflects the fiercely independent, but sometimes ideologically uncertain, attitudes of Government.

The very presence of *The Nationalist* also seems to have acted as a restraint on the *Standard*, if not on the third Tanzania daily, *Ngrumo*. *Ngrumo* is, since the death of *Mwafrika*, the only Swahili daily, owned and edited by an Asian, R. B. Thaker. It is a poor production job, but more lively, and sometimes also more politically radical, than any other Dar-es-Salaam paper. It specialises in sensation, political or personal, and since it occasionally dares to print first and check afterwards, if at all, it sometimes comes up with the kind of scoop that endears a popular newspaper to its public. It is passionately anti-colonial, rather than nationalist, and seems to speak for an unorganised, and not solely African left wing.

Since the Zanzibar revolution in 1964, and the subsequent union with Tanganyika, the Tanzania Press has increasingly found itself forced into a posture of defending Government policy against hostile foreign criticism: the United Republic is alleged to be harbouring Chinese communist 'infiltrators,' to be training revolutionaries from the countries of the South as guerrillas; and even, on occasion, to be plotting the overthrow of neighbouring African governments. These complaints have been made in Britain, the United States and West Germany—and they have provoked a strenuous reaction. *The Nationalist*, as Government spokesman, has not only roundly denounced foreign imperialists in terms far stronger than any used during the struggle for independence, but had to explain Government's policy of non-alignment in the cold war, and full commitment to the freedom fighters in Southern Africa, in analytical terms which are comparatively new to Tanganyika. Another reaction has been the appearance of a small but immensely colourful fortnightly called *Vigilance Africa* in English and Swahili, dedicated to "Scientific socialism and African Unity, against Colonialism and Imperialism." This devotes considerable space to documentation, to activities of co-operatives and trade unions, and analyses of the role of international institutions such as the World Bank, in addition to the predictable preoccupations of Congo, Rhodesia and South Africa.

Most Dar-es-Salaam papers also circulate in Zanzibar, where resources for ambitious newspaper ventures are simply not available. But the Zanzibar Government does publish a weekly information broadsheet called *Kweupe*, which contains analysis and exhortation as well as local information; and apart from the well-established *Samachar* and *Zanzibar Voice*, there are two other Swahili weeklies, one independent—*Afrika Kwetu*—and the other published by the Afro-Shirazi Youth League. The Federation of Revolutionary Trade Unions publishes a fortnightly, *Mfanya Kazi*.

Uganda, which followed Tanganyika to Independence, also embarked on a new newspaper venture, this time not by the ruling party, but by Government itself. The Government Information Service started a daily newspaper, *Omukulembeze*, and a series of vernacular weeklies. It is interesting that it should have been decided to put what finance was available into what must only be a local paper (Luganda is not widely spoken outside Buganda)—whether the decision reflects dissatisfaction with the two existing Luganda dailies, *Munno* and *Taifa Empya*, or simply a conviction that publication in a local language would mean closer contact with the people, or at least an influential section, has never been explained. But *Omukulembeze* has not been a success. It remains the smallest of the Luganda dailies, and has no influence on a national level.

The two most significant developments in the Uganda Press since independence have in fact not involved Government directly, nor even, formally, the ruling U.P.C. They are faction papers, in that each represents a trend within the party rather than the party itself. The first was the *African Pilot*, started just after Independence, in December 1962, in Katwe—as if to confound all generalisations about the future of Kampala's one-time Fleet Street. Though the *Pilot* supports the

U.P.C., it is generally regarded as a spokesman for the party's left wing, and one of the most frequent contributors has been John Kakonge, General Secretary of the U.P.C. until he was ousted in 1965.

Much closer to the attitudes of the present leadership is the English weekly *The People*, published for the first time in March 1964. It is owned by the Uganda Press Trust Ltd., which in turn was promoted by the Milton Obote Foundation, Peace with Freedom Incorporated, New York, and an organisation called World Wide Partnership, Bonn. Chairman of the Trust is Erisa Kironde, a senior U.P.C. man, and the directors include three U.P.C. Members of Parliament representing the Foundation, and three representatives of each of the overseas organisations. Although at one stage there was an idea that *The People* might be an official party paper, it is not, as it seems that the capital would have been more difficult to raise if final control had rested with the U.P.C.

In its first two years, the paper has tended to find itself trapped between two roles—on the one hand as unofficial spokesman for Government, and on the other as independent 'popular' paper. It has too much of the staid quality of a Government organ—static photographs of foreign visitors on official occasions, cautious comment, big headlines reserved for Ministerial Statements. But it also strives for popularity with too many of the trivia of the commercial Press. Old-fashioned lay-out and type faces make matters worse. Features, in contrast to those in *The Nationalist*, are often culled from foreign agencies; the 'pop' charts are reported; and half a page is occasionally devoted to undistinguished columns such as one entitled 'Wonders of Humanity', which collects items reading "Ho! What a big stomach—Philip Vazonir, U.S.A., ate seventy-seven hamburgers at one sitting." The paper also apparently keeps half an eye on its foreign backers, for though international news is sparse, space is found for a picture of Dr. Adenauer writing his memoirs, and for lengthy treatment of visits by German delegations.

One issue, however, has stirred *The People* with that sense of political commitment that pervades *The Nationalist*, and *Pan-Africa* in Nairobi. This is the Congo. Editorials do not appear in every issue, but when they did, in the period January to March 1965, nearly every one was on the Congo. Their main content has been an impassioned plea for an end to foreign intervention, and, in spite of the American financial involvement in the paper, attacks on U.S. policy there. So strongly does *The People* feel that comment often invades the news columns, and at least one report on mercenary activities ended with two paragraphs demanding their immediate expulsion and an end to the fighting!

A letter column is not as regular a feature as it is in the *Uganda Argus*, but when it appears, it also contains genuine conflict of opinion.

Only in Kenya, then, of the four East African territories, was there by the end of 1965 no official Government or party newspaper. Kenya was the first East African country to take broadcasting under State control, and the first to start a national news agency. Afterwards, the Government seemed content to let the matter rest, at least as long as the existing Press remained 'responsible.' Foreign newspaper attacks, which for a time made a strong case for a Government organ that would be able effectively to counter them, have abated since a series of political setbacks for the Kenya 'left' in mid-1965. And perhaps the strongest argument against investment in a Government paper (which would have to be a daily if, in competition with the Standard and the Nation, it were to be effective at all) is the cost, which *The Nationalist* has already proved to be inevitable. But the gap left is a large one, only inadequately filled by the brave but haphazard fortnightly, *Pan Africa*, and its companion Swahili weekly, *Sauti ya Mwafrika* (the voice of the African). These have been published since Independence by the Pan-African Press, with which is also now associated Odinga's *Nyanza Times*. Kenyatta was himself originally a main shareholder, and so were his daughter Margaret, and Oginga Odinga; but the main energy behind the project was Pio Pinto. These papers are turned out, according to one of those who helped set up the press, on machinery that "has seen fifty years of local history." Full-time editorial staff has seldom consisted of more than the editors of the three newspapers, and such voluntary help as they can command, so neither production nor the standard of journalism is of a very professional level. Pinto's death in February 1965 was a blow that was expected to kill the scheme altogether.

But a young Australian replaced him, who has managed to retain that refreshing spirit of belief in a new Kenya and a new Africa, of indignation at injustice and oppression, that is missing in all the other Kenya papers. Foreign news is sparse, partly because the paper cannot afford to pay outside contributors. Editorial policy is still unobtrusively left of Government.

So independence has brought to East Africa as a whole some new African-controlled newspapers, notably *The Nationalist*, *The People*, and *Pan-Africa*. But none of these is anything but an economic liability; and all find competition with the big groups a heavy burden. None can afford correspondents abroad (though *The Nationalist* had a part-time correspondent in London for a while), which leaves them at a disadvantage especially in relation to the *Standard*, which has a well established London office.

The big groups, for their part, have been treading very warily. More radical policies by the African Governments, however, which could be forced upon them by the needs of economic development alone, or by Pan-African pressures, could end the honeymoon at any time; and then the Kenya and Uganda leadership would feel the want of an effective African-owned daily Press. The very lack of such a voice could lead Governments to restriction, or even suppression, of existing papers, which they might not otherwise find necessary.

CHAPTER 8

THE CONGO

THE CONGO, AS in other matters, is an exceptional case. Belgium's extreme paternalism there expressed itself in social development—workers' housing and welfare services—that was a model to the continent; and in a disregard for political progress so complete that a proposed thirty-year-programme towards independence, published in 1955, was greeted as a revolutionary document. Primary education was widespread enough to produce a literacy rate of between 35 and 40 per cent by 1961; but secondary education was neglected, and by the date of Independence in 1960 there were no more than twenty-six African graduates in the entire territory.[1] Trade unions on a purely industrial basis, were encouraged to develop after the last war; but political institutions of any kind were totally forbidden (the vote was used for the first time in local government elections in 1957). And with strict colour impartiality, the Belgian Government excluded white settlers as well as black Africans from all participation in political decisions. These were made by what Colin Legum[2] has called the "Trinity of Power" in the Congo—the Administration, Big Business (the great companies exploiting the Congo's mineral resources), and the Church (which until 1946 had a monopoly over education throughout the country).

These are not conditions in which a vigorous local Press is likely to grow. In fact, Press freedom was not included in the rights detailed by the "Charte Coloniale" of 1908 under which the Belgian Government assumed responsibility for the administration of the colony, after the public scandal of King Léopold's personal rule. In 1922 a Government ordinance made the publication and distribution of any journal subject to official permission, and this situation was not changed until the eve of Independence. Information was to be developed as a virtual Government monopoly.

[1] Catherine Hoskyns, *The Congo Since Independence*, O.U.P., 1965.
[2] Colin Legum, *Congo Disaster*, Penguin Special, 1961.

This was done through Inforcongo, which Legum has described[1] as "perhaps the most brilliant—and in some ways the most intelligent—propaganda machine ever created. This Information Service of the Congo encouraged the Belgians to believe—and they honestly, if uncritically, did believe—that their colonisation of the Congo was a cause for national pride, and that the Africans loved and honoured them for their civilising mission. Nobody knows how much was spent on Inforcongo. It must have been considerable. But its success was not because of the money spent on it. It had a good story to tell, of solid economic achievement and of steady social development. It had a consistent policy in which it believed— benevolent paternalism. Its tone was positive, unfailingly courteous, severely practical and high-minded, like the man who inspired it, Pierre Ryckmans, for long the Congo's most legendary Governor-General. 'Rule in order to serve . . . this is the sole excuse for conquest. It is also its complete justification'."

This eccentric policy paid off by creating a favourable public image for Belgian colonialism; and as far as Belgian interests were concerned, a fund of propaganda experience to be drawn on in the crises of 1960 and afterwards. But the cost was the extraordinary, almost total isolation of this great and populous country at the heart of the African continent. Nowhere in English-speaking or French-ruled Africa—or even, arguably, in the Portuguese colonies—were perspectives so rigidly confined. English-speaking Africa lived within the context of the Commonwealth, and its Press reflected, with all its shortcomings, world events and the evolution of public opinion abroad; Africans, however few, travelled to Britain and the United States, and elsewhere. French-ruled Africa, strictly orientated as it often was to Paris alone, developed as part of a French empire, and African leaders were absorbed into the structures of French culture and French governmental institutions. But the Congo, until the very last minute, knew only itself. No habit of public discussion on the one hand accustomed the people to question what they heard on the radio or read in the Press; no open lines of communication on the other enabled them to put their own views to the outside world. These grotesque circumstances had not a little to do with the tragedies that followed Independence.

[1] Op. cit.

Considering the restrictions hedging all publications but official ones, however, there have been a remarkable number in the Congo, some of them dating from the days of Léopold himself. In 1958, 354 publications were counted, including nine dailies; and the oldest monthly among them, *Minsamu Miayenge*, was founded by the Swedish Missionary Society at Matadi in 1891. By 1919 Katanga, home of the Union Minière and the major mineral exploitations in the Congo, already had a daily paper, *Le Journal du Katanga*, founded as a weekly in 1911; and predecessor of *L'Echo du Katanga*, which ceased publication only in 1962. In 1927 *Le Journal* was joined in Elizabethville by *L'Essor du Congo*, which in 1961, as a gesture to Katangese 'independence', changed its name to *L'Essor du Katanga*.

The first Léopoldville daily was *Le Courrier d'Afrique*, established in January 1930, followed by *L'Avenir Colonial Belge*, a weekly founded in 1920 which turned over to daily publication ten years later. It was not until after the war, however, that other provincial centres had their own daily papers: *La Feuille de Chou* (a Jadotville supplement for *L'Echo de Katanga*) started in 1952; *Le Stanleyvillois* (1952) and *L'Echo de Stan* (1954), Stanleyville; *Centre Afrique* (which became a daily in 1953), published in Bukavu; and *La Chronique de l'Ouest* published in Kolwezi in 1958.

All these were publishing just before Independence. All were run by settlers, though in several cases, notably those of the two Léopoldville papers, they also retained close links with newspaper groups in Belgium: *Courraf*, financed in part by Belgian Christian Democrats, was associated with *La Cité*, Brussels, and *L'Avenir* used matrices sent out by the La Meuse Press group in Belgium. None of them appear to have been viable economic ventures, and those that had no links with backers abroad were usually secondary enterprises of printing companies—according to a study made in 1958 by the Centre d'Etudes Liberales de Liège, "most of the newspapers of the Congo should be seen as visiting cards by which the printers could recommend themselves periodically to the kind attention of their clients."[1]

As settler papers, then, all could be said to defend the

---

[1] Quoted in the weekly broadsheet of the Centre de Recherche et d'Information Socio-Politiques, Brussels, July 1959.

interests of their white readers; *Le Stanleyvillois* in particular did
so to such effect that it was widely accused of racialism. Apart
from *Courraf*, whose Christian Democratic policy may be
assumed to have been laid down for it by its backers, the only
exception to the rule was *L'Essor*, which rather than reflecting
settler preoccupations, was reputed to be the voice of "certain
industrial circles in Katanga."[1] Its high production standards,
wide news coverage and its subsequent record during the
secession of Katanga, would certainly be consistent with
backing from business interests operating there—but no
inquiries made through the Union Minière have received a
reply.

Until 1959, however, when the main restrictions on publication were lifted in preparation for Independence, expression of
policy was so limited that no newspaper could expect to have a
serious impact on the political development of the country.
As Helen Kitchen remarks in her 1956 survey, "the political
role of the Press in a country without any legislative bodies is a
somewhat anomalous one," and when Congo papers dealt
with political or social issues, they tended to be Belgian, and
not Congo, issues. A copy of *Le Courrier d'Afrique* in 1944, for
instance, deals exclusively with European news—the war,
international conferences, items on the resistance movement
against the Nazi occupation—with the exception of a column
of brief items on French Equatorial Africa, and a report on a
road programme for Orientale Province.

Apart from a few earlier mission papers, the first African
newspapers seem to have been stimulated by the trade union
activity permitted after the war. *Le Syndicalisme Indigène* was
founded in 1946, and *Mbandaka* in 1947. The first editor of
Le Syndicalisme Indigène was José Lobeya, who later took over
a Léopoldville Catholic fortnightly, *La Croix du Congo*, when
in 1954 it expanded into a general information paper. And the
first editor of *Mbandaka* was Justin Bomboko, later Foreign
Minister in both the Lumumba and Ileo governments.

In the 1950's, the Belgians took pains to see that the newly
literate masses, products of the extensive primary school
system, should be served with 'suitable' newspapers. The
Catholic Church (which co-operated closely with the Adminis-

[1] Weekly broadsheet of C.R.I.S.P., 10th July, 1959.

tration in most things) started some of them, including *La Croix du Congo*, a Léopoldville fortnightly in Lingala, *Kongo ya Sika* in Kikongo, *Conscience Africaine*, whose one-time editor was future Premier Joseph Ileo, and *Présence Congolaise*, founded in 1956 as a weekly supplement to *Le Courrier d'Afrique*. African editors were appointed, in the hope that this as yet highly restricted outlet would act as a safety valve against more radical demands. By 1959, *Présence Congolaise* was entirely African run, under the editorship of a leader of Lumumba's Mouvement National Congolais (M.N.C.), Joseph N'Galula. Its rival in Léopoldville, however, *Les Actualités Africaines*, a weekly supplement to *L'Avenir* also started in 1956, seems to have enjoyed less freedom of comment, and to have been more closely supervised by the parent paper.

Inforcongo itself published several papers: *Nos Images*, an illustrated fortnightly in Léopoldville, published in four local languages and French; *La Voix du Congolais*, a Léopoldville monthly, and *L'Etoile Nyota*, an Elizabethville bi-monthly in French, Lingala and Swahili. *Nos Images* had an African editor by 1955, and a one-time editor of *La Voix* was Michel Colin, Minister of Information after Independence.

All these were of course cautious publications—Mrs. Kitchen says that they all stressed "progress through diligence and hard work." And even such independent papers as did emerge were no less timid. *Le Congo Prâtique* (subtitled 'The Congo Practises what it learns from the Europeans'), was an early example, boasting of being "an entirely independent and free newspaper published by Africans without distinction as to race, language or religion", and "not supervised by mission or Government."

Like the tribal and cultural associations which, outside the trade unions, were the only form of organisation permitted by Government, these newspapers, and the journalistic training provided at the University of Lovanium from October 1958, performed two significant functions. First, they brought into prominence and gave some professional experience to many future Congolese leaders. Apart from those already mentioned, Jean Bolikango, later a candidate for the Presidency, was actually Assistant Commissioner-General for Information before he roughly repudiated Inforcongo at the Brussels Round Table Conference in 1960; and the future General Mobutu, Chief of Staff of the Armed Forces and maker and breaker of governments, is a former editor of *L'Avenir's Les Actualités Africaines*. Mobutu was sent to Brussels on a training course in journalism and public relations in 1959. Second, they provided the primitive forms of later national institutions. For they quickly began to burst out of their strait-jackets. The first and most celebrated example is that of the Catholic *Conscience Africaine*, which in 1956 spoke for the first time of political independence for the Congo, warning that "the concept of a Belgian-Congolese Community was deeply suspect in African minds." The Community idea was being canvassed at the time as an alternative to self-government. But the paper carefully qualified this outburst by adding that it felt no hostility towards Belgium, provided that it undertook sincerely and unequivocally to co-operate in achieving independence "within thirty years." This was a year after Professor von Bilsen had presented his "Thirty-year Plan for the Political Emancipation of Belgian Africa."

It was *Conscience Africaine's* manifesto that sparked off the Abako (Bakongo tribal association) leader Kasavubu's public statement that the Congo would not wait thirty years, and the events that led in 1958 to the formation of Patrice Lumumba's M.N.C., the first national political party. A year after the manifesto, permission was given for the publication of two new independent weeklies in Léopoldville, *Quinze*, and *Congo* (which called itself the first African-owned weekly), and the way was at last open to the relaxation of the Press regulations of 1959.

Since the lifting of the licensing regulations was also accompanied by the introduction of other freedoms, including the freedom to form political parties, it led to a mushroom growth of African political newspapers. These, the first real journals of opinion in the country, resembled the campaigning nationalist organs that have been characteristic of political struggles everywhere in Africa. One of the most important was Lumumba's *Independance*, published in Léopoldville. Catherine Hoskyns, in '*The Congo Since Independence*', remarks on the impression of "activity, youth and excitement" which the paper was able to communicate. It was first of all an organising instrument—two pages were devoted to party activity, formation of branches, accounts of meetings and appeals for assistance—and a vehicle for projecting the personality of the leader, through pictures, poems and eulogies.

She also remarks on the influence of Ghana stamped on photographs, comment and letters—for Lumumba had developed a close relationship with Ghana and Nkrumah since his visit to the Accra All African Peoples' Conference in 1958.

The M.N.C. had another paper, *Uhuru*, which ran for a while as a daily in Stanleyville, until it collapsed for financial reasons. Abako had a weekly in Léopoldville, *L'Echo du Bas-Congo*, and two bi-monthlies, *Notre Kongo* and *Kongo Dieto* (in Kikongo). Antoine Gizenga's Parti de Solidarité Africaine had a weekly in Stanleyville, *Solidarité Africaine*, and Justin Bomboko's UNIMO had two weeklies in Coquilatville, *Alerte* and *Equateur Mambaza*, in Mongo. While Anicet Kashamura's left-wing CEREA, for a while published *Verité* as a party organ.

It was a brave but a brief flowering. Whereas in most parts of Africa, independence has brought the consolidation of at least some nationalist papers, in the Congo it has brought their virtual extinction. Although West German and Israeli sources are reputed to have financed for a while a paper to support the Adoula Government of 1962, *Afrique Réelle*, none of the African political papers seems to have been able to command sufficient resources to survive the stresses of the five years of independence. With the decline of the political parties themselves, their organs disappeared, and only the Abako papers have remained. The 'settler' papers, however, seem to have found financial backing. They have undergone a metamorphosis, and emerged in full command of the Congo Press scene.

The mass emigration of Belgians in 1960 made the survival of these papers, never in any case economically viable concerns, problematical. The white population had been no more than 100,000 at its peak. So they turned their attention to attracting African readers, reporting on political events, photographing African leaders, publishing pages in vernacular languages. The effect occasionally verged on the comic, as when *L'Essor du Katanga* in 1962 added a picture of an African woman to the masthead of its Woman's Page (Plaisirs de Femme), without altering a word of the content, which dealt exclusively with Paris fashions, cosmetics and (European) cooking.

L'Echo and *L'Essor* published in Elizabethville throughout the period of Katanga secession, but once secession was ended, Decoster, the publisher of *L'Echo*, was expelled. He continued

to publish his paper in Belgium for the ex-colons, and its place
was taken in Katanga by two new papers, *La Voix du Katanga*,
and *La Dépêche*, both still publishing in 1965.

The most important Katanga newspaper without doubt
remains *L'Essor*. It is one of Mr. Tshombe's oldest admirers,
having cheered him on throughout the secession, and lent
itself enthusiastically to the Katanga campaign to discredit
the United Nations. Catherine Hoskyns[1] describes an issue of
September 12th, 1961, just before the outbreak of hostilities
between the U.N. and Katanga, which features a speech by
Sir Roy Welensky, then Prime Minister of the Federation of
the Rhodesias and Nyasaland, attacking the United Nations,
quoted in full; an interview with M. Evariste Kimba, Katanga
Minister of Foreign Affairs, headlined 'Katanga est Prêt a se
Défendre'; two articles entitled 'Katanga—Bastion du Monde
Libre' and 'Sauver le Katanga' (reprinted from the conservative *La Libre Belgique*, Brussels); and an editorial that read
in part: "Our reason for fighting, and we are ready to fight, is
our absolute refusal to bow our heads and yield to intimidation
from foreigners, who are as ambitious as they are grasping.
Our glory is in our spiritual and material birthright, our
Katanga, sacred heritage of our fathers."

L'Essor in 1965 is still reprinting editorials from *La Libre
Belgique*, still running an all-white fashion page, and still
cheering on Mr. Tshombe. Its Katanga parochialism is still
there, though it does indulge in a 'Coup d'Oeil sur le Monde.'
Main foreign stories in a fortnight in October and November
1965 showed a heavy slant, however, not towards African
affairs, but anti-communist propaganda: a picture of a small
girl is captioned 'The Vietcong have made her an orphan';
there are reports on refugees from North Korea, on the Berlin
Wall, and a setback to the Soviet agricultural programme. By
contrast, a series carried over several days featured sport in
West Germany.

In Léopoldville, three dailies were publishing in 1965: *Le
Courrier d'Afrique*, *Le Progrès* (successor to *L'Avenir*) and a new
paper, *L'Etoile du Congo*. *Courraf* and *Le Progrès* still have their
companion weeklies, *Présence Congolaise* and *Les Actualités
Africaines*. *Courraf*, the biggest and most powerful of the three,
is a Kasavubu paper. Its editor, Gabriel Makoso, was jailed in

[1] Op. cit.

1960, and the paper itself closed down for a month, when he accused the Lumumba Government of allowing the country to fall "under a second kind of slavery." But it has acquired the status of the principal voice of established power since then. There is no regular editorial, but an effort has been made to give it an African, even Pan-African image (in November 1965 portraits of the thirty-six Heads of State of the Organisation of African Unity appeared on the front page, and Kasavubu was praised for "brilliantly defending the cause of his country" in face of threatened isolation by the O.A.U.).

But *L'Etoile* is politically the most interesting. What political conflict is reflected in the Congo Press, tends to be expressed here. Headlines are dramatic — "Scandale au sein de l'Assemblée d'E'ville"—and interviews with political leaders are sometimes healthily disrespectful. An interview with Prime Minister Tshombe in October 1965 was obviously designed to embarrass, and included the blunt accusation that his Government had squandered public funds. The paper appears to favour former Prime Minister Cyrille Adoula; and it covers African affairs—Algeria, South Africa, Rhodesia—more generously than the other dailies.

The forces that dominate the Congo Press today, then, are very little different from those that dominated it under Belgian rule. The indigenous products of 1959 and 1960 have nearly all vanished, and there seems little chance of revival. Editors of the established papers are now of course all African, and policies are aligned around current political personalities, so that in appearance none of them bears much resemblance to its predecessors in the 1950's. But there is no evidence that financial control has passed into new hands. The biggest enigma remains the position of the Union Minière, which has answered no enquiries about its connections, if any, with the Press, but is still the greatest single economic force in the territory.

It was the Union Minière that had the forethought to make 'President' Tshombe a present of a radio station at the time of Katanga secession. And it was through the Union Minière that the world received the scare story, during the UN-Katanga fighting of 1961, that an Irish company had been exterminated at Jadotville. U.M.H.K. had at the time the only reliable

communications system linking Kolwezi, Jadotville, Elizabethville and Ndola, while the U.N. had only field telephones.
The Union Minière could thus communicate across battle
lines, the Press knew that it could, and depended upon it for
information, and also, incidentally, on its facilities to transmit
their cables through Ndola to the outside world. Dr Conor
Cruise O'Brien, in charge of the U.N. Katanga operation at the
time, credits the Jadotville incident with having been instru-
mental in inducing Hammarskjöld eventually to "backtrack"
on his previous instructions to secure the end of Katanga
secession by force.

The past record of the U.M.H.K. in the field of political
manipulation is not such as to suggest that it is likely to be
ignoring the field of information today.

CHAPTER 9

L'AFRIQUE NOIRE

THE PRESS IN French-speaking 'black Africa' has never been as highly developed as that in the English-speaking countries. In part, this fact is linked with the generally low level of economic development, and the more selective, though intensive, system of African education, which produced so small a percentage of literates that figures were never published—except for the former United Nations Trust Territory of Cameroun, where literacy was estimated in 1950 as between five and ten per cent. And in part it was a consequence of French colonial policy, which by favouring direct rule from Paris, and drawing the African leadership into the machinery of metropolitan government, managed to shift the arena of conflict from Africa itself to Europe. It is consistent with this policy that there should have been a tax on the import of newsprint and printing machinery into the African colonies, but none on the import of newspapers, so that local newspaper production was penalised and the circulation of French papers encouraged.

There were a few newspapers in Senegal towards the end of the nineteenth century. This was the only West African country with a considerable white population, mainly of traders and colonial administrators. *Le Rèveil du Sènègalais* was founded in 1885; *Le Petit Sènègalais*, in Saint Louis, in 1886, and *L'Union Africaine* in 1896. M. Raymond d'Auriac, proprietor, editor and printer of *L'Union Africaine*, explained in an editorial that "Our expansion in Africa has for some years been such a preoccupation of our metropolitan press, that it would be useful to possess a newspaper on the West Coast that would serve on the one hand as a link between the traders of the metropolitan country and those of the colonies, and on the other among those of the colonies themselves."[1]

[1] Quoted by M. Ekani Onambélé, in a thesis on L'Exploitation de l'Entreprise de la Presse en Afrique au Sud du Sahara, 1965.

These were papers produced by Frenchmen for Frenchmen. D'Auriac in fact makes clear that he intends to circulate his paper in France as well as on the coast. No effort seems to have been made to reach African readers, and even mission publications seem to have been slow in establishing themselves, except in those territories—Togo and Cameroun—ruled before the First World War by Germany. A few of the early German mission papers were actually produced in vernacular languages, and most were printed in Germany. *Der Evangelische Monatblatt*, printed in Stuttgart, was already appearing in Cameroun in 1903, to be followed by *Mwendi ma Musoge* (Message of Peace) in 1906; *Elolombe ya Kamerun* (The Cameroun Sun—the first paper in Equatorial Africa to be edited by an African, M'pondo Akwa) in 1908; *Mulea-Ngea* in 1910; and *P'oa Mudi* (Sword of the Spirit) in 1914. There was also an official gazette, printed in Buea from 1908, and a fortnightly, the *Kamerun Post*, edited in Douala but printed in Germany, intended for the German commercial community.

Mia Holo, a Catholic monthly still published in Togo in 1965, also dates back to the German days before 1918.

Newspapers before 1930, however, were few and small. In Cameroun, *L'Eveil des Camerounais*, ancestor of the country's one daily today, *La Presse du Cameroun*, was founded around 1919, to circulate among French traders and civil servants. In Senegal, a spasmodic weekly, *L'A.O.F.*, appeared in 1907, as organ of the local section of the French Socialist Party, and as an early political paper, was not without significance. Among its subsequent editors was Lamine Gueye, one of the first African members of the French Parliament. And in Dahomey, several papers sprang up in the 1920's, among them *La Voix du Dahomey*, started in 1926, *Le Cri Nègre* and *La Phare du Dahomey*, which survived for 20 years. The latter two were remarkable for being both African-controlled and run, and they contributed greatly to the gradual national awakening that took place throughout French West Africa in the 1930's.

This was the decade of the first African elections to the French Parliament. They were limited to Senegal, but their repercussions were felt throughout West Africa, and in Senegal itself the campaigns led to a spate of news-sheets, most of them merely broadsheets, in support of one candidate or another. The campaign of 1932 between Blaise Diagne and Galandou

Diouf produced three newspapers, *La Bastille* for Diagne, and, for Diouf, *Le Périscope Africain* in Dakar and *L'Echo de Rufisque* in Rufisque. Although only a duplicated broadsheet, *Le Périscope* had a correspondent in Paris, and became a major source of news in the country. None of the three publications, however, had a long life. Diagne closed his down immediately after winning the election, when he thanked his readers warmly for their votes, and bade them farewell. But they had introduced a new public to newspapers, and more political papers followed, more or less long-lived, such as *L'Ouest Africain*, *Le Journal de Dakar*, *La Sirène Sénégalaise* (in St. Louis), and *Rumeur Africaine*, founded by Ibrahim Sow, who had collaborated with Diouf on *Le Périscope*.

The Ivory Coast had seen its first paper, *L'Indépendant*, in 1910; but the real journalistic awakening came around 1930, with the expression of nationalist ideas in print for the first time. A report of the official Documentation Française lists eleven publications, settler, missionary and African, between 1928 and 1938. In spite of the strict control exercised over the colonial Press, some of these papers attacked consistently both the colonial Government and collaborationist African chiefs: *L'Indépendant Colonial* and *Le Trait d'Union*, both established in 1930, *Deci Dela*, 1931, *L'Eclaireur*, 1935 and *Le Flambeau de la Côte d'Ivoire*, 1937.

Another development of the 1930's was the beginning of the only newspaper chain in French-speaking Africa: the establishment in 1933 of a weekly, *Paris-Dakar*, in Senegal, the enterprise of a French businessman, Charles de Breteuil, who had already started newspapers in Tangier and Casablanca (Morocco). By 1935, *Paris-Dakar* had become a daily. In 1938, it was joined by a paper in the Ivory Coast, *France-Afrique*, which changed its name in 1954 to *Abidjan-Matin*; in 1954 by *La Presse de Guinée* in Conakry, and in 1955 by *La Presse du Cameroun*. *La Presse de Guinée* was suppressed in 1958, when Guinea voted 'non' in the de Gaulle referendum, and became independent outside the French Community.

The de Breteuil papers were all originally intended for a predominantly European readership, with the exception of *Bingo*, a popular picture monthly of not very high technical standard started in Dakar in 1952, and intended to entertain the urban African youth.

In the rest of French West Africa, and the whole of Equatorial Africa outside Cameroun, there was apparently silence, though some of the Senegal papers had a circulation in other territories. And with the censorship imposed during the war, growth was halted even in those areas where a publishing tradition had been established.

But though the war and its aftermath brought no direct benefit to the African Press, it did bring a new political consciousness to thousands of Africans. Many had fought in the North African campaigns; others may have been made aware of the issues involved by the propaganda war between Radio Dakar (pro-Vichy) and Radio Brazzaville (Free French); and yet others by the campaign around the 1946 Constitution for the French Union, which promised extension of the franchise to Africans in the French possessions, and opened the way for African politicians to election to the French Senate and Chamber of Deputies. It was in the same year, 1946, that the first major African political party was formed, the Rassemblement Démocratique Africaine, at a Congress at Bamako in the Soudan (now Mali). The R.D.A. was an inter-territorial party, with sections in most of the West African and some of the Equatorial territories. Many of these, including the Parti Démocratique de Guinée and the Union Soudanaise (Mali), later formed the Governments of independent States.

Public opinion was therefore evolving; but Ekani Onambélé, in his thesis on the African Press already quoted, remarks on the paradox that in spite of this evolution, the Press did not seem to benefit—even after 1945, African newspapers sprang up only to die away again, as political parties formed and re-formed. He estimates the average life of the political papers of the 1940's as between two months and two years. In Dahomey, he points out, the Union Progressiste Dahoméenne alone published eight different papers between 1939 and 1959, to say nothing of two R.D.A. papers, five published by other parties, and nine trade union bulletins. The paradox can perhaps only be understood if one takes into account the structure of French administration, centralised in Paris, where African Members of Parliament had to operate within the machinery of French politics. This system tended to direct African political energies away from any single, specifically African, objective—independence of France was a minority

cry until after 1958—and towards alliances with French
political parties. The contrast with the history of parties of
national liberation in the English-speaking countries, which
had been founded on the demand for self-rule, is obvious. In
the British colonies, the objective was clear and defined:
independence. And its achievement demanded popular
agitation, and mass organisation. In the French colonies, the
role of the parties even after 1946, tended to be largely that of
mobilising votes for the elections. A continuous dialogue went
on among the leadership, the élite who were deputies and
senators, on the question of reform. But they did not feel the
need for a stable mass organisation to back them up, and
comparatively little of the sustained grass-roots campaigning
took place that could have demanded, or supported, the
establishment of serious party newspapers.[1]

These, on the whole, came later, in the 1950's, and notable
among them were *L'A.E.F.-Nouvelle*, Brazzaville, published
as an organ of the Parti Progressiste Congolais, by Felix
Tchikaya; *Afrique Noire*, published in Dakar to serve both
Senegal and the Ivory Coast, as official organ of the R.D.A.,
and edited by the future Ivory Coast President, Félix
Houphouet-Boigny; and *La Condition Humaine*, also published
in Dakar by a future President, Léopold Sédar-Senghor, as
mouthpiece for his political party. These were all party
political papers, established in the early 'fifties. Only
Cameroun had any variety of privately owned African papers:
L'Echo du Cameroun, Douala, *Dialogue*, *Le Petit Camerounais* (a
one-man venture run by one of the best known of the African
journalists of the time, M. Kala Lobe, who now works in Paris
for the political and cultural review, *Présence Africaine*), and
Les Nouvelles du Mungo were among the most successful. Unhappily, the political repression that followed the banning of
the major political party, the Union des Populations du
Cameroun, in 1955, and the consequent guerrilla war, put an
end to the growth of the independent Press; and stringent
Press control by the Ahidjo Government since independence
has prevented any resurgence. Many of the Cameroun's finest
journalists now work abroad.

A private Press in non-African hands, however, was growing.
In 1947 the Catholic White Fathers at Dakar started an

[1] Nor were there literate populations to sustain them.

information weekly, *Afrique Nouvelle*, printed on their own mission press. This was the first of the West African papers to aim at an inter-territorial distribution, and international news coverage. Under the liberal editorship of Père Joseph de Benoist, it developed first-class news coverage of French-speaking Africa, and maintained enough independence of administrative policy to ensure a steadily rising circulation among African readers.

In 1947, too, an eccentric publication was set up in Dakar, which had started in Conakry as *Les Echos Guinéens*. Now, as *Les Echos d'Afrique Noire*, it launched into a strident political career under the direction of a French couple, Anne and Maurice Voisin. Voisin was secretary of a local Producers' Co-operative. He is said to have faced libel suits under the colonial regime, but after 1960 left Dakar for Bordeaux, whence he attacked "arrogant and racialist" leaders in Africa.

By the end of the 1950's, the de Breteuil group comprised *Dakar-Matin* (formerly *Paris-Dakar*), *Abidjan-Matin*, *La Presse du Cameroun*, and *Bingo*. These were by far the most sophisticated newspapers in French-speaking black Africa. They were well illustrated (the press in Dakar had its own photographic laboratories, a rarity), and included international news coverage, and sporting and other special features. But in spite of the changes of titles, they had not accommodated themselves to an African environment, beyond the concession of a letter-page in *Dakar-Matin* of 'Opinions Africaines.' Although the most powerful force in the Press of French Africa—and the only daily newspapers in the region—they were still essentially European papers that happened to publish in Africa.

When between 1960 and 1962 all the French-ruled countries of West and Equatorial Africa gained formal independence, there were only three daily papers in the entire region, all of them belonging to de Breteuil. The new Governments had to make themselves heard through their party papers, which after struggling through the 'fifties as ill-printed or even duplicated broadsheets, acquired a new dignity as organs of governing parties. Senegal had *L'Unité*, Mali *L'Essor*, Ivory Coast *Fraternité*, Guinea *Horaya*, Congo (until the fall of the Youlou government in 1963) *L'Homme Nouveau*, Dahomey *L'Aube Nouvelle*, Central African Republic *La Terre Africaine*, Cameroun *L'Unité*, Upper Volta *Carrefour Africain*, Niger *Le*

Niger, Tchad *L'Unité*, Gabon *La Patrie Gabonaise*, and Mauritania *Mauritanie Nouvelle*—which was printed in Senegal, since Mauritania had not even a press of its own. Most of these were weeklies, except for *La Terre Africaine* and *La Patrie Gabonaise*, which were fortnightlies.

The difficulties in the way of turning any of these papers into dailies were enormous. There were far too few trained journalists, so that extra staff would have to be imported or specially trained. There was no reservoir of African-owned private capital, so the full burden of investment would fall either on Government or on the political parties. And except in Senegal, literate populations were so small that a daily paper could only be at best a doubtful commercial proposition. Only those countries that saw the venture as a political priority could be expected to make the effort. Mali, where *L'Essor* was turned into a daily in 1962, and Guinea, where *Horaya* became a daily in 1964, are predictable examples, since both regard mass political education as an essential function of government. But Niger too established a daily, *Le Temps du Niger*, as early as 1960; Togo founded *Togo-Presse* (*Denyigba*) in 1962; and at the end of 1964 the Ivory Coast Government bought *Abidjan-Matin* from de Breteuil, and turned it into *Fraternité-Matin*.

But seven countries—Central African Republic, Congo, Dahomey, Gabon, Upper Volta, Mauritania and Tchad,— still have no daily newspaper, except the duplicated bulletin of Agence France Presse or the local news agency (itself simply the distributor of A.F.P. news). However, *La Terre Africaine* in Central Africa, which in 1962 was a fortnightly, is now a weekly, and Gabon too has a weekly, *Gabon d'Aujourdui*. It is worth remarking that all these publications are in French, and that only in Togo (where *Togo-Presse* contains a page in the vernacular) and Cameroun is there any attempt at publishing in local languages. This again is a heritage of the French policy of 'direct rule', for education in colonial times was in French only, whereas in British territories primary education was frequently in a local language.

In spite of advances over the past few years, then, the Press in French-speaking Africa is weak. A glance at any of their newspapers will betray their poverty of production, of foreign and local news coverage, and of feature material. The de Breteuil papers have been an exception to this rule, in that they have had access to better machinery than the others (la Grande Imprimerie Africaine, Dakar, which printed *Dakar-Matin*, had until recently the only rotary machines in French West Africa). *Dakar-Matin* was able to publish a full page of photographs every day, and an illustrated supplement fortnightly; and all the papers in the group benefited from the services of correspondents in other African centres, in Paris and in London. But they failed in that they neglected to Africanise their staff—even now senior posts are held by Europeans—and to adapt themselves to the needs of an African readership, although by 1960 70 per cent of the readers of *Paris-Dakar*, for instance, were already estimated to be African. Even in 1965, their coverage of African news was inferior to that of *Afrique Nouvelle*, which from the beginning has aimed to identify itself with African interests. It has had senior African editorial staff for some time, and successfully established the image of a thoroughly based local paper, though it retains a clear Catholic ideological bias.

The problem for the African papers, on the other hand, all of them official organs of party or Government, is not one of orientation, but of presentation—and finance. They are descended—*Horaya*, *L'Essor*, *L'Unité*—not from the metropolitan 'information' tradition, but from a propagandist past, in the days of anti-colonial struggle. Then, their chief function was one of comment and exhortation. Reporting would normally be limited to party activities, and the speeches of party leaders. Professionalism was the last concern of their editors, who were often not journalists but politicians. And these papers were all the more important to the political parties they supported when African opinions and activities were so poorly reflected in other papers. Now they have a far wider role to fulfil, as information media as well as official exponents of Government policy.

For papers in French-speaking Africa, even more clearly than in English-speaking Africa, the choice has been between continuing to suffer from lack of professional experience and financial backing, and settling for foreign capital, foreign journalists, and agency material from abroad. The Ivory Coast has chosen the latter alternative with *Fraternité*, in that it still uses some French journalists, and foreign sources of feature material, although the paper is now owned by Government.

5*

The result is one of the most professional and informative papers in the region—but not one of the most politically exciting. *Horaya* (which has the advantage of a first class East German press capable of printing a sixteen-page paper at the rate of 15,000 copies an hour) and *L'Essor* prefer to rely on their own efforts. As a result, the papers are small, with only occasional pictures and few features. They are trimmed ruthlessly to necessities. *Horaya*, which is usually only four pages long, devotes the first page to Government news and policy statements, page two to national news (La Vie dans la Nation), and page three to Africa (La Guinée, l'Afrique). Its very economy is purposeful, and the analytical treatment of news gives the paper a tension which *Fraternité* lacks; but all feature material must be sacrificed. There is no room for the women's features, agricultural advice, educational material for children, and cultural matter that the richer papers of Ghana regard as essential to their role as mass educators. A very large part of the problem is still lack of skilled journalists, who would know how to make the best possible use of little space, and to make lay-out and presentation attractive.

But the biggest problem is that of news collection. No newspaper, apart from *Afrique Nouvelle* and the de Breteuil chain, has an efficient system even of domestic news collection, though *L'Essor* has some advantage in the highly developed local organisation of the Union Soudanaise (the national political party). The national news agencies fare very little better since nearly all of them were set up as distributing agents for A.F.P. rather than as collectors of news themselves. Guinea and Mali have received technical aid from Tass, the Soviet news agency, and Ceteka, the Czechoslovakian agency, and the Ivory Coast and Congo from Reuters, which has gone some way towards improving internal news collection over the past year or so; but none of them has anything like an adequate system of local correspondents, nor apparently sub-editorial and journalistic staff equipped to provide enough interpretive stories on international affairs. Letter columns too are few, and seldom play the part of opinion forum.

A development of the past two years, however, has been an effort by French concerns to repair the omissions of colonial days, and to give some active assistance to African newspapers. In Niger and the Ivory Coast, for instance, a French enterprise,

La Societé Nationale d'Editions Industrielles, has been brought in to help develop what is conceived to be eventually a chain of newspapers in French-speaking Africa. *Le Temps du Niger* and *Fraternité-Matin* have both had assistance from S.N.E.I., which sets up and runs printing works, and provides technical advice, and trains printers and journalists. Purchase of modern plant can be financed through La Societé de Financement de Materiel d'Imprimérie. Both S.N.E.I. and SOFIMA are subsidiaries of La Societé Nationale des Enterprises de Presse (S.N.E.P.), a state enterprise, with Press representation, originally set up in France after the last war to dispose of the confiscated assets of newspapers that had collaborated with the Nazis.

One of the directors representing the Press on S.N.E.P. is M. Max Jalade, a Member of Parliament, and former journalist on *Paris-Presse* and Paris correspondent of de Breteuil's *Paris-Dakar*. M. Jalade is the essential link with yet another venture, set up in Paris by M. Jalade and a young journalist called Jean Watrinet, who worked for a time in Madagascar on the main Malagasy daily, *Le Courrier de Madagascar*. M. Watrinet explains that his time on *Le Courrier* showed him how difficult it is for African newspapers to obtain suitable feature material, especially on foreign affairs, since the cost of a permanent Paris correspondent is prohibitive. He and his colleagues therefore conceived the idea of an agency in Paris that would deal exclusively with African and Malagasy papers, and act as a sort of 'own correspondent' for each of them. This agency is La Nouvelle Agence de Presse (N.A.P.), which already had in mid-1965 some fourteen regular subscribers in French-speaking Africa, and a total of twenty-seven or twenty-eight papers receiving occasional material. Among the newspapers making regular use of N.A.P. material were *Fraternité-Matin*, Abidjan, and *Le Temps du Niger*, Niamey; *Le Carrefour Africain*, Upper Volta; *La Semaine Africaine* and *La Voix Africaine*, Brazzaville; *Togo-Presse*, Lomé; *L'Aube Nouvelle*, Dahomey, and *La Terre Africaine*, Central African Republic. N.A.P. offers a weekly bulletin of news and comment, and undertakes special articles or assignments, such as covering the visit of an African dignitary to Paris. It has correspondents in main centres in France, and an office staff of nine, six of them journalists, and some of these Africans.

The bulletin is over forty pages in length, with separate sections for general information (political background and analysis), popular science, educational features (for instance on careers guidance, or advice to mothers), culture and sport. The scientific material is practical and simple, and so is the educational advice. It is in the pieces of political interpretation that the essentially French, rather than African, bias of the service is betrayed. An item on "re-establishing Peace in South East Asia," for instance, in the bulletin of 23rd February, 1965, is not so much factual, as an explanation and apology for French policy in South East Asia: "General de Gaulle's aim is in fact the true independence of Viet Nam, Laos and Cambodia. Africans and Malagasies should not wonder at this. Since his return to power in Paris, the President of the French Republic has based his whole policy on respect for the independence of every country." Such an article would not be out of place in an official government information service.

Additional features sent out from N.A.P.'s Paris office range from photographic strip stories from the cinema, picture puzzles and cartoons, to articles on fashion and cosmetics.

It is difficult at this early stage to estimate the long-term effect of a service such as this one on the development of the African Press. Already those papers that subscribe are the more varied and attractive for it. N.A.P. prefers to minimise its connections with the French State enterprises, S.N.E.P., S.N.E.I. and SOFIMA; but it is clear that they are far from irrelevant. The service is potentially an immensely powerful influence, and there is some real danger that subscribing papers may become virtual appendages to the French Press, rather than indigenous products. The only alternative is for African newspapers themselves to co-operate in the provision of foreign correspondent services. But this will prove far more expensive than a subscription of approximately £10 a month to N.A.P.'s weekly bulletin, and involves a degree of international co-operation that has so far proved difficult to achieve.

To some extent also, use of a foreign correspondent service in Paris tends to perpetuate the great language division in the African Press: the division between the French-language papers whose news is orientated towards the French-speaking world, and the English (and other language) papers that emphasise news of the English-speaking world. This is a barrier recognised in independent Africa as an obstacle in the way of African unity, a barrier which many African-controlled papers consciously strive to overcome,—by attempting a genuinely Pan-African news coverage. *L'Essor* and *Horaya*, and incidentally *Afrique Nouvelle*, are among the papers where this attempt is most obvious, just as in other regions of the continent the Press of Ghana, Algeria and Tanzania is outstanding for similar efforts. It is a problem constantly before the relevant commissions of the Organisation of African Unity, and probably soluble only in an international context.

CHAPTER 10

NORTH AFRICA

THE MOST ANCIENT Press in Africa fittingly belongs to its
oldest civilisation—that of Egypt. Egyptian historians date the
earliest newspapers as appearing in the eighteenth century.
There are records of periodicals published in French, during
the Napoleonic occupation of 1797; and certainly by the mid-
nineteenth century several regular newspapers were flourishing,
most of them the creatures of the Turkish regency. The
Egyptian Press, however, soon established itself as lively,
political and rebellious. Journalists of the time apparently
played a major role in the Arabi[1] revolt against the Turks in
1881, and Abdulla Nadim, the leading nationalist journalist of
his day, is credited with having taken his paper, printing press
and all, to publish 'from the battlefield' in the war with
Britain that followed in 1882.

The Egyptian Press was also from early times an international Press, in the sense both that it covered international
events, and that side by side with popular papers in Arabic
there existed newspapers in English and French. These were
intended to serve the growing foreign commercial community
that had settled itself at one of the great cross-roads of the
world's trade routes. *The Egyptian Gazette* (still appearing, in
1965, its eighty-sixth year) was publishing in the 1880's, in
English and French, news from Reuters and Havas on
revolutionary activity in Paris, sabotage in Dublin, Belgian
expeditions to the Congo, and the siege of Omdurman in the
Sudan. *The Gazette* did not fail to record the rebellion, from the
indignant point of view of the foreigners. An account from
"our own correspondent" in Suez ("delayed in transmission")
printed on August 18th, 1882, rather neatly recalls the flavour
of the time: "Some inquietude is felt today by the two or three
Europeans still left in this almost deserted town of Suez. Cut
off from free communications with the outer world, the Bazaar

[1] So called because it was led by Colonel Ahmed Arabi, Egypt's first modern
nationalist hero.

is now our chief source of information, and rumours of the most extraordinary description seem to increase in inverse ratio with the supply of our comestibles, which is daily becoming more meagre and costly." The correspondent goes on to describe the mass exodus of Egyptians from the town following a rumour that the British are to bombard it, and he concludes with evident disgust that they are all going "to join Araby."

It was in the late nineteenth century, too, that *Al Misr*, *Al Watan* and *Al Ahram*—all destined to play a part in twentieth century Egyptian politics—were founded. *Al Misr*, as organ of the liberal Wafd party, was one of the first papers to give publicity to the Free Officers Movement led by the Colonels Nasser and Neguib, between 1950 and 1953. Neguib himself wrote, anonymously, for *Rose el Yusuf*, a paper founded by a celebrated actress of that name, and edited by her son, Ihsan Abdul Qudus, still one of the country's foremost journalists. *Al Misr*, however, was banned by Nasser when he became Prime Minister in 1954, together with the Wafd party itself, because it had opposed the Nasser revolution, and advocated instead a return to parliamentary government. The editor of *Al Misr*, according to the International Press Institute's report 'Government Pressures on the Press', 1955, had been accepting bribes from the Farouk Government.

Nasser's reimposition of censorship (which had been lifted under Neguib), however, did not destroy the vitality of the Press. In 1956 Jean and Simonne Lacouture, in their study 'L'Egypte en Mouvement', were still able to say that "the Egyptian Press has lost none of its dash, although it is held in check by censorship", and to remark on the heated cultural debate—on the role of the writer in society, the virtues and failings of social realism—conducted even in the pages of official newspapers such as *Al Goumhuriya* and *Al Sha'b*. The political cartoons, for which Egyptian papers have been famous, may be both 'less scurrilous and less funny' than before the revolution. But except where Egyptian interests are directly involved (where Government policy must be reflected, and explained), it is probably little appreciated outside Egypt how wide is the range of editorial comment: there was in 1965, for example, a whole range of editorial opinion on the Indian-Pakistani war.

Most newspapers in Egypt were privately owned, until 1961,

when a new Press law was passed to bring all the main papers under the direction of the National Union, predecessor of the Arab Socialist Union, Egypt's single political party. According to the journalist Yusuf Seba'i,[1] "The Bill was drawn up for the people who believe in the Press as an instructive and directive cultural instrument, which may not be misused for commercial interests." The Constitution for the Press states in part that "the Press must be a mission rather than a commodity or commercial goods . . . it is not only the right of the Press to criticise, it is the duty of the Press to do so."

In theory, the party is supposed to supervise only, and not to interfere with the day-to-day running of newspapers, which is the responsibility of the journalists themselves. President Nasser, speaking at a Press conference held in October 1963, for delegates at an international journalists' conference, elaborated on the rights and duties of the United Arab Republic Press. "The Press is now owned by the Socialist Union," he said, "and the papers are run by boards of directors. The boards of directors, the editors and the staff have full freedom to express themselves in accordance with the provisions of the National Charter. No one has the right to demand the abolition of socialism, because this is against the Charter. Within the framework of the Charter, every journalist has the right to criticise and express his opinion in full. This guarantees a 100 per cent freedom of the Press."

There may be some difference of opinion over the President's definition of '100 per cent Press freedom;' but there is no doubt that the Press in Egypt today is a formidable force not only in the U.A.R. but throughout the Arab world. There are nearly 100 national and local publications in the country, led by four major national dailies: *Al Ahram* (The Pyramids), *Al Akhbar* and its sister papers *Akhbar el Youm*, and *Al Goumhuriya* (The Revolution). *Al Akhbar* is a popular paper, concentrating on foreign affairs, seeking out the sensational and strange; *Al Goumhuriya* is the paper of the Egyptian revolution, concerned first of all with domestic matters; but the most powerful, and the oldest, of the dailies is *Al Ahram*. *Al Ahram* is a paper of international standing, with wide news coverage (of the Arab world, Africa and Asia, East and West), and considerable space devoted to analysis and comment. Production is relatively

[1] Writing in *The Afro-Asian Journalist*, Jakarta.

poor—pictures are small, though numerous, and lay-out unexciting. But when *Al Ahram* speaks, it speaks with authority. It is edited by one of the rising stars of Egyptian politics, Mohammed Hasanain Haykal, who towards the end of 1965 took over the chairmanship of the Akhbar papers, and was expected to take over the Goumhuriya group as well (which includes, significantly, the English and French-language dailies).

One of the major achievements of the Egyptian Press to date is its news service. The Middle East News Agency was established as a co-operative concern by the papers themselves in 1956, and is now the biggest in Africa, run under the direction of the Socialist Union. It has not only a large staff within the U.A.R., covering all main centres with trained correspondents, but bureaux in thirteen cities abroad (principal coverage being in the Middle East, where are also the main buyers of the service), and thirty-five correspondents in four continents.

The second major achievement has been educational. Newspapers are expected to play a role in literacy campaigns, and to provide an outlet for creative writers in their cultural pages; and background information, articles on subjects ranging from health and social questions, to political analyses, are a regular feature of all newspapers. *Al Ahram*, for example, publishes a weekly supplement which includes a full page analysis, by the editor, of a current political, economic or social problem.

However, with the single exception of the Sudan, where the Press is also almost exclusively Arabic, Egypt remains the only country in Africa whose major dailies are neither in English nor in French. (The English and French-language papers published at present are intended for foreign communities inside the country, and are of only marginal importance). This means that their international influence is limited to the Arabic-speaking world, and in particular it means that they are isolated from the rest of Africa. But there is some evidence that this problem is not escaping the attention of the Egyptian leadership, and Heykal himself is reputed to be anxious to produce an English paper. He is already planning an organisation to distribute news and feature material in English and French, and putting one of his most talented assistants in charge of the project. If this is intended as a potential 'bridge' across the Sahara, it may prove an important one, for there is scarcely a newspaper in Sub-Saharan African that does not suffer from an acute shortage of suitable feature material.

Arabic has survived in Egypt as the language both of the masses and of the élite, partly because Cairo has been for centuries the main centre of Arabic learning; and partly because European domination in the colonial period was nearly always indirect. In the French colony of Algeria, however, and the Protectorates of Tunisia and Morocco, the influence of the European culture was more profound, producing a French-educated élite; and the first newspapers, established by settlers around the turn of this century, were in French.

The most powerful settler Press was that of Algeria, where most settlement took place, and by the 1950's there were eight daily newspapers in the country. The two biggest were also the loudest voices advocating 'L'Algérie Française—*La Dépêche Quotidienne* was controlled by the great land-owner, financier and settler politician Henri Borgeaud (and partly financed by the French industrialist, ship-owner and arms manufacturer, Schiafino); and *L'Echo d'Alger*, was run by Alain Vicomte de Serigny, landowner, wine-farmer, businessman, associate of Jacques Soustelle, and later of the army mutineers under General Salan who attempted a putsch in April 1961.'[1]

There were two other dailies in the capital, *Le Journal d'Alger*, which made some overtures to 'moderate' Muslims and was identified with the conciliatory policies of Pierre Mendes-France; and *Alger Républicain*, organ of the Algerian Communist Party. *Alger Républicain* was the only popular voice among the dailies, but it was banned at the beginning of the war of liberation, and its editor, Henri Alleg, arrested and tortured by the French authorities.

Oran had two daily newspapers, *L'Echo d'Oran*, an extreme right: t paper, and *Oran Républicain*, a Socialist organ linked in the days of the popular front with *Alger Républicain*. Constantine had one—*La Dépêche de Constantine*—and Bône *La Dépêche de l'Est*.

The nationalist movements on the other hand had only weeklies: *Algérie Libre*, organ of the Mouvement pour la Triomphe des Libertes Démocratiques (M.T.L.D.) under Messali Hadj; *La République Algérienne*, voice of Ferhat Abbas'

[1] De Serigny was actually tried with the army rebel Lagaillande in 1961, but acquitted. Cf. *Political Africa*, editor Ronald Segal, London 1961.

Union Démocratique du Manifeste Algérien; and *Al Bassair*, published by Ulema, the Muslim cultural organisation. During the war of liberation, which broke out in 1954, the Communist Party continued to publish its weekly *Liberté* underground, and the new Front de Libération Nationale, embodying militant elements from all the popular organisations, set up an Information Bureau in Tunis, where it published *El Moudjahid*, which also circulated clandestinely in Algeria. The F.L.N.'s underground system of communications enabled it, throughout the war, to counter French propaganda with its own, and so to lay the foundations for its own news agency, now the Algérie Presse Service.

None of the settler papers has survived. *L'Echo d'Alger* was suppressed by the French Government after the Salan putsch in 1961; *Le Journal d'Alger* fell victim to an O.A.S.[1] 'plastique' the same year: and after Independence most of the others decided to pack up and go. Only Borgeaud and his *Dépêche Quotidienne*, which effected a dramatic switch of policy in favour of democratic rule, decided to remain, together with *La Dépêche de Constantine*,[2] and the Oran papers. All these were nationalised after the Programme of Socialist Orientation was adopted in March 1963, providing for the nationalisation of French assets in Algeria. *Oran Républicain* was taken over as an F.L.N. journal, *Alger Mouriha*; *La Dépêche de Constantine* became *Al Nasr*; while the offices, plant and machinery of *La Dépêche Quotidienne* were commandeered to produce the main Algiers papers. With the seizure of his paper, his factories and his lands, Borgeaud's power was at last broken—a fact which to Algerians symbolised a liberation almost more important than the Constitution itself.

Alger Républicain—which the intrepid Alleg had brought out again immediately after Independence, apparently working from a hotel bathroom in Algiers—became an F.L.N. organ, too, in 1964, when the Communist Party was absorbed into the national party. The paper retained the leading members of its original staff, and remained in many ways the best of all the Algerian dailies. It was thoroughly professional, and was able

[1] Organisation de l'Armée Secrète, the settler rebel force that attempted to keep Algeria French through terrorism.

[2] According to popular legend, *La Dépêche de Constantine* had paid so much to the F.L.N. during the war for "protection" of newspaper and plant, that its owner, Morel, felt disinclined to abandon the investment!

to identify itself with popular opinion through a lively correspondence column in which political issues were argued out in
a manner rare among official newspapers anywhere.

There were, during the time of the Ben Bella Government,
three Algiers dailies: *Alger Républicain*, the F.L.N. daily *Le
Peuple* (which had an Arabic edition, *Al Chaab*), and *Alger ce Soir*,
an evening paper established in 1964 when the International
Organisation of Journalists helped to set up a new training
course for journalists in the capital. There were also dailies in
Constantine and Oran, and three national weeklies—*Révolution
Africaine*, *Révolution et Travail* (organ of the trade union movement) and *Jeunesse* (organ of the F.L.N. youth)—in addition to
L'Algérien, distributed among the Algerian community in
France. *El Moudjahid* became the party analytical monthly,
and *El Djaich* and *Révolution l'Université* appeared as monthlies
for the army, and the students. All these publications were the
responsibility of a special committee of the F.L.N.

The June 19th Movement, which overthrew President
Ben Bella in mid-1965, and established Colonel Boumedienne
at the head of a new government, seems to have put an end to
the extraordinary expansion of the Algerian Press between
1963 and 1965. *Alger Républicain* ceased publication, and Alleg
fled to Paris. *Le Peuple* and *Alger ce Soir* closed down, and *Al
Chaab*, which continued to appear in Arabic, and *El Moudjahid*,
now the main national newspaper, were at the end of the year
the only two remaining dailies. *El Moudjahid* also had a weekly
edition, in which F.L.N. news appeared, and *Révolution
Africaine* and *Révolution et Travail* were still publishing, though
the latter was by no means secure, since it had been highly
critical of the Boumedienne regime.

Révolution Africaine is probably the most interesting of the
remaining Algerian newspapers. It was established at the
beginning of 1963, as an international weekly, a voice for the
African revolution, whch, it was hoped, would circulate
throughout French-speaking Africa, and eventually have an
English edition as well. The idea was to produce a 'quality'
paper, with striking lay-out and liberal use of photographs and
original cartoons. Bureaux were set up in Paris, London and
Dar-es-Salaam to help ensure continental news and feature
coverage, and early issues featured liberation struggles in
Southern Africa, the economic programme of Algeria, the war

in Viet Nam, and the negro movement in America. However, for political as well as economic reasons, the international ambitions of the first numbers were never fulfilled. The English edition came out only once or twice, before disagreement between Jacques Vergès, first director of the paper, and the party, led to a split, after which Vergès published his own *Révolution* from Paris. *Révolution Africaine* in Algeria reconciled itself to being a national rather than an international paper, as far as correspondents and distribution abroad were concerned; but its mission remained that of keeping the continental struggle before the Algerian people.

What was striking about the Algerian Press in the first two years after Independence was not only its pan-African consciousness, but the sheer extent of its operation. Five dailies and three weeklies, all supported by the single political party, are an extraordinary undertaking in a country where 90 per cent of the people are illiterate, and the biggest circulation of a daily (that of *Alger Républicain*) was no more than 40,000. The Algerian Government is proud of the fact that it has been spending up to 25 per cent of its national budget on education, and it is clearly in the same spirit that this enormous investment was made in the Press, which is expected to play a primarily educational role.

But the change of government has meant, temporarily at least, a setback for the ambitions of the Press, and has lost to it not only the two most successful daily newspapers, but some of the most experienced journalists in the country, since they opposed Boumedienne.

The Press of neither Tunisia nor Morocco can match that of Algeria in vitality, in range, or in sense of purpose. Morocco had until 1964 a wide variety of newspapers, some of them outspoken in their criticism of the Government of King Hassan. In 1964, however, a number of newspapers were suppressed, including the organs of the left-wing opposition, the Union Nationale des Forces Populaires, and of the Istiqlal party itself, which had led the struggle for Moroccan independence. Those that remain are largely subservient to the Government, several of the biggest—among the most important are *Le Petit Morocain*, and *Maroc Informations*, Casablanca, Rabat—being the non-controversial descendants of papers founded by French companies during the Protectorate. As 'information' papers

which carefully avoid political involvement, and incidentally
select their news from a Mediterranean rather than an African
or even markedly Arab viewpoint, these have no parallels in the
'committed' Press of Egypt or Algeria; but they do have something in common with the independent commercial papers of
Tunisia. There are five daily newspapers in Tunis, of which
two—*Le Petit Matin* and *La Presse*—are French-language
'information' papers, largely non-controversial in character.
An Italian-language weekly, *Il Corriere di Tunisi*, is similarly
uncommitted, and serves the local Italian community. But
Tunisia also has its political Press, led by *El Amal* (Arabic),
organ of the ruling Neo-Destour party, and its sister paper in
French, *L'Action*. *L'Action* is the paper founded by Bourguiba
himself in 1934, as the instrument of his radical breakaway
movement from the more ancient and conservative nationalist
party, the Destour. There is in addition a second national daily
in Arabic, *Es Sabah*. *Es Sabah* supported the 'rebel' Secretary
General of the Neo-Destour, Saleh ben Youssef, against
Bourguiba in 1956, but after the rebellion had been crushed,
tempered its criticisms, and retained enough popularity to be
in 1965 the third biggest national paper.

By far the most important Tunisian paper today, however, is
not printed there, although it has editorial offices in Tunis, and
in Paris. This is *Jeune Afrique*, an illustrated weekly, and
probably the best produced publication on the continent. It is
printed in Rome, by photogravure, and compares, as its editor
intends it should, with the most expensively produced
European photo-magazines.

Bechir ben Yahmed, owner and editor of *Jeune Afrique*, is a
former Chef du Cabinet in the government that negotiated
Tunisian independence, Minister of Information after independence, and editor first of *L'Action*, and later of his own independent Tunis weekly, *Afrique Action*. *Jeune Afrique*, he says, is
Afrique Action under a new name, since the President opposed
the use of the name 'Action' without permission. Ben Yahmed
defines his policy as "for the *real* independence of African
countries; for the economic progress and education of the
African peoples; for the participation of young people in the
direction of their countries, which is now in the hands of
dépassé politicians; and against conservatism and dictatorship,
even of the left."

He publishes abroad because he finds himself free of political presses there—nowhere in Africa, he says, is there a really free Press. Because of the centralisation of airline routes in Europe, he is also in a position to distribute quickly and efficiently throughout French-speaking Africa. *Jeune Afrique* has a Maghreb edition, and one for Afrique Noire, and boasts a circulation of 100,000 built up over a mere six years.

Like the Algerian papers, *Jeune Afrique* stresses the unity of Arab and black Africa, and prides itself on helping to build a 'bridge' across the Sahara. Activities of the Organisation of African Unity are fully reported, and all of Africa's leaders, of north and south, receive space, and varying degrees of sympathy. Main attention of course is paid to the French-speaking areas, where the paper's influence is such that former Prime Minister Adoula chose to make his new proposals for a 'solution' in the Congo in 1964, through *Jeune Afrique*. There is also generous coverage of the United States and of main international events in the West, and some coverage of the Socialist world. The paper has a full-time staff of fifteen, and staff correspondents in Tunisia, Algeria, Morocco, Libya and Egypt, as well as travelling correspondents to cover Dakar, Abidjan, Yaoundé, Léopoldville, New York and Tokyo. In 1965 a correspondent was appointed to deal with South Africa.

So ambitious a venture has obviously required large financial backing of a kind not normally available in Africa. M. ben Yahmed explains that this has been obtained entirely on the basis of personal loans, which he has been able to repay, so that the magazine is self-supporting. It does get a good proportion of advertising—about eight pages, at approximately £300 per page, in a 40-page paper—most of which comes from large international concerns such as airline companies, and motor manufacturers in Germany, Japan, the United States or Rumania.

But *Jeune Afrique* is a paper for the intelligentsia. Neither it, nor any other north African publication, can reach across the Sahara to touch the consciousness of Africa's masses. In as far as this bridge has been built at all effectively, it has been done through another means of communication altogether—the radio.

CHAPTER II

RADIO

IN AFRICA, WHERE rates of illiteracy are among the highest in the world, radio is practically indispensable to modern life. Newspapers may reach the educated in the cities and the towns, but few in the villages. Television, where it exists, may excite those within the radius of a transmitter, if they have access to a set. But for the mass of the people, workers in the towns and peasants in the countryside, radio is the one sure means of contact with the rest of the country, and with the outside world. Access to a radio station is thus, next to control of armed forces, the most urgent necessity of Government. Domestically, it is an instrument of power: in the Congo, the fate of Patrice Lumumba was virtually sealed when he was banned from Léopoldville radio, while his rival President Kasavubu could broadcast from across the river in Brazzaville; the first act of John Okello's revolutionary forces in Zanzibar was to seize the radio station to announce the overthrow of the Sultan and the formation of a revolutionary council; and even in Nigeria, during the constitutional crisis at the end of 1964, the fate of the coalition government hinged for a time on whether or not President Azikiwe was to make a post-election broadcast. And internationally, radio has become so much a weapon in the struggle of conflicting ideologies that journalists refer to a "propaganda war of the air," in which the external services of the leading African States compete with those of white South Africa on the one hand, and of foreign countries on the other, to influence the thinking of the continent. The "war" is about all the main issues that affect Africa today—African unity, commitment in the struggle between capitalism and communism, and the liberation of those countries still under white rule.

Radio is therefore an intensely serious affair, and not an entertaining luxury. In rural Africa, it is often the single means of receiving news—news of regional, national or world events, of Government activities and policy decisions. It is also the main vehicle for social education: advice on health, on farming methods, on civic responsibilities and voting procedures. It is an instrument for the extension of education in the schools, and for the learning of languages. No development programme in tropical Africa would be possible without it. And because African villagers depend so much upon radio as a bearer of news and as an instructor, they listen with an attention almost forgotten in Europe, where the medium has largely degenerated into a casual background for other activities. Francis Bebey, whose *La Radio-diffusion en Afrique Noire*[1] is one of the few recent studies of the role of radio in Africa, emphasises the psychological impact of a medium that speaks with authority, and yet to the individual.

But radio seen as an essential instrument of national development is a comparatively new phenomenon. For a long time, its role in Africa was confined to the information and entertainment of European minorities.

The earliest broadcasts were made in South Africa, nearly fifty years ago, very soon after the first successful attempts had been made in Europe and the United States. The first regular programmes came from Johannesburg in 1924, three years before the incorporation in London of the British Broadcasting Corporation; and in 1936, the formation of the South African Broadcasting Corporation, as a statutory public corporation along B.B.C. lines, took the control of radio out of private hands. There were by then some 120,000 receiving licences issued in South Africa.

Aimed as it was at Europeans, literate and well served with newspapers, the S.A.B.C. had no exclusive role as distributor of news, though it took the services of the South African Press Association and relayed B.B.C. news broadcasts twice daily. Its main task was to entertain—it provided music on two channels, one English and one Afrikaans,—and in due course discussion, variety and drama, very much on the B.B.C. pattern. Even when programmes in African languages were started, they aimed at little more than musical entertainment. After the last war, a commercial programme entitled 'Springbok Radio' was set up under S.A.B.C. auspices, to compete with the popular commercial channel broadcasting from

[1] Editions Saint-Paul, France, 1963.

Lourenço-Marques in Moçambique. But until the advent of the Nationalist Government in 1948, the pattern of broadcasting in the Union did not greatly change.

The first modest venture in Kenya, in 1927, also took the B.B.C. as its model. Leaning heavily on relays from London, the Kenya station sought to brighten the evenings of settlers on the farms in the Highlands. Another service for settlers started in Salisbury in 1932, then wired services in Sierra Leone in 1934, on the Gold Coast in 1935, and in Nigeria in 1936. Meanwhile, private radio clubs had started broadcasting in Moçambique in 1933, and in Congo (Brazzaville) in 1935. The Jesuit College, Léopoldville, started the earliest religious radio service in 1936.

It was in 1936—when some nine radio stations were on the air, none of them commanding a range much wider than the radius of a city—that the British colonial authorities took a policy decision that was to be of some moment to the future of communications in Africa: they decided to develop radio in the British colonies as a public service. The wired services in West Africa had been a success, and Britain alone among the colonial powers was able at the time to appreciate the potential of the new medium in African conditions.

The outbreak of war in 1939 forced plans for extending the existing wired services, and establishing new transmitters elsewhere, to be abandoned; but it also brought an urgent need for quick and efficient communication that proved a unique stimulant to African radio, which was used to keep British troops stationed on the continent or en route by ship round the coast, in touch with the progress of the war. Thus in Lusaka, Northern Rhodesia, a station was set up to keep the small European community informed, and this station was destined after the war to pioneer broadcasting to Africans in Southern Africa. In the Belgian Congo, not only was an official Radio Congo-Belge established, but the free Belgian Government in London set up a National Broadcasting Service in Léopoldville equipped with shortwave transmitters beamed to Belgium itself. In the French Congo, the old Radio Club station was taken over by the Free French administration to counter broadcasts from Dakar by the pro-Vichy Radio Afrique Occidentale Française. And Radio Douala was established as a Free French mouthpiece in Cameroun. After the war, Radio

Afrique became Radio Dakar, run by the local administration; and the Brazzaville station served to transmit the overseas service of Radio-diffusion Française.

The Gold Coast, too, benefited by the acquisition of a short-wave transmitter, which was used for Free French broadcasts. And the post-war British administration of Somalia inherited the equipment of Radio Kudu, run by the military for troops in the territory after its capture from the Italians in 1941.

After the war, radio in English-speaking Africa advanced fairly rapidly, on the basis of separate territorial systems. In 1949, two Government Commissions examined projects for single inter-territorial services for West and East Africa, but each rejected the idea, for technical reasons (difficulty in covering large areas and separated territories adequately and economically), and political reasons (because it was felt important to adapt broadcasting to varying local needs). In 1949 Tanganyika went on the air; in 1951 Zanzibar, and in 1954 Uganda.

Broadcasts in African languages had begun during the war, in the Gold Coast, Kenya and Northern Rhodesia. In 1946, an agreement between the governments of Northern and Southern Rhodesia and Nyasaland provided for Lusaka radio to cover the other two territories as well, and this arrangement persisted through the ten years when the three countries were federated (1953-1963). Although Southern Rhodesia (for Central Africa) and Kenya continued to provide services especially for Europeans, British policy on broadcasting was, by the early fifties, clearly committed to developing national networks whose primary purpose would be to inform and educate the African population. Tiny Gambia, and the three High Commission Territories in South Africa, were the only exceptions. Civil service commissions were sent out to several countries in East and West Africa in the 1950's, headed by senior B.B.C. personnel, to advise on development, and all made recommendations on broadly similar lines. Systems were to be operated first under departments of information, then as separate government departments, and eventually as independent statutory corporations on the lines of the B.B.C. Finance could not be adequately raised from receiver licences, not only because so few would be able to afford them, but also because the administration of fee collecting and checking would be almost impossible. Even today, most African countries have no radio licensing system. Thus funds had to come either from Government (which was usually the case while broadcasting was run by government departments), or at least in part from advertising, which was the eventual solution chosen for most of the independent broadcasting corporations in tropical Africa, and has been retained in all countries except Ghana, and Zanzibar. In most cases, advertising is limited to 'spot' advertising, although in East Africa there are a certain number of sponsored programmes.

The main funds for expansion, however, came originally from Colonial Development and Welfare Fund grants, and through assistance from the B.B.C. in the shape of seconded staff to occupy senior positions, of advisers and training officers to work on the spot, and training courses in Britain for African personnel. Studios were built, and transmitters varying in power from 5Kw. to 20Kw. according to the extent of the area to be covered. Machinery for news collection had to be set up, for local news was regarded as an essential part of broadcasting as a public service, although B.B.C. relays remained the main source of foreign news. And elaborate arrangements were made to cover as many vernacular languages as possible. In order to reach rural audiences, it was recognised from the beginning that radio must speak in the languages of the people, and by 1960 an American communications expert, Dr. Arno G. Huth, could count 109 African languages and dialects used by radio in tropical Africa, the majority of them used by stations in British—or formerly British—territories.[1] The French had been much slower in recognising the value of vernacular broadcasting.

No figures are available for the total sums involved in this extensive development scheme, but in Uganda, for example, a Colonial Development Fund grant of £294,000 was made in 1960-61, following recommendations made by a Committee of Enquiry into the Organisation, Policy and Operations of the Government's Information Services. The report of this Committee throws some light on the political thinking of the colonial power which led it to invest so heavily in radio development.

[1] *Communications in Tropical Africa*, 1960, a study by Arno G. Huth, for the U.S. International Co-operation Agency, now the Agency for International Development (A.I.D.).

"The value of a broadcasting service to the economy of a country," it asserts, "cannot be estimated in shillings and cents; the cost must be looked at in terms of the contribution broadcasting can make to the education of people, the prevention of the spread of disease, improvements in the methods of agriculture and better living standards. It can draw the ear away from hostile propaganda from abroad; it can, perhaps above all, cultivate a spirit of unity, and evoke an awareness of political issues."[1]

By the time of independence, Uganda (1962) was broadcasting 22½ hours weekly in English, and 45½ hours in vernaculars. Schools programmes amounted to three hours a week. Sierra Leone (independent 1961) was broadcasting 63½ hours a week; Tanganyika (1962) 63 hours in Swahili and 40 hours in English and Asian languages; Nigeria (Federal Service, not including the regional systems; independent 1960) was broadcasting 96 hours per week; and Ghana, at the time of independence in 1957, was already broadcasting 145 hours, of which over 120 were in local languages. Material sent out on the air included B.B.C. relays, and transcription material from the B.B.C., the Canadian Broadcasting Corporation, the United Nations, Voice of America, Radio Nederlands, Radio-Televisione Italiana, R.T.F. (France) and the radio services of Israel and West Germany. But local programmes, live or recorded, in nearly all cases took the major part of air time: 63 hours out of 68 in Uganda; 36 hours out of 63½ in Sierra Leone; 35 hours out of 103 in Tanganyika; 88½ hours out of 96 in Nigeria, and 63½ hours out of 145 in Ghana. In Northern Rhodesia, by 1957 locally produced programmes already occupied 70 transmitting hours out of 77.

Local programmes often consisted largely of musical requests —but they also involved local news services, in English and vernacular languages. In Nigeria, particularly, the studios showed great enterprise in producing features from 1954 onwards: religious and sports broadcasts, news reviews and ʝalks, children's programmes, quizzes, a Brains Trust (introduced in 1955), a nightly summary of proceedings in Parliament, Party Political Broadcasts (started in 1954), and a series of Lugard Lectures, inspired by the B.B.C.'s Reith Lectures,

[1] Report of the Committee of Enquiry into the Organisation, Policy and Operations of the Government's Information Services, Uganda, 1958.

launched in 1954 as an annual event. There was even one hour-long historical feature broadcast in 1955, called 'Nigeria's Story,' based on recordings in the N.B.S. library, and live interviews and comment. A monthly *Radio Times*, reprinting talks and publishing programmes and profiles of radio 'personalities', appeared at the beginning of 1954.

Thus in the early sixties, the B.B.C. could look with some satisfaction on a whole brood of more or less dutiful offspring in East and West Africa, all fashioned in the maternal image, and all schooled in the sacred principles of 'balance' and 'impartiality' that govern the mother organisation in matters controversial.

The French, however, had a quite different approach. Theirs was conditioned partly by the fact that French West and Equatorial Africa, unlike the British possessions, were contiguous, forming a land link all the way from Morocco to the Congo, enabling the use of numbers of low-powered relay stations to retransmit centrally produced programmes. But it was also consistent with the basic distinctions between French and British colonial policy, between direct and indirect rule. Education in the French territories, geared to French standards and French examinations, was in French only, and used French text-books; in British territories, vernacular languages were frequently used at primary school level, and colleges for higher education were set up on the spot in preference to sending all students abroad for higher degrees. Political advance in the French territories meant the election of African representatives to the Metropolitan Parliament, while in British territories it meant elections to a local Legislative body, destined for eventual independence. Not until 1958 was the principle of independence conceded for French Africa.

French policy on broadcasting, accordingly, did not at the beginning envisage the development of African-controlled national networks. Direction was to be centralised in France, through La Societé de Radio-diffusion de la France d'outre-mer (SORAFOM). SORAFOM was set up in 1956, as a semi-statutory body, but its roots lay in an inter-ministerial commission of 1950, which formulated three main problems of overseas broadcasting: adoption of a comprehensive plan for broadcasting development in the colonies; provision of programmes; and research into reception conditions and availability of receiving sets. SORAFOM was intended to assume all these responsibilities. Its charter defined its aim, "to facilitate the development of radio broadcasting in the territories under the responsibility of the Ministére de la France d'outre-mer, by setting up equipment for a network, and ensuring that it eventually functions." After 1956, broadcasting in the French territories, which had lagged sadly behind development elsewhere, was to grow more quickly. Bad, inadequate equipment was replaced, and a serious programme of technical training initiated. SORAFOM immediately took over the management of Radio Dakar, which became Radio Inter-A.O.F., to serve the whole of French West Africa; and a second station at St. Louis, which became Radio Senegal, to serve Senegal and Mauritania. New stations were set up in Niamey, Yaoundé, Bamako, Fort-Lamy, and Nouakshott. Existing stations at Douala, Conakry, Abidjan, Lomé, Cotonou, and Brazzaville (which was to be Radio A.E.F.), came under SORAFOM's control, and by 1957 the only radio station in Afrique Noire not controlled by SORAFOM was the second Brazzaville station, Radio Brazzaville, which remained (until the revolt against the Youlou Government in 1964) a 'poste nationale Française' directly administered by the R.T.F.

The policy of centralisation, by which two inter-connecting networks covering West and Equatorial Africa respectively, were to be co-ordinated through SORAFOM, allowed the radio experts to install comparatively low-powered transmitters: 1 Kw to cover the main town and its environs, 4 Kw to cover, in theory, the rest of the country. In 1962, only a few countries had transmitters that were more powerful: Senegal had installed a 100 Kw. transmitter in 1960, at the time of the short-lived federation with Mali, because existing equipment could not produce good reception throughout the two territories; Guinea invested in a 100 Kw transmitter in the same year; and the Ivory Coast in 1962.

With the change in political policy in 1958, when the French Union gave way to de Gaulle's Community of separate nations, the idea of two inter-connecting networks fell away, and a programme of national networks replaced it. And with the collapse of the Community in turn, when the French-speaking States demanded a status no less dignified than that of their neighbours, the concept of direct supervision of broadcasting from Paris had itself to be dropped. SORAFOM changed both its name and its function, when in 1962 it was replaced by the Office de Co-opération Radiophonique, known as OCORA. OCORA describes itself as a "technical cooperation agency of the French Republic, specialising in problems of assistance in the fields of radio broadcasting and television." It took over from SORAFOM the unique Studio-Ecole in the forest of St. Germain outside Paris, and provision of technical assistance to African stations. It offers radio programmes, and facilities for research in the extensive documentation centre in Paris—OCORA's tape and record library of African music and folk-tales is one of the finest in the world—; and acts as news agency and foreign correspondent. This extraordinary range of functions, though without doubt it has been of invaluable assistance in extending the horizons of radio in French-speaking Africa, also tends to perpetuate the centralisation planned under SORAFOM, so that Paris remains the source of nearly all foreign material, and many of the cultural, social and educational features which on the English-speaking stations would be locally produced. It is possible that the very existence of highly professional material offered by OCORA inhibits attempts at production on the spot, and so delays the development of a truly national broadcasting service in those countries making most use of OCORA co-operation.

French-speaking stations in Africa have however made several significant advances over the past five years: in educational, vernacular and external broadcasting. Educational broadcasting was already well established in some territories by 1962, when OCORA took over from SORAFOM. Cameroun had launched an educational programme as early as 1955, including instruction to the illiterate and courses in French. Central Africa had in 1962 daily programmes for farmers, and weekly programmes for women on health and hygiene, as well as question-and-answer services. The Ivory Coast ran a 'Popular University of the Air', addressed mainly to teachers in rural areas, as well as French language courses, and talks on hygiene and social affairs. Upper Volta had a course in English, in addition to literacy and French-language instruction. And Senegal had a special educational network broadcasting seventy-two hours per week, mostly in vernacular languages, to farmers, co-operators, housewives and young people. This service was broadcast on a 200 Kw. medium wave transmitter, so that good reception was possible throughout the country. While Mali, which takes mass education by radio very seriously indeed, had developed a unique system of 'feedback' to consolidate the learning process started by the broadcast itself. Villagers in Mali meet to hear educational programmes together, under the supervision of an administrative officer, who transmits comments and suggestions to the Ministry of Co-operation for possible inclusion in future programmes. This system not only reinforces the lesson, but serves also to help listeners to feel part of the creative process themselves, as they find their suggestions, or those of their neighbours, dealt with on the air.

Vernacular broadcasting, which had not been much encouraged under French rule, had already by 1962 been incorporated in the programmes of nearly all the formerly French States, though the proportion of vernacular programmes was usually low: 10 per cent on Radio Douala, 40 per cent on Radio Garoua, both in Cameroun; 12 per cent in the Central African Republic; 15 per cent in Dahomey, 30 per cent in Upper Volta. The highest percentage was on the Niger station, which transmitted more than 50 per cent of its programmes in vernacular languages. These percentages have been increased since 1962, in order to cover not only most of the languages and dialects spoken at home, but also several spoken in neighbouring countries. These have grown with the growth of foreign broadcasting: nearly all French-speaking countries now have an external broadcasting service, where only seven (Congo, Ivory Coast, Upper Volta, Dahomey, Mali and Guinea) had one in 1962.

The Governments of black Africa thus inherited in the early sixties national radio systems of more or less technical efficiency —usually able to cover the country, but often not designed to broadcast abroad. The two most technically advanced services were not in black Africa at all, but at the two extremes of the continent—in Egypt in the north, and South Africa in the South.

The Cairo Broadcasting Service, started before the last war

6

and developed during the war to broadcast news to the troops in North Africa and the Mediterranean, has expanded dramatically since the Nasser revolution in 1953. Broadcasting capacity has increased from 72 Kw before 1953 to 2,000 Kw in 1964, with 4,000 Kw capacity planned for 1965. Transmission time has increased from fifteen hours daily to over 100 hours in 1965. Cairo Radio produces programmes in eighty-two languages, and claims to be second only to the Voice of America in the number of languages used in its broadcasts.

U.A.R. radio services comprise a General Programme, producing entertainment and cultural material, and a series of special programmes, of which the most important is probably the Voice of the Arabs, founded just after the Nasser Revolution, and broadcast for twenty-two hours daily to the Arab World "from the Atlantic Ocean to the Persian Gulf." The Voice of the Arabs is one of the principal instruments of Egyptian foreign policy, its theme Arab solidarity against colonialism. A special Palestine Service beamed to Israel was started as a sub-division of the Voice of the Arabs in 1960; and in 1962, following the Evian Agreements between France and the Algerian nationalists, an Algeria Programme was added, beamed to Algeria.

Internal services, apart from the General Programme, included a special cultural network, known as the Second Programme, set up in 1957 to promote science and culture, in accordance with the Government's policy of using radio as a medium of formal and informal education; a Peoples' Broadcasting Programme, founded in 1959, which promotes mass cultural and political education, including literacy education, and provides special programmes for young people, the Army, the Police and other social groups; and the Chanted Koran Station, started in 1964 to broadcast readings from the Koran for fourteen hours daily.

International services include a European Programme, in addition to the Voice of the Arabs; and many programmes are beamed all over the world. Some are programmes of instruction in the Arabic language, but most foreign programmes have some political content, and are intended to project the image of the U.A.R. abroad and to further the struggle against colonialism, in the Arab world, in Africa and elsewhere. The tone and content of these broadcasts has on occasion laid the U.A.R.

open to charges of interference in the affairs of neighbouring States whose regimes the Egyptian Government regards as inimical to the Arab, or the Afro-Asian, cause. Israel is of course the first victim of Egyptian hostility, but governments in Syria, Iraq and the Yemen have also had frequent cause to protest. And the Swahili programmes beamed to East Africa before independence gave the British Colonial authorities no little cause for concern. These were often run by militant political leaders in exile, to whom Cairo radio was an invaluable link with their people; and in the same way broadcasting time is now made available to African leaders from Southern Africa. Cairo radio can be heard in Rhodesia, in the Portuguese territories and in South Africa, and though no direct evidence of its impact is available, white governments pay it no little attention.

The spread of anti-colonial propaganda from Cairo, from Accra, from Radio Moscow, which has an extensive African programme, and Peking Radio, whose beam is so powerful that it can be heard in some areas more clearly than the local station itself, is one of the excuses for the recent expansion of the External Services of the South African Broadcasting Corporation. The S.A.B.C. announced in 1965 that it would spend approximately £70,000 on the expansion of overseas services, in English, Afrikaans, French, Portuguese, Swahili, Dutch, Spanish and German. The aim is eventually to cover not only Africa (an Africa Service was started in 1958) but Europe, the United States and the Far East.

The content of these broadcasts is unlikely to contribute to peace in Africa, for the S.A.B.C. is now an unashamed mouth-piece of the extremist Nationalist Secret Society, the Broeder-bond, of which Dr. Verwoerd himself has been a member, and which already controls many aspects of South African life. Since the Nationalists came to power, Broederbonders have been promoted over the heads of other staff, so that in 1965 not only is Dr. Albert Hertzog, the Minister of Posts and Telegraphs (who is responsible for Broadcasting), a member of the Broeder-bond, but Dr. P. J. Meyer, Chairman of the S.A.B.C., is Chairman of the Bond; and one of the regional advisers for the Witwatersrand, Dr. Piet Koornhof, is the Bond's Secretary. The Corporation has departed so far from its original responsi-bility under its Charter to act as "an impartial public body serving all the peoples of South Africa," that the *Rand Daily Mail* referred to it in December 1965 as "a branch of the Government's propaganda machine as partial and as biassed as the Government Press." The S.A.B.C. itself provoked this outburst, by a series of violent attacks on English-speaking newspapers, accusing them of 'un-South African' conduct for criticising the government. It also indulges in personal abuse of opponents of apartheid both in South Africa and abroad, particularly in a daily 'Current Affairs' programme written by the editor of *Die Vaderland*, a leading Nationalist newspaper. And the Corporation has gone so far in its commitment to apartheid that it actually refused to broadcast the customary commentary on the South African Grand Prix golf tournament in 1964 because a non-white golfer, Papwa Sewgolum, was playing in it. The bias is not limited to domestic affairs, for during the 1964 elections in Britain and the United States, the S.A.B.C.'s support for the Conservatives in Britain and Senator Barry Goldwater in America led the Johannesburg *Sunday Times* to refer to the "S.A. Barrycasting Corporation."

But perhaps the simplest way of conveying the bias and racialism expressed in South African radio is to quote from a satirical programme broadcast on the English-language service on November 13th, 1965. This programme is a weekly feature, and can be heard clearly on medium and short-wave over half of Africa. It purports to be a skit on radio in independent black African States, and African accents are crudely mimicked throughout:[1]

First Voice: Greeting, listeners, this is Station Ublumbublu of the Mazintoland Broadcasting Corporation, radiating on long wave, short wave and permanent wave. When you hear the time-giving drum, the time will be thirteen o'clock. When your clock strikes thirteen, time to have your clock mended ... Have you got the road report, Mr. Magaziti?

Second Voice: Oh yes, Mr. Nkosa. Now, the road report of the Mazintoland Automobile Club reports that the road between Uukanti and Tushblashi is not quite so good as the surrounding countryside. For the motorists, I advise to avoid the road wherever possible ...

First Voice: I have a nice letter from a regular listener who

---

[1] The programme was monitored in South Africa, and published in *Anti-Apartheid News*, London, December 1965/January 1966.

gives the same address for over three years—cell 124, Central Jail, Utabanu, who wants to hear a poem specially for his girl friend Petunia, and he adds—"she was so sweet and tender, I thought I could eat her up, but she was much better cooked in butter." Oh well—it's better to have cooked your love in butter than never to have loved her at all. Oh, and I have received a very nice original song from Mr. Daniel Sloppogahli, Banana City, Wooziland South:

Chorus: Oh, I love my big fat Sarah,
   She is my love and life,
   No girlfriend could be dearer
   Than my fuzzy-wuzzy Sarah,
   I love the ring stuck through her nose,
   I love her big black eyes,
   To keep my pin-up girl true to me,
   I spear her with assegais!

The men who permit this programme to go out on the air, also broadcast day-long programmes for Africans, in seven languages. That this service is regarded as a means of indoctrination was admitted by the Minister of Finance in 1964, when he said in Cape Town that the S.A.B.C., and "Radio Bantu in particular,"[1] were used to counter overseas propaganda aimed at South Africa. Present policy is to develop F.M. services, which can be received on comparatively cheap and simple receivers—that is, receivers not strong enough to receive short-wave broadcasts from abroad. The Republic now boasts the most modern FM network in the world.

In white Rhodesia, policy is similarly aimed at isolating the public from 'hostile' foreign broadcasts, and developing radio as an instrument of Government propaganda. The R.B.C. is a statutorily independent corporation (it succeeded the Federal Broadcasting Corporation which was disbanded in 1963), but even before the emergency regulation introduced after the Unilateral Declaration of Independence by the Smith cabinet, the government increasingly intervened in the Corporation's

[1] So much resented is the apartheid indoctrination of Bantu Radio, that on Black Monday, the day of mourning following the Sharpeville massacre in 1960, rediffusion sets in the African townships were stripped off the walls of the City Council houses and burnt in the public squares. These sets were broadcasting anti-strike propaganda.

affairs. News "obviously designed to exert political pressure on the Government and the public" could be banned, according to the Chairman of the R.B.C. Board in explanation of the banning in September 1964 of a news item reporting the opinion of a group of white academics that Africans should be allowed to vote on the independence issue. Three senior members of the Corporation staff handed in their resignations in protest.

But censorship has become more rigorous since then, extending after U.D.I. to legislation imposing a fine of up to £500 or two years' imprisonment on anyone who "causes or permits" any hostile broadcast to be heard "in public." Before U.D.I., the R.B.C. had already discontinued one of its relays of B.B.C. news, and replaced it with the news broadcasts of Radio South Africa. After U.D.I. all B.B.C. relays were discontinued, and B.B.C. programme schedules were banned from the daily Press, though full details of South African programmes continued to be published.

Rhodesia also has developed extensive services in African languages (about sixteen-and-a-half hours daily), since the break-up of the Federation. Until 1963, Lusaka Radio had been responsible for broadcasting to Africans throughout Central Africa, while Salisbury controlled broadcasting to Europeans.

It is clear, then, that radio has become a crucial—and in many ways the most powerful—weapon in what 'Prime Minister' Ian Smith of Rhodesia has revealingly called the "war for men's minds" in Africa.[1] And it is all the more powerful because it is so easily available not only to protagonists on the continent itself, but to interested foreign parties as well.

The biggest efforts in broadcasting to Africa, in terms of hours transmitted, have been made by the United States and

---

[1] The teams of Moral Re-armament broadcasters who hastened to the Congo immediately after independence in 1960 would have agreed with this formulation. They set about attempting to capture the minds of the Congolese for the war against communism, neutralism and Pan-Africanism. "Neutralism is no solution for Africa," one speaker told his radio audience, "neutralism means co-existence with evil . . . neutralism is communist strategy for infiltrating our countries and taking power"; and another proclaimed that "Pan-Africanism has become an instrument of communist penetration in Africa, quite as destructive as imperialism." Lumumba's Government suspended these broadcasts after a fortnight, but on his fall from power, M.R.A. returned, to continue on the air until Aug. 1961.

the Soviet Union, though the B.B.C., for historical reasons, and through its transcription services which offer finished programmes to African stations at small cost, is still probably the service most widely heard, in English-speaking Africa at least. The Soviet Union was broadcasting about 125 hours a week to Africa in 1965, mainly in English, French, and Swahili, but also in a variety of smaller languages including Amharic, Bambara, Lingala and Zulu. The Voice of America also concentrates on English, French and Swahili, but it has in addition programmes in many other local languages, and its total of only about fifty hours in 1965 of broadcasting specifically intended for Africa, is supplemented by another sixty hours of the World Service clearly audible on the continent. China broadcasts about sixty-six hours, in English, French, Swahili, Hausa and Portuguese; West Germany about fifty-three hours, in English, French, Swahili, Hausa and Kinyawanda (spoken in Rwanda); and East Germany about sixty-six hours in English, French and Swahili. France's programmes for Africa are difficult to extract from almost round-the-clock 'Services d'outre-mer'; and the B.B.C.'s General Overseas Programmes are audible in Africa as well as the special Africa services for West, East and Southern Africa. Finally, there are three other European stations with smaller programmes for Africa— Belgium, Italy and Holland—and to all the totals must be added Arabic services to the Middle East and North Africa. These many voices are daily competing with local services, and with the only three African independent States which have as yet considerable external services of their own: the U.A.R., Ghana and Nigeria. The U.A.R. broadcast about eighty-eight hours a week to Africa in 1965, in English, French, Portugese and seven vernacular languages, in addition to the services of the Voice of the Arabs beamed to Arabic-speaking areas; Ghana produced about 84 hours, in five languages, and Nigeria about sixty-three in four languages.

Although in mid-1965 both the Soviet Union and China were reported to be setting up short-wave transmitting stations on the continent, near Nairobi and Dar-es-Salaam respectively, it is still the Western stations that play the dominating role in broadcasting to Africa. They have numerous advantages—the former colonial links which tie African broadcasting traditions with those of Britain and France; the extensive transcription services offered by Britain, France, and the United States (language alone inhibits any of the Communist countries from competing); financial ties, such as the agreement whereby Overseas Rediffusion, London, operates Liberia's radio service for the Liberian Government; and the sheer extent of the operations of the U.S. Information Agency, the biggest in the world, of which the Voice of America is only a part.

Although it broadcasts fewer hours per week specifically for Africa than the Soviet Union, the V.O.A. has the additional advantage of two established broadcasting stations on African soil: 35 Kw, 50 Kw and 100 Kw relay transmitters at Tangier, Morocco, and a complex of six 250 Kw and two 50 Kw transmitters near Monrovia, Liberia. The Liberia station, until the 1965 expansion of Cairo Radio, was the most powerful broadcasting complex on the continent, and primary V.O.A. broadcasts are made there.

Unlike the B.B.C., the V.O.A. is an integral part of the U.S.I.A., which is directly responsible to the President, and explicitly an arm of U.S. foreign policy. According to a Presidential directive, "The mission of the U.S.I.A. is to help achieve U.S. policy objectives . . . (Agency) activities should emphasise the ways in which U.S. policies harmonise with those of other peoples and governments, and those aspects of American life and culture which facilitate sympathetic understanding of United States policies." In accordance with this directive, of some 1,300 transmitter hours disseminated weekly by the V.O.A., an official briefing on the organisation's work and history estimates that 60 per cent is material "of a political nature." News features prominently—seven 15-minute news broadcasts daily, two 30-minute programmes on 'issues in the news', four 30-minute news and comment programmes on Africa, and a daily World Press Round-Up or Opinion Round-Up were included in English-language schedules for Africa in 1964. The V.O.A.'s authorised appropriation for 1963 was $26,776,855—nearly £9mn—and the U.S.I.A.'s total appropriation for that year was $133,996,031, or nearly £50mn. Total information expenditure by the British Government, for instance, was less than half this amount.

The main distinction between the task of the B.B.C. and that of the V.O.A. arises from the difference in structure of the two information services. The B.B.C. is a semi-autonomous statutory corporation, which expects to be treated by Government rather as the Press is treated. It has no formal links with the Government's information agency, the Central Office of Information (C.O.I.). External Services are in fact not paid for out of licence fees, like the Home Services, but by Foreign Office, Commonwealth Relations Office or Colonial Office grants, but the Government Ministries are supposed to do no more than specify the number of hours broadcast to what region, and not to influence the nature of the programmes, which are the responsibility of B.B.C. staff. Other Government information efforts are directly, but separately, controlled by Ministries, and only the production of material is the responsibility of the C.O.I., which acts as an agent, and not as an executive. The U.S.I.A. on the other hand is responsible for all United States information effort abroad, it co-ordinates, controls and directs a planned programme round specific objectives. At the end of 1963, for instance, it swung into action through all its media (press and publications, radio and television) with two policy objectives in mind: first to focus world attention on the heroic qualities of the assassinated President Kennedy; and second, to transfer as far as possible the sentiment stirred by Kennedy's image to the new President Johnson, whose loyalty to Kennedy's policies was to be stressed from the beginning.[1]

The B.B.C. by contrast is proud of its reputation for the 'impartial' reporting of news, and for 'balancing' controversial subjects by presenting different points of view. It is on the definition of 'balance' or 'controversy' that disagreement may arise in Africa. A number of African independent States, including Ghana, Kenya, Tanzania and Zambia,[2] have discontinued relays of B.B.C. news broadcasts in their national programmes, because of such disagreement. For example, a B.B.C. comment on Rhodesia might strive to 'balance' the points of view of the British and Smith Governments more carefully than either of these as opposed to the view of the

---

[1] See the U.S.I.A.'s own account of its coverage of "The Assassination and the Succession", U.S.I.A. 21st Review of Operations, July 1st– December 31st, 1963.

[2] Zambia resumed these relays in December 1965, by agreement with Britain, when the rebel Government in Rhodesia cut off all B.B.C. transmissions. The Zambia Broadcasting Corporation beamed its own B.B.C. programmes into Rhodesia in order to keep the people there informed of events at home and abroad censored within the country.

6*

African nationalists, which nearly all African States fully support; or a report on the issue of economic sanctions against South Africa, a controversial question in Britain, might well be weighted against sanctions, while the African States have all adopted them as a matter of policy; and throughout the fighting in the Congo in 1964 and 1965, the B.B.C. referred to the Stanleyville forces as 'rebels', a definition which few of the African States could concede. The point is that there is a fundamental disagreement between the foreign policies of all the Western States—and above all of those whose broadcasting to Africa is most extensive—and that of the African States, as expressed through the Organisation of African Unity. The O.A.U. is committed to two main principles of foreign policy: anti-colonialism, and non-alignment in the East-West power struggle. The West is by definition aligned, and the embodiment of colonialism.

The objective of anti-colonialism, on the other hand, is shared by Africa with the Communist countries; a fact which explains the permission granted by Kenya and Tanzania for Russian and Chinese transmitting stations on their soil, at a time when no similar permission has recently been granted to a Western country.

The problems facing African radio in the 1960's, then, are problems partly of orientation, and partly of inadequate equipment and know-how. Except in Ghana and Nigeria, where the most highly developed systems were, and Guinea, which had lost all its French personnel when it voted 'non' in the 1958 referendum, nearly all senior broadcasting posts in tropical Africa were still held by European ex-patriates as lately as 1962. In 1959, according to Dr. Huth,[1] estimates of the total number of receiving sets in the area varied between 550,000 and 1,750,000 and these were concentrated mainly in the cities of Ghana, Nigeria, Kenya and the Central African Federation. And above all, the close links with the B.B.C. and with OCORA of the past had left African services heavily orientated towards the outlook of the former imperialist power. It was the B.B.C., for instance, that provided foreign news for the English-language countries; B.B.C. relay and transcription material that made up large proportions of broadcasting time. OCORA provided similar material; and in both cases, foreign

[1] In the study on Communications Media in Tropical Africa already quoted.

material was not merely the main or only source of news and comment on foreign affairs, but also on African affairs, since no African radio station had—or has to this day—its own network of regular correspondents in the capitals of Africa. It was also the B.B.C. or OCORA that had provided the planners to set up the services in the first place, laid down the basic structure and policies for the running of the services, and continued to train nearly all staff.

The main aims of radio in Africa today (outside the white south, where entertainment is still the basic ingredient), could probably be summarised much as the Colonial report on broadcasting in Uganda defined them in 1958: dissemination of news, particularly political news and analysis; education; and the building of national unity. Several countries have already replaced B.B.C. news services, but only the few (U.A.R., Ghana and Algeria, in effect) that have national news agencies developed enough to do their own foreign news collection are in a position to do anything but compile their own bulletins from the services of the international news agencies. In 1965, most of the countries of North Africa, and the English-speaking independent countries, were doing this, and supplementing the news with their own comment. Most French-speaking countries, including the Congo (Léopoldville), Rwanda and Burundi, on the other hand, were leaning heavily on the assistance of OCORA, the principal exceptions being Mali and Guinea.

Even educational programmes, which had been developed under colonial rule, required fundamental reassessment with independence. The aim is no longer to help educate a few, but to raise the general educational level of an entire population in order to meet the needs of economic development, so far more stress needs to be put on literacy and social education. Here, the experience of developed countries such as Britain and France is likely to be far less useful than that of countries such as the Soviet Union, Cuba, or even Australia, which have had to force the pace of their own development through the mass media. Experts from other countries are now advising on the educational uses of radio, in Ghana, Guinea, Mali, Kenya, Tanzania and elsewhere, often through the agency of UNESCO. The whole orientation of broadcasting is nearly everywhere shifting from the concept of 'entertainment'—which has a place in any 'European' definition of the medium—to that of education in the broadest possible sense of the word. Schools broadcasting is now a relatively small part of educational broadcasting. And the fact that Ghana has replaced the traditional 'Ministry of Information and Tourism' with a 'Ministry of Information and Education' which controls broadcasting, indicates the extent to which the two ideas are becoming identified. Zambia, Tanzania and Kenya have all embarked on schemes for expanding educational radio, Uganda's is already well advanced, and in Algeria, the U.A.R. and Ghana literacy education through radio has been developed on the basis of monitored group listening, supplemented with written material on radio lessons published in the Press.

But it is in the development of an independent national consciousness, pride in a national culture and history, that radio has perhaps the most urgent role to play in the first years after independence. Dr. Don R. Browne, of Boston University, who made a study of broadcasting in Guinea in 1962, sees the cultivation of national unity as the first concern of Radio Guinea. "Internal consolidation and development of national consciousness are evident goals," he writes,[1] "when one considers that all news and important statements are given in the six chief tribal languages as well as in French, and when one considers that Guinean music is played far more often than that of any other nation or area. Similar evidence is noted in the broadcast of such programmes as 'Advice to Mothers' and 'Aminata and her Home' (which attempt to dissipate the influence of tribal traditions), 'Guinean Folklore' (which seeks to make the country conscious of its pre-colonial-era past), etc. . . . There is every indication that the Guinean Government has been successful in its efforts to develop a 'national feeling' among its people. Travellers in remote parts of the country report that the people in the villages and towns know something of the Central Government and what it is doing, and give every evidence of being loyal to, and proud of, Guinea as a nation. Since radio is the one instrument of mass communication that can reach almost everywhere and everyone (literate or not), it would seem that Radio Guinea deserves a fair amount of credit for this development."

Ghana's *Radio Review* also reveals a great deal about the

[1] Don R. Browne, "Radio Guinea: a Voice of Independent Africa," Journal of Broadcasting, Spring 1963.

new orientation of African broadcasting. Ghana and Guinea
are not typical examples, but they are important because they
are among the countries where change has been taken furthest.
Ghana's *Review* is thus very different from the Nigerian *Radio
Times* of 1954 and 1955, which was modelled on Britain's *Radio
Times*. The number for 12th December, 1964 has a Congo
picture on the cover, captioned 'Colonialism, threat to world
peace.' Inside, are features on the Role of the African Press,
the Rise of Nationalism in Kenya, Ghanaian Culture, Instruments of the Orchestra, the Automatic Camera, the Pope's
circular 'Pacem in Terris,' and a short story. Some, but not all,
of these articles are reproductions of radio talks. There is a
feature, 'Talking about Teaching', on teaching methods, and
another of Farmers' Questions and Answers; there are also
texts for radio lessons in French. The programmes themselves
include plenty of music, mainly African; news three times a day
in six vernaculars and English; features on Sunday with titles
such as 'From the Ghana papers', 'The African Scene' (on the
Congo), 'Voices from Abroad', 'Sports Round-Up', 'Radio
Doctor', 'Ghana Newsreel', and 'Pictures in Sound' (President
Nkrumah's address to a Science-for-Peace Conference at the
Ghana Academy of Sciences). In addition, during the week,
specialist programmes are listed for farmers, fishermen, women,
and a 'Young Pioneers' Corner.' There are religious programmes in several languages, a half-hour magazine programme in Akan and another in Dagbani, and a serial in Ewe.
These programmes are selected from one week's schedules, but
they give a fair picture of Ghana's policy for radio. There are
no B.B.C. relays, and in this programme at least no foreign
transcription material.

Ghana now has the most extensive external service of any
radio in black Africa. It broadcasts over four 100 Kw transmitters to eleven areas (ten in Africa, the eleventh service being
to Europe), in English, Arabic, French, Hausa, Portuguese and
Swahili. Like most of the African States, Ghana wants its voice
to be heard among the myriads on the air; and in particular it
wants its policies on African unity, on the Congo, on apartheid,
and on Portuguese colonialism to be heard and understood.
Guinea, though its station is less well equipped, has similar
aims. In 1960 Czechoslovakia installed a 100 Kw. transmitter
at Conakry, after which foreign broadcasts in French,

Portuguese (for Portuguese-ruled Guinea), Arabic and English were expanded. And M. Alassane Diop, Minister of Information, on opening the new centre, said that the expanded service would enable "the voice of truth to go throughout the world to combat colonialism and neo-colonialism, the voice of rehabilitation will go to the African people and to all oppressed peoples, and the voice of friendship and peace will go to people everywhere."

Internally, Guinea was able to increase the number of vernacular programmes, to produce features for the first time, emphasising social education, African history and culture; and a special series on the life, geography and politics of foreign countries. News stresses Guinea first, then African news, but strives to cover the world, East and West.

Nearly all changes in African broadcasting so far described tend away from the concept of broadcasting as a function independent of Government, such as was envisaged by the British (though not by the French) in colonial days. The tasks of radio have emerged as so much part of, and essential to, the policies of Government, that many of the countries that inherited with independence a statutory corporation in charge of broadcasting, have legislated to bring radio—and television—back under direct Ministerial control. Ghana and Kenya each did so soon after independence; Tanzania announced its intention to do so in 1965; and as yet indecisive moves have been made in both Nigeria and Uganda to bring broadcasting more closely under Government's eye.

The biggest remaining problem in reorientating radio services to new needs is that of technical, journalistic and production training for broadcasters. Both Ghana and Guinea have fully 'Africanised' their services, but in 1965 Guinea was still without a full complement of adequately trained personnel able to use the medium as it might be used. Guinea's broadcasting staff numbered a mere thirty in 1961, and receivers throughout the country numbered less than 50,000 (representing about 300,000 listeners). Ghana had as many listeners by 1957, and a total administrative, technical and programming staff of 815! Most systems in Africa are in fact short of staff—according to Dr. Huth, Uganda Radio alone needed ninety-four extra staff in 1962, a number which he calculates it would have taken existing B.B.C. training facilities twenty-three years to produce. Nigeria, Ghana, Senegal, Uganda, U.A.R. and Algeria now have their own training schools; and the B.B.C. has expanded its training facilities under a former director of Nigerian and Tanganyika radio, Mr. Tom Chalmers. But B.B.C. courses can still take only about half a dozen African trainees a year, plus a few more experienced broadcasters for periods at Bush House. Some African governments are sending students abroad on special grants: by 1965 Moscow, Prague, Warsaw, Berlin and Bonn, and occasionally Scandinavian broadcasting stations were among those offering scholarships abroad, or staff to train young people on the spot. OCORA's scale of operation remains the largest. Some 250 radio and television broadcasters and technicians have, up to 1965, been trained by the Studio-Ecole; but this figure includes French students, who because of their better educational background, often get the senior posts in African stations.[1]

OCORA's first Director-General, M. Robert Pontillon, who was also formerly Director of SORAFOM, told a conference of African and Malagasy radio representatives in April 1963 that "we see ourselves achieving a new concept which goes beyond the notion of technical assistance and henceforth sets our relations on the level of real co-operation." That OCORA's function goes beyond that of mere assistance is true, but whether 'co-operation', if the word implies co-operation among equals, is the precise word is less certain. A British broadcasting expert who remarked that OCORA is "very political" had in mind both the organisation's jealousy of its influence, its unwillingness to allow its students to accept experience elsewhere, and the sheer extent of its activities, which if fully utilised could actually stifle the growth of independent broadcasting in Africa. It not only produces programmes for Africa, buys R.T.F. and other material for African stations, and acts as a news agency with its own international correspondents; but, although originally intended not to be an administrator of African stations, it was still in 1964 jointly financing and controlling stations in Dahomey, Gabon and the Ivory Coast. It thus assumes in certain cases the role of agent with powers of representation.

In the end, it will only be co-operation among African radio stations themselves that will be able to effect the additional

[1] cf. Francis Bebey, *La Radio-diffusion en Afrique Noire*.

training, the news and production facilities and programme exchanges which can produce broadcasting services fully adapted for Africa. It was with these objectives in view that the Union des Radio-diffusions et Télévisions Nationales Africaines (URTNA) was set up in Dakar in 1963. President of URTNA is M. Diallo Alpha, Director General of Information and Tourism, Republic of Guinea, and the organisation's headquarters is at Dakar. Nearly all African independent States are now members. But programme exchanges have been slow to start, though they, and the creation of an African news and programmes agency, are under discussion, as part of the overall project of an All-African News Agency.

CHAPTER 12

TELEVISION

Viewed from one of the so-called 'developed' countries, where a television set is the latest luxury, and jokes are made about the couple who bought a telly before a cooker, the prospect of television in Africa, where millions are under-nourished and live in grass huts, seems frivolous, if not grossly irresponsible. Africans themselves sometimes sneer at the idea of millions spent on television when the development of agriculture and the establishment of local industry should have first calls on Government investment. Communications are necessary for development, they concede, but why television?

The highly developed countries, where television followed an already complex information-system, including daily Press and radio, tend to regard television primarily as an entertainment medium, a rival for theatre and cinema, something to relax over in the evening after a day's work. Such a view presupposes a population with spare cash as well as spare time for luxuries. Either private sets must be bought in such numbers that licence fees can subsidise the station (as in the case of the B.B.C.), or commercial advertising must provide the money (as with American television). Advertising on this scale again assumes an established and competitive commercial system. In very few African countries—the U.A.R., South Africa, Rhodesia, and among the Europeans of Kenya, perhaps—can these conditions be met.

The U.A.R., Rhodesia and Kenya were all among the earliest African countries to set up a television system. In Kenya, there were some 5,100 sets in 1963, most of them owned by European and Asian traders and officials in Nairobi, and farmers within the 25-mile range of a transmitter. There were 150 community viewing-sets in schools and social centres. According to the Colonial Office Report on Sound and Television Broadcasting for that year, the average price per set, including a 25 per cent import tax, was £85, and the estimated price that would have been "within the means of the average citizen" £10. Hence, of a weekly 31½ hours' broad-casting, 26¾ hours were in English, that is for Europeans, the major proportion of time being taken up with showings of British and American feature films, and 'entertainment' series. The main cost of operating the station was apparently to be met by licence fees at £3 per year (£15,400 in that year), and advertising revenue (£32,600), since the cost to Government, following the installation of television in October 1962, was not supposed to exceed the cost at that time of running the radio service alone. This arrangement meant that the full television staff was a spartan thirty-seven, eleven only being programme staff, and that a mere 7¾ hours of local material could be produced per week. In spite of these economies, the service spent £140,000 in the year in which it was set up.

Clearly, the burden of running a television system for the sake of entertainment only would be intolerable for African States. The capital expenditure and recurrent expenses would both be enormous, finance by licence would be limited by the public's inability to afford sets (unless Government were prepared not only to lift import taxes but actually to subsidise receivers), and by administrative difficulties in collection. Finance by advertising on the other hand carries with it certain obvious disadvantages. The big advertising could only be expected to come from abroad, and to deal with consumer goods that must in the end be paid for in foreign currency. Not all Governments would wish to lay their peoples open, more than absolutely necessary, to the competitive values of consumer advertising. This tends to play on jealousies, rivalries and snobberies, and to emphasise the divisions between the cumulative economies of the cities and the subsistence living of the villages. Most Governments of emergent States would say that they wished their communications system to promote national unity. Those television systems that have resorted to commercial advertising as a source of revenue—and most have —must feel that they have a greater advantage to gain, to balance the account, than the mere entertainment of a few.

This greater advantage is simply defined as education. "To the illiterate," wrote the projects director of Thomson Television (International) in 1964,[1] "the screen can become a

[1] "Television for Emergent Nations," by A. Becker, British Kinematography, May 1964.

miraculous blackboard; to the isolated it opens a window on the world; to the new nation seeking identity it becomes a mirror of its new reality. The thinner the lines of communication, the less educated the mind, the fewer teachers and guides, the more television can do.

"It is not the closely knit, affluent, educated and advanced civilisation of Europe and America which needs television. For them it may be a nice and pleasant extra. The emergent nations need it as their daily bread."

This is the attitude to television expressed by most African governments. Opening Uganda's television service in October 1963, the Minister of Information, Broadcasting and Tourism said that, "Television in Uganda—indeed television in Africa—must be used mainly to expedite development." And President Nkrumah told Ghanaians in 1964 that, "Television will be used to supplement our education programme and to foster a lively interest in the world around us. It will not cater to cheap entertainment nor commercialism. Its paramount objective will be education in the broadest and purest sense."

The word 'education' was used, practically without exception, by every delegate to the UNESCO Meeting on the Introduction and Development of Television in Africa, held in Lagos in November 1964. Participants came from Algeria, Congo (Brazzaville), Gabon, the Ivory Coast, Kenya, Liberia, Mauritius, Morocco, Nigeria (Federal, and all three regions), Senegal, Sierra Leone, Sudan, Uganda, U.A.R., and Upper Volta, with observers from Cameroun and Dahomey. All agreed on the great potential of television for education in Africa.

The meeting recommended, in summary, that television in Africa should be used as a force for national unity, and for social and economic development; that it should regard its educational role as a priority, and make its resources available to schools, for the training of teachers, for literacy programmes, and for programmes on national development projects. Use should be made not only of studios, but of videotape recordings and film units in order to portray the life of the people throughout the country; and teachers should be adequately trained both to use educational television and to take part in planning educational programmes.

In May 1965, twenty-one African countries had television

systems on the air or shortly to start broadcasting. In 1961 there were only three, the U.A.R., Nigeria and Rhodesia (Morocco had launched a short-lived service in 1956). Television is thus still new, too new perhaps to have settled into a pattern on which it can properly be judged. But there are many African journalists who profoundly mistrust the rush to install the telly, suspecting it to be motivated more by ambition for prestige than the serious intention to use it, as recommended by the UNESCO conference, as an integral part of a national programme of development. Many journalists would prefer to see Governments invest in newspapers by financing new ones, installing modern printing presses and improving distribution facilities. Neither radio nor television, they argue, can replace the permanence of the printed word, which is something that can be examined at leisure, read in a group, discussed, and passed from hand to hand. "The only excuse for television in Africa, is education," said one African newspaper-editor sternly, and he thinks that frequently it is only an excuse.

The Ivory Coast, for instance, in 1964, was broadcasting more programmes on sport than on anything else (5½ hours out of 17 hours per week); the Sudan labelled 52 per cent of its programmes 'entertainment'; and even the comparatively sophisticated U.A.R. networks gave an estimate of 20.9 per cent as entertainment, though in this category it could count productions of the work of indigenous playwrights and film-makers. The existence of a flourishing Egyptian film industry, which has long provided the bulk of Arabic cinema to the Middle East, was obviously a unique source of strength to U.A.R. television, and today Egyptians can boast that the medium has already provided a major outlet for local creative writers. It can draw on a strong literary culture, and is learning how to feed it in return.

Those countries without either a film industry or an institutionalised theatre to fall back on, however, find themselves starting from scratch in a visual medium. They must not only obtain technical help from abroad in setting up their stations, but also in running them. The B.B.C. gave this help to Nigeria; Rediffusion, London, to Western Regional Television; and Granada Television, also a British firm, to the Northern Regional network there. The Thomson Organisation set up the

Kenya station in 1962, the Sudan one in 1963, and a new station in Ethiopia in 1964, and is running the systems in Ivory Coast and Sierra Leone; Overseas Rediffusion (London) did the same job in Liberia at the beginning of 1964. The Canadian Broadcasting Corporation has advised, and helped to train Ghanaian staff for Ghana's station, which started broadcasting in September 1965. And in most of the French-speaking States it is OCORA that has been called in to set up the stations, train staff and assist in administration. Senior posts, in spite of crash training programmes for Africans (usually in-service), have often remained for some time in the hands of foreigners: in 1965 OCORA men managed most of the French-speaking stations, Granada staff were largely responsible for Northern Nigeria, and a senior Thomson expert was still with Ethiopian television six months after the station went on the air.

This reliance on foreign expertise is not simply hurtful to African pride, though it may be irksome; nor is it only a question of foreign exchange (though this too is a serious consideration: Lord Thomson referred in his Chairman's Review in 1964 to his organisation's technical help abroad as "invisible exports" for Britain). It is a political question.

"Many European countries have awakened to the realisation that television is a significant political factor in the new countries", writes Thomson's Mr. Becker, "and Government action has often resulted in gifts and loans to get a television service on the air. In terms of major projects such as hydro-electric dams, this is often a comparatively cheap way of making friends and influencing people. Britain has been comparatively slow in this field and there has been only gradual awareness by Government of its significance.

"Private capital has shown greater readiness to come to the rescue and many television networks owe their existence to long-term bank loans backed by guarantees from the local Governments, provided that the efficient performance of these stations is assured by managerial advice. It is generally felt, however, that an increasing participation by the British Government would be needed to preserve British influence in mass communications in the emerging countries."[1]

The political aspects have not in fact escaped the attention of

[1] Becker, op. cit.

the Foreign Office, which sets great store by the presence of British experts in key positions in communications. Final political and programming control of course rests with the local Broadcasting Corporation or the relevant Ministry, but the personnel involved in the execution of policy are not without influence—"it is all a question of a cast of mind", as a senior Foreign Office official remarked to me. And the French Government takes equally seriously the role of OCORA, which does far more than train staff for African television and provide experts at executive levels. It also acts as a programming agent, and as news and features agency providing televised international news coverage from its headquarters in Paris.

The full extent of Africa's problem can perhaps only be brought home by looking at programme schedules. One list of foreign programmes, bought by a London agent for a station that undoubtedly wishes to make responsible use of television, looks something like this: *The Alvin Show, The Avengers, Beverly Hillbillies, Bonanza, The Three Stooges, Defenders, Deputy Dawg, The Dick Powell Theatre, Gunsmoke, The Lucy Show, Sir Francis Drake, December Bride, Rin Tin Tin, Wagon Train, The Jack Benny Show, Alfred Hitchcock Hour, Wonders of Man or The Magic Atom, The Invisible Man, Whirley Birds, Animal Land, Perry Mason, Rawhide, Ben Casey or Dr. Kildare, Beachcomber, Watch Mr. Wizard, Science Fiction Theatre, Broadway Goes Latin, Popeye, Tales of the Vikings, Adventures in Paradise, Match of the Day.*

Watch Mr. Wizard is an educational cartoon programme for children. *Animal Land* and *The Wonders of Man* are both informative. But as far as "education" is concerned, no great claims can be made for the rest, and some of the series on the list—*Alfred Hitchcock, Sir Francis Drake, The Invisible Man* and *Broadway Goes Latin,* for instance—would surely appear on most people's list of the ten worst programmes on television. And though *The Avengers* and *The Defenders* have been among the more positive achievements of British and American television respectively, they hardly retrieve the mediocrity of the rest. A thousand hours a year are bought abroad by this station, at an average fee of perhaps £25 an hour (compared with about £3,000 paid by British companies).

I asked this programming company why no current-affairs programmes and not a single documentary appeared on the

list. *World in Action*, and other current-affairs programmes had
in fact been offered, and refused. The only documentaries
bought for Africa through this firm were the Independent
Television coverage of Sir Winston Churchill's funeral (which
won an international award in 1965), and *The Valiant Years* (a
series on the last war based on Churchill's memoirs). The
difficulty is that current-affairs programmes involve political
comment. They are made, inevitably, from a point of view that
is foreign to that of Africa, and frequently unacceptable there.
As an example, British and American coverage of the Congo
has almost always been filmed from the point of view of the
white refugees, and would hardly be sympathetically viewed
in Kenya, while President Kenyatta was head of an Organisation of African Unity's conciliation commission. Western
treatment of the Berlin wall would go down no better in a
country that preserves friendly relations with the German
Democratic Republic. Even the best of the British or American
documentaries, such as the N.B.C. film made on Viet Nam in
1964, are orientated by the nationality of their makers: the
Viet Nam film was critical of American policy in Viet Nam,
but it did not question the assumptions behind that policy, and
it is the assumptions that are inconsistent with the policy of
non-alignment, adopted by the Organisation of African Unity
on behalf of the African States. That so powerful a medium as
television should show programmes that run counter to the
basic tenets of Government policy would be unusual anywhere.

Africans are thus faced with the difficulty that foreign
documentary material is felt to be unsuitable, and local
facilities are simply not available for features on any ambitious
scale (the Sudan has outside broadcast units, and so of course
has the U.A.R., but they are a rarity in Africa, though videotape recording equipment is more frequently used. To send
staff correspondents to cover events abroad is almost incon-
ceivable, though Uganda sent a man to the Congo and to the
O.A.U. Heads of State Meeting in 1964). It is not surprising
then that most stations find themselves stuck with 'entertainment' after all. Some try to lay down a policy that will exclude
what they regard as the most corrupting aspects of the commercial material. Uganda boasts that it has never screened a
crime film or a Western. And Ethiopia, to the dismay of its
London representatives, Television International Enterprises,

has stipulated "absolutely no guns." Since some of the most imaginative of British series have been crime series—*Z-Cars*, *Maigret*, *It's Dark Outside*, *Sergeant Cork*, *Public Eye*—which involve violence at one time or another, these policies tend to limit the range of choice. *Maigret* has been shown in Kenya, however, and so has *Z-Cars*.

Other Governments, by contrast, have apparently given no moral or political directives to programme contractors. Thus Liberia, though it has expressed the desire to use its station (ELTV, established in January 1964) for mainly educational purposes, has apparently given Overseas Rediffusion no specific instructions to expand educational programmes, and the company has devoted itself over the year and a half of the station's operation to providing a balanced and varied *entertainment* schedule. It draws a good deal on material from the U.K. Central Office of Information, and a little on French and American information-programmes, as well as commercial sources (from which come *The Flintstones*, *The Dick Powell Theatre* and *Maigret*, among other series). In Liberia, the British Independent Television News programme *Roving Report* has been regularly screened; and so has *Les Français Chez Vous*, a French-language teaching series, the only educational venture so far.

ELTV in 1965 produced only 20 per cent of its programmes locally, including news and newsreel (filmed, with sound superimposed), features for women, and interview-programmes on which visitors to the country, or Government Ministers, are questioned mainly in the studio. There is a toddlers' *Rumpus Room*—a play programme, rather like the American-originated *Romper Room*—*Teenage Dance Time*, a Quiz, and a single local cultural venture, *Songs and Legends of Liberia*.

Uganda's indigenous output, on the other hand, is one of the biggest in Africa, amounting to some 60 per cent of all programmes, and whereas most local material in Liberia is live, much of Uganda's is recorded on videotape. Apart from *Night Club* (a teenage 'pop' show), and football matches, Uganda makes its own documentary programmes about great Ugandans; *Weekend Report* on general and political news; *Woman's Page*; and *1965*, on social advance in Uganda in the fields of agriculture, or industry, or schools.

The Ivory Coast actually claimed in 1964 to produce 80 per

cent of its material locally (one of the only existing arrangements for exchange of programmes between African stations
has been negotiated between the Ivory Coast and Uganda).
It is a new station, however, and at the time of this estimate
was screening only seventeen hours per week. In 1965, it
expected to increase broadcasting time to sixty hours per week.
Staff were undergoing three year training courses at the
OCORA training school. The station has the special advantages
of two outside-broadcast units, and the proximity of a National
School of Dramatic Art which already enriches cultural
programmes. The Director of Television hopes to set up Television Clubs in the villages, whose viewing will be guided by a
trained monitor.

It is clear that, in Africa, local production is the key to an
educational role for television, and its use for national development as envisaged by the Lagos conference. Development
needs seem to fall into four main categories.

The first is for literacy training. UNESCO experts (such as
Wilbur Schramm) and African leaders agree that television
can hasten literacy campaigns, as indeed it has already done in
Italy and elsewhere. What is required is first a programme-
staff trained not only in televisual but also in educational
techniques; facilities for group viewing (in schools and social
centres); and local monitors or teaching staff to follow up
lessons in practice. Algeria and the U.A.R. have already
embarked on programmes along these lines, and Ghana
intends to do so.

In Zambia, an Educational Television Research Project was
conducted in 1964-65, among African miners in the Copper
Belt. The experiment was sponsored by the two main mining
groups, Anglo-American and the Rhodesian Selection Trust,
and was intended to carry literacy training a little further than
the mere ability to read and write. Under the direction of the
University College of Rhodesia and Nyasaland, the project
sought to demonstrate how television could most effectively be
used in the teaching of English and arithmetic to adults with
less than three years' formal education. An experimental
television studio was set up in Kitwe, and telelessons evolved
to follow a Primary School syllabus. Mr. Kenneth Cripwell,
director of the project, feels that these telelessons have proved
their effectiveness, and that they could certainly be used with

correspondence courses, where monitors were not available. He was engaged at the end of 1965 in a further project monitoring television and the teaching of skills to African workers, for the Union Minière in Katanga.

Second, come projects for 'social education'—programmes on hygiene and child care, on farming, on co-operatives, or even on mechanical techniques. Shirley Graham, Director of Television in Ghana, speaks with enthusiasm of this aspect of adult education. "Television can save lives!" she told workers at the new centre in January 1965, "Let me give one example. One in eight of the babies born in Ghana are afflicted with incurable trachoma before they are a year old. Why? Is this an inherited disease in West Africa? Not at all. Science found the answer some time ago, but science has as yet been able to do little with this knowledge. It is an ancient and time-honoured custom at the time of birth, before cutting the cord uniting mother and child, to plunge the knife deep into Mother Earth. It is possible that in the old days when people lived uncrowded on grassy glades, beside rivers or in shaded forests, this custom was not harmful . . . Today, when too many of our villagers crowd into shacks to which water must be brought from some distant tap, the trampled earth is impure, and a knife plunged into it picks up the germs of trachoma and the new-born baby is doomed.

"With television, this fact can be shown in every village and crowded area. The knife, the germs (enlarged through a microscope), the effects on the infant can all be plainly seen. When mothers and prospective mothers *see* these things, when women know the dangers, how long do you think it will be before this custom goes out of practise—along with the crowded huts and the surrounding rubbish?"

This type of programme has been part of nearly every African service from the beginning, as it was of radio programmes from their beginning. Uganda, Kenya, Ivory Coast, Sierra Leone, Nigeria, U.A.R., and Algeria all list them among their regular features. OCORA, and the British Centre for Educational Television Overseas (CETO, a private organisation run under the auspices of the Nuffield Foundation, in London), both produce basic material for social education programmes. CETO prepares a 'package' programme contained in a box, which includes notes for producers and teachers, scripts for the complete series, and visual material such as diagrams, title-cards and photographs, to illustrate them. Some filming may be done on the spot to localise the illustrations as far as possible, and the rest is produced live in the studio, requiring only minimal studio resources and production experience, and a suitable 'teacher' to present the programme. A series on infant feeding is among those already available.

Third among the educational purposes of television is the more formal programme for schools, and more advanced technical or even academic education. Schools television is used widely in Northern Nigeria, to some extent in Kenya, Uganda, and in the U.A.R. But it has been regarded as less a priority than might be expected, partly because in most countries radio broadcasting to schools is already well-established. Schools television is likely to grow, however, and again CETO's package-programmes (there are series available on science and on electricity) may help. Problems exist in providing sufficient numbers of schools with sets, in maintaining the sets, and in checking that the programmes are in fact being used. But shortage of adequately trained teachers is bound to encourage further extension of existing schemes, so that the best possible use may be made of the best teachers available.

More widely used at present than the strictly schools-programmes (which are in any case, as in Uganda, often repeated in the evening for adult viewers), are language lessons, such as the B.B.C. series on learning English, which has been bought by the Foreign Office and offered to African networks. And the use of television for technical training has been discussed. Experience in the Soviet Union, and to some extent in Japan, has shown that television can be used effectively together with correspondence courses for purposes of higher education, including academic education. Though the idea has not been implemented in Africa, it is clearly a logical extension of other educational uses for the medium.

Another important function for African television, as for radio, is the stimulation of indigenous culture. Liberia produces its series on songs and folktales; Nigeria and the Ivory Coast present African drama; all the stations make liberal use of local music, whether traditional, or modern urban jazz. Uganda has already attempted historical reconstruction, and the Ghanaians have similar plans. Presentation on television has given new life to dance and drama groups which might never otherwise have survived the social changes now taking place.

Finally, the medium is potentially the most powerful of all instruments of political education. Already, Government Ministers and officials in all countries with television systems, have been enabled to present themselves for the first time to remote villages they might never hope to visit. Interviews, and discussions on government policies and projects, help to bring the rulers and their thinking nearer to the ruled. And feature programmes on life in other countries can be expected to grow in future. At present, the main source must be information services including that of the United Nations, and independent travel-film-type productions.

But most African services would like to find a way of presenting an African view of the world, and of international politics, to their viewers. These are programmes which foreigners cannot provide, and existing African resources cannot hope to meet, except possibly on a co-operative basis.

This central problem of inter-African co-operation came up at the Lagos conference, where Liberia proposed, and the conference recommended, that UNESCO and the Union de Radio-diffusion et Télévision Nationales Africains (URTNA) set up a single centre in Africa for research into programmes, a television and tape library, exchange of radio and television programmes among existing stations, and training of personnel.

Algeria made the first concrete contribution to the idea of pooled resources when its delegate announced that R.T.A. (Radio-Télévision Algérienne) proposed to mark the year of international co-operation with a filmed magazine series on Africa, which would be made available to any service that wanted to show it. Provisional titles of programmes included one on literacy teaching, one on African history, one on African women, and others on the flight to the cities, industrial and agricultural development, and the great civilisations of Africa as they are today.

There is no doubt that it is only through regional or Pan-African co-operation that African television can break away eventually from total dependence on foreign sources of programme material and technical help. Only by sharing costs can African stations afford their own correspondents to cover news stories abroad and in other parts of Africa, or make their own documentary programmes. There are major obstacles in the way, including existing contracts, and political rivalries that may make even the siting of a research centre hard to agree. But there are signs that the O.A.U. is itself setting a high priority on communications development, and that it will make considerable efforts to find solutions to the problems.

There remain problems of training of African personnel; and of the supply of receiving sets. Egypt, Algeria, Nigeria and Ghana now have their own training facilities, but only Egypt can offer a significant number of places to students from other countries. UNESCO is prepared to help in finding training officers to help on the spot, and several countries in East and Western Europe are offering places for African students to train in their own schools or in their own television systems. The B.B.C. offers comprehensive courses at its own training school, and so does OCORA. It will be some time, however, before all training can be done in Africa, and before all stations have a full African staff.

The U.A.R. had by far the greatest number of viewing sets in Africa in 1964—it claims about one and a half million viewers—and sold 200,000 sets in that year alone. Algeria came next with a total of 53,000 sets, most of them inherited from colonial times. Sudan claimed 10,000 sets, Liberia had 2,000 early in 1965, after only one year on the air, and Ethiopia, after less than six months, 300, and 2,000 after a year. In some countries, Government has taken the step of buying sets for community viewing—U.A.R. has bought 2,000 for distribution among the villages since coverage was extended to rural areas (television in Egypt covers most of the country, and not, as in most countries, only the main towns). And in Gabon, the Government offered credits to buy private sets, and has set up collective viewing centres. The number of sets in any given country, however, is only a rough guide to the number of viewers, as the average number of viewers per set may vary from six to ten or more, and in some cases be nearly 30.

Television in Africa thus remains a potential, rather than a realised force. Its fulfilment awaits training schemes, and the political co-operation necessary to develop African news and feature production. Only the U.A.R., with its advanced economy, has as yet a television service able to stand on its own feet. Arab Television, started in 1960, was broadcasting twenty-three hours a day by 1965, on three channels, supporting ten theatrical troupes, and selling programmes abroad to other Arabic-speaking countries. But the language barrier prevents it, along with other sympathetic networks in other parts of the world, from playing an appreciable part in aiding television services in black Africa.

It is one of the ironies of the African situation that the only other country on the continent with the financial, technical and production resources to support a television service on so advanced a level, is the Republic of South Africa, where the Government has obstinately refused to sanction its development. Dr. Albert Hertzog, Minister of Posts and Telegraphs, regards television as "a deadly weapon" that has been used to "undermine the morale of the white man and even to destroy great empires," and he will have nothing to do with it. He fears in fact two main consequences of the introduction of television: first that the availability of comparatively cheap material from abroad, in English, will mean the eclipse of whatever modest productions are possible at home in Afrikaans, and therefore that 'Afrikaans culture' will suffer; and second, that the ideological content of foreign material, which he complains is "drenched with liberal and demoralising propaganda," will undermine the apartheid propaganda which now dominates radio. His fears, and those of his party, are no doubt well grounded, but a substantial lobby, supported by powerful economic interests in the country, is allowing no opportunity to pass, for pressing for a television licence. A crisis might well develop should any of the present High Commission Territories, due to become independent in 1966, decide to inaugurate a television service, which would inevitably be visible inside the Republic. South Africa has already taken precautions against such eventuality by forbidding any citizen of the Republic from taking part in, or advertising on, any broadcast, by radio or television, designated 'hostile' to the Republic.

CHAPTER 13

A COLONIAL LEGACY

DEVELOPMENT OF MASS communications in Africa in
the future will depend on the development of other communications—on rail, road and air transport (for mail, quick
distribution of newspapers, and for carrying journalists and
cameramen quickly and easily about the continent); and above
all on telecommunications. These are the basic requirements
not only for the mass media, but for any economic development programme, and the African States have recognised the
fact. But the extent of the problem requires some explanation.

The colonial period did bring a system of telecommunications
to Africa. Cairo was linked first with Malta, in 1868, and then
with the English terminal at Porthcurno in 1870. A submarine
cable was laid round the East Coast, via Aden, to Durban, and
thence by landline to the Cape, as early as 1879. And in 1885 a
direct link between West Africa and Europe followed, connect-
ing Bathurst with Cape Verde and Porthcurno. Domestic
overland telegraphic systems were established afterwards, and,
much later, telephones, and eventually international links by
radio-telegraph and radio-telephone circuits. By the time that
independence was won by most of Africa in the 1960's, this
was in some respects a highly sophisticated network. But it had
one characteristic that considerably affected its usefulness to
the new States—the main lines of communication were all with
Europe. Accra, Nairobi, Pretoria, and Johannesburg were all
linked with London by radio circuit; Dakar, and the North
African capitals, with Paris; Léopoldville with Brussels. But no
direct line connected Dakar with Lagos, Accra with Conakry,
or Nairobi with any West Coast city. A telegram or telephone-
call between any of these centres had still to go first all the way
to Paris or London or both, before the connection could be
made.

At the time of independence, Africa's internal communications network consisted of one telegraphic undersea cable (part
of the Commonwealth Common User system, that skimmed

the coast of the continent from Ascension Island off the West Coast, round the Cape to Port Sudan and Aden); no telephone cable at all; overland, and often inadequate, telegraphic and telephone systems that crossed national boundaries only in exceptional cases (such as between South Africa and Rhodesia; between the East African territories of Kenya, Uganda and Tanganyika; and between the groups of countries formerly French West and French Equatorial Africa); and, most important, radio circuits, that look on the map rather like two great fans, their bases on London and Paris.

While all important decisions were being made in Whitehall and on the Quai d'Orsay, this somewhat eccentric pattern of communications was no doubt practical enough, and certainly no more idiosyncratic than the colonial divisions themselves. But Africa today is concerned to rediscover continental unity, and to break down the divisions forced upon it by foreign rule. Lagos cannot speak to Addis Ababa, nor Kampala to Algiers, without a costly and time-wasting detour via a European capital. Even airline routes follow the same well-beaten longitudinal tracks, forcing air-letters from East to West, from English-speaking to French-speaking countries, through the sorting offices of Europe.

This pattern has many political implications: until April 1964, for instance, Government Ministers in Northern Rhodesia (now Zambia) had no means of telephoning or telegraphing abroad except via Salisbury, and the undoubtedly inquisitive ears of a settler government. On April 1st, 1964 a direct line linking Lusaka and Nairobi was opened; and in November a new line between Lusaka and London. But there is still no direct line between Central Africa and West Africa, just as there is none between East and West. Again, the three small High Commission Territories in Southern Africa—Basutoland (Lesotho), Swaziland and Bechuanaland (Botswana)—find themselves in the anomalous position, just before independence, of having their telecommunications operated by a foreign country, because the South African Department of Posts and Telegraph took over the responsibilities of Cable and Wireless there when the British firm was nationalised in 1948.

Lack of adequate inter-African communication affects the mass media mainly from the point of view of news collection, by raising costs and wasting time. An acute example of what was referred to as 'cable colonialism' was cited at the UNESCO-sponsored conference on African news agencies in 1963, when the delegate of the Middle East News Agency (Cairo) demonstrated that certain messages from Cairo to Accra, Moçambique or Monrovia had to go via New York, a detour of at least 3,000 miles. Other delegates alleged that press rates within Africa could vary by as much as 600 per cent over equal distances.

The following are 1956 figures, published by UNESCO, for telephone and telegraphic rates affecting Africa. Although many are by now out of date, they give a fair picture of the problem.

Press cables from the (then) Belgian Congo to Brussels cost 2c (U.S.) per word, and the same rate applied in the opposite direction. The rate to Congo from France, however, was 18.9c, and from the U.S.S.R. 27.8c. Although the rate from the U.K. was only 6.7c, from Congo to U.K. cost 16c per word.

Rates between Europe and French West and Equatorial Africa were generally higher than for traffic with the Congo, although the French territories are geographically closer to Europe. Only rates with France were a uniform 4.9c per word both ways.

British territories were by far the best served, for within the Commonwealth they all benefited (and in 1965 they still do) from the Special Commonwealth Press Rate of 1d (1.2c) per word. This applies to all press telegrams within the Commonwealth, by a Commonwealth Agreement of 1942, as a concession to the right of the peoples of the Commonwealth to full and immediate information on the progress of the war. The postal authorities have made frequent attempts to raise the rate, but thanks mainly to the efforts of the British Press, and of the Commonwealth Press Union, they have failed.

Once outside the Commonwealth, the same high rates apply: a cable to Kenya from France cost 24.6c per word in 1956, from the U.S.S.R. 32c, from the U.S.A. 6.5c.

These rates might be compared with transatlantic routes, where comparable distances are involved. Press cables from the U.S. to the U.K. cost 5.5c per word, and from the U.K. to the U.S. only 2c. The rate from Moscow to New York was 6.3c per word.

Inside Africa, charges were even more irrational. Rates among Commonwealth countries on the one hand, and the French possessions on the other, are comparatively cheap

7

and uniform; but a cable from French West Africa to Kenya in 1956 cost no less than 42.5c per word; and even from French West Africa to Gambia (which might be a distance of less than 100 miles) cost 19.6c. Similar discrepancies affected 'urgent' press rates; and, to a lesser extent, telephone charges, though these on the whole appear more explicable than cable rates, partly because, though telephone calls between some countries can still not be made at all, calls from French-speaking to English-speaking Africa that go via London are charged at the standard British charge for Africa of £1 a minute, from there.

The immediate task in this maze of apparent inconsistency is to attempt by agreement to standardise cable charges within Africa, by placing a limit on the handling charge any one country can make, as is done in Europe. This should have the effect of eliminating large variations in charges over similar distances, and also of reducing rates in general. Consideration might eventually be given to reducing still more press rates within Africa, as an encouragement to the exchange of African news.

Other services that affect the work of news media are 'collect' facilities on press cables, which are available in most African countries, although in 1964 special permits were required in twenty-four countries before a journalist could avail himself of them. Photo-telegraphy services were available only from London to Accra, Cairo, Cape Town, Durban, Johannesburg, Lagos, Léopoldville, Nairobi, Port Elizabeth and Salisbury; but since these are in any case expensive (a minimum fee of £5 per picture is chargeable from London) only the large white-owned papers make regular use of them.

It is self-evident that high cable and telephone costs affect the transmission of news. If costs are high from Europe to Africa, press agency fees may rise, and the work of correspondents of African papers be inhibited. Within Africa, high costs impede the free flow of information between States. And if costs are high from Africa to Europe, news about Africa in the foreign Press may be affected. Lack of 'collect' facilities for journalists is similarly inhibiting, and so may be the bad quality of radio circuits for telegraph or telephone.

The Organisation of African Unity, meeting in Cairo in July 1964, decided for the first time to tackle the problems of Africa's communications, and resolved to establish a "Transport and Communications Commission." This commission met in

Cairo three months later, to recommend, *inter alia*, the establishment of three offices within the Secretariat to be responsible for Postal Services, Telecommunications and Transport respectively. It asked that member States should request an additional three seats on the Administrative Council of the International Telecommunications Union, to bring African representation up to a total of seven seats among 28; and suggested that direct telegraph-telephone communications between member States be established as soon as possible, that the provision of further co-axial submarine cables linking West and Central African States be studied, as well as the possibility of using space satellites in Africa, that preferential telegraph and telephone rates be arranged among member States. The Dakar and Rome plans of the I.T.U. Plan Sub-Committee for Africa, said the Commission, should be implemented as soon as possible.

The problems facing the planners are considerable. A start has been made through the O.A.U. on planning rationalisation of inter-African telegraphic and postal rates, and the existence of an O.A.U. body to negotiate on behalf of all with the big powers that still control the main circuits, must strengthen their hand. But the establishment of new lines of communication is the main problem. Here, radio has probably the main immediate role to play, since overland cables would have to be laid, at great expense, underground. But radio is subject to disturbance, and particularly so in the equatorial regions. It so happens that the East-West beams required to link East and West Africa are more open to such disturbance than the north-south beams that already exist. And a second, equally important, problem is the world shortage of frequencies, especially of the shortwave frequencies needed to span long distances.

However, H.F. radio does offer for the moment the only relatively cheap means of implementing a 'crash' development programme for Africa. The I.T.U.'s Plan Sub-Committee at its meeting in Dakar in January 1962, and its meeting in Rome in November-December 1963, came regretfully to this conclusion, while advocating "the widest possible use of overhead wire carrier circuits, radio relay links and cables." The Dakar plan in fact foresaw two stages, during the first of which H.F. links would connect countries, and at a later stage be expanded with multi-channel equipment. It envisaged a whole network of new channels, particularly across the 'language barriers', and many of these new lines are already in service: Lagos to Porto Novo and Cotonou, Dakar to Rabat, Léopoldville to Accra and to Nairobi, Stanleyville to Kampala and to Yei, in the Sudan, Accra to Abidjan, Tamale (Ghana) to Ougadougou, Nairobi to Addis Ababa, Monrovia to Abidjan, Bamako to Freetown. But by far the most important of the new links will be the trans-continental ones, that will connect Accra with Addis Ababa, Addis with Cairo and Dakar, Lagos with Cairo and Khartoum, and Morocco with West Africa. Of these, only a few have been implemented, and the project for an undersea cable which will eventually link West and East Africa directly has been held up indefinitely since it requires the participation of the Republic of South Africa, with which the African States feel unable to co-operate.

The Rome conference looked forward, beyond the immediate plan, to another form of communication for Africa, space communication by artificial satellite.

"For the developing countries particularly," comments a booklet on *Space Communications and the Mass Media* published by UNESCO in 1963, "satellites could generally provide greater security and flexibility, both by making alternative routes available, and if appropriate satellites were used, by assuring direct access to areas which have only limited links by cable or radio with the outside world . . . Especially in regions such as Asia and Africa where distances are great and communications facilities very limited, space communications would bring their first completely dependable contact with the rest of the world."

Although the use of satellites is, in 1965, barely three years old, and in its earliest stage of development, experts are already looking forward to their use not only to transmit sound and pictures throughout the world, but to connect with receivers small enough and cheap to be within the reach of the average daily newspaper. And once highly developed and sufficiently used, satellite communications are expected to prove more efficient and more economical than any other.

There are two basic types of satellite. The first is non-synchronous, like the American Telstar which transmitted pictures across the Atlantic in 1962, and which requires extremely complex tracking devices skilfully operated to track it across the sky during the limited period when it is 'visible' from any given spot. The synchronous satellite, on the other hand, like the Early Bird launched above the Atlantic in April 1965, orbits the earth on a constant orbit at a speed to make it appear stationary in the sky. The ground station can then be set at a constant angle, and need be far less complex, requiring less technical skill in operation. The orbit is much higher than Telstar's, however, so the signal is weaker, though means may in due course be found to boost it. So the ground station is still far from cheap, but it should be within the range of the national budget of a moderately rich country, or of a group of neighbouring countries. It is this prospect—of a series of synchronous satellites, three of which it is calculated could cover the entire earth's surface—that could open up many new possibilities for Africa.

The technical advantages include the fact that the frequencies on which they operate are not subject either to the interference or the 'fading' which bedevil present radio communications. But among the problems, apart from immediate capital outlay, is the 'political' one of the allocation of wave bands, and the assignment of radio frequencies for satellite transmissions. Since there is at present a world shortage of radio frequencies, the I.T.U. has had to approach some of the 'developed' countries to sacrifice frequencies for the use of newer communications systems, or to sanction the use of the same frequency by different countries suitably separated geographically. Satellites will extend the range of frequencies available; and they are also relatively economical in frequency usage. But diplomatic difficulties will undoubtedly arise: countries with highly developed radio systems need to expand, and those with less developed systems need to develop. UNESCO, the I.T.U. and Economic Commission for Africa have all urged that frequencies be allocated "in a manner which would give all nations and diverse cultures adequate facilities for expression," and international Allocations Conferences have already taken place.

A further complication is the fact that space satellites are being developed in the West not by international agencies, nor even by Governments, but by private enterprise in co-operation with Governments. Early Bird was developed by the Communications Satellite Corporation—COMSAT—a Congress-chartered U.S. consortium, which co-operated with forty-four other nations. Participation in the space race must thus be limited to those countries that can afford public or private funds for investment running into millions of dollars. Fourteen nations that met in Washington in 1964 to reach agreement on establishing a global telecommunications system by 1967, included no African, Asian or Latin-American country; although among the forty-five nations eventually co-operating over Early Bird, there were seven representatives of Africa: Algeria, Ethiopia, Libya, Sengal, South Africa, Tunisia and the U.A.R. The 1964 meeting set up an Interim Communications Satellite Committee, to operate until 1969, and to have jurisdiction over ground stations; and established proportions of an estimated total cost of $200mn to be invested by signatory nations, ranging from .2 per cent by Austria to 61 per cent by the U.S., through COMSAT, the American share never to fall below 50.6 per cent.

The hope for any single African State of participating effectively in the direction of a satellite system is thus remote. Only co-operation between several countries could possibly make available sufficient capital for an African stake in the venture, and it is doubtful that any States, outside South Africa (where a series of tracking stations for Early Bird have been sited, by agreement with the U.S.) could justify the sacrifice necessary even for joint investment. It is far more likely that Africa will for a very long time be only a customer, renting channels and receiving transmissions from abroad.

In the long run, satellite channels will bring reliable telegraphic, telephone and telex services where they do not at present exist; transmit news more quickly and more economically (for example, by the processes of data transmission now being developed); link continents by television; and eventually possibly revolutionise the Press by enabling newspapers to be printed simultaneously in several countries by facsimile transmission of whole pages. These new techniques could be used to hasten dramatically the development of Africa; but they could also increase rather than reduce the continent's dependence on material from abroad—lead to a new centralisation in the developed countries of newspaper production, or television production, and turning the less developed peoples into permanent consumers. This is only one of the problems of the future.

CHAPTER 14

THE NEWS AGENCIES

FOR THE COLLECTION and dissemination of news, as in its communications system, Africa still looks to Europe, and to a lesser extent to America, and to the East. In very few African countries indeed—in Southern Africa, and in Egypt—have national newspapers developed to the point at which they could finance alone their own network of correspondents abroad, or even (in many cases) internally, so that they lean even more heavily than the Press of more advanced countries on the services of the international news agencies.

Before the last war, news agency activity on the continent was negligible outside South Africa, Rhodesia and Kenya, homes of the main white-run newspapers. Papers elsewhere had to shift as best they could, gleaning something from the colonial administration (which controlled the only reliable information channels with Brussels, Paris or London, or with government posts in the interior of the country) and more through their own ingenuity.

Ingenuity was not lacking. Back in the nineteenth century, West African newspapers were apparently informed of events far beyond their own borders. The *Observer*, Monrovia, could editorialise in 1880 on the scramble for Africa and the war between the British and the Zulus in Natal. In 1883, the *Eagle and Lagos Critic* was publishing extracts from debates in 'The Imperial Parliament: House of Lords', while local news, and local grievances, poured into the correspondence columns. By 1910, the by-line 'Telegraphic Intelligence, Reuters Agency' begins to make its appearance, probably obtained through a service of multi-addressed cables operated by the news agency at the time. And by the time Dr. J. B. Danquah's daily *West African Times* was launched in March 1931, foreign news was reaching the Gold Coast readers within hours of the event.

Reuters is of course the oldest of the international agencies, and it was the first in the field in Africa. It started a news service in South Africa in 1912 in association with local news-

papers, Reuters South African News Agency, and after the
First World War it encouraged the South African newspapers
to combine and run it themselves. It was not until 1938, however, that the South African Press Agency (SAPA) was born,
and took over Reuters existing news machine.

By agreement, SAPA supplied domestic news, on South
Africa, the Rhodesias and the Portuguese territories of Angola
and Moçambique, and Reuters supplied international coverage
(about 334,000 words per month, or 10,000 words per day).
This was Reuters 'Africa Service' at the time, designed for the
'white' dailies of South Africa and Rhodesia, and serving also
the *Standard* papers of East Africa, which were able to 'leak'
Reuters beam on its route to the south. This common use of a
news service helped to forge a link between the Press of East,
South and Central Africa that is even now reflected in some
co-operation, and in the past did a great deal to make sure that
the 'European' point of view in each territory was well expressed
in the others.

In West Africa, the first regular subscriber to Reuters was
Dr. Azikiwe's *West African Pilot*, in 1945. The West African
service had been started during the war as a service to passing
troops, and it amounted to little more than 800 words a day,
received by radio in morse. It soon went on to 'hellschreiber'
which was the precursor of the modern teleprinter.

Reuters, though the biggest of the world news agencies, has
the smallest budget (about £3½m a year, compared with the
American Associated Press' £17m). Partly for this reason, and
partly because colonial governments did not look upon the
presence of independent Press correspondents with particular
favour, the organisation had very few men in Africa before
1960. A staffman might be sent to cover an event of world
significance, such as Mau Mau, and for the rest such news as
was collected came from non-professional stringers. (Zik was
himself for a while a Reuters correspondent, though far from
an unprofessional one). So when between 1956 and 1963 one
former colony after another emerged as an independent State,
Reuters found itself caught napping. Not so Agence France
Presse.

The newest of the world agencies, A.F.P. was set up in
Algiers in 1944, while France was still under Nazi occupation.
Directors of the agency were appointed by the Free French

Ministry of Information. But in 1957, the organisation became
a statutory corporation, by Act of the Legislative Assembly. Its
Governing Council was to include a member of the Conseil
d'Etat as President, and *two members chosen for their experience of
the overseas territories.*

Financed in part by subscription from the French Government, A.F.P. is not, according to M. Sabattier, Director of the
Africa Service, a co-operative, though it functions "in the spirit
of a co-operative." It is, except for Tass, the only one of the big
five international agencies directly supported by the State.
There is no doubt that its quasi-official status made possible the
position it came to occupy in the French African territories.

It inherited in 1944 bureaux in Rabat, Algiers, Tunis and
Cairo, and correspondents in Dakar and Tananarive (Madagascar). In 1945, a permanent office was established in Dakar,
intended to centralise operations in French West and Equatorial Africa. Efforts were made gradually to appoint correspondents in most of the colonies—editors of local papers, staff
members of the radio station, local businessmen. And some
exchange took place with Reuters to supply news of the
British territories. In the period 1950-55, however, part-time
correspondents were replaced by full staff members, trained
journalists from France. These were busy people, each of
whom had to be his own typist, telegraphist and reporter,
and occasionally, it seems, Government Information Officer
as well (this was the case in the Soudan [now Mali], Upper
Volta and Togo). And so A.F.P. built up its position of virtual
monopoly over the flow of news in the territories of France
Outre Mer.

As early as 1950, A.F.P. had also taken some interest in
English-speaking Africa. In 1950, a bureau was opened in
Johannesburg; and in 1956 the South African Broadcasting
Corporation became a subscriber, in accordance with its policy
under the Nationalist Government of developing its own news
services in competition with SAPA. A one-hour service by radio
to Liberia followed, and in 1958 a service to Kenya.

In 1960, then, Reuters was caught with a series of unsatis-
factory stringers in English-speaking black Africa, and no
correspondents at all in the French-speaking areas. It had some
contact with North Africa through its service to the Middle
East; but for the rest, only the SAPA-Reuter linkup could be

7*

said to be working satisfactorily. A.F.P. on the other hand was in a virtually impregnable position in French-speaking territories, and was already battering at the doors of Reuters strongholds. Mr. Patrick Cross, now General Manager of Reuters Africa Service, was sent to carry out a full survey on the spot. He visited most of the independent countries, and concluded that existing news media were in general so little developed, and so short of skilled staff, that Reuters existing World Service of about 60,000 words daily would be totally unsuitable. What was needed was a specially designed Africa Service, which would need minimal sub-editing, heavily condensed to about 16,000 words a day at most. It would also have to be written in such a way as to reflect the non-aligned policies of African governments. At present, 60–70 per cent of the news sent on this service is African, the rest international news and sport. Each day's report also includes a special feature, such as a profile of a personality in the news.

This specialised service costs hundreds of thousands of pounds a year to maintain, but Mr. Cross told me, the reward is in the reporting coverage. The organisation had by 1965 twenty-four staff correspondents on the continent, and more than fifty stringers.

It was clear that revenue to cover expenditure on this scale (a single correspondent might cost £10,000 a year to maintain, in salary, travel expenses and cable charges), would never be raised from subscriptions from newspapers which more often than not could not afford a decent printing press. The only institution that could be expected to afford the service was Government. And so it was that, in spite of the misgivings of members to whom the total independence of the Fourth Estate was a sacred principle, the organisation found itself signing contracts with African governments, and encouraging them to set up Government news agencies which would buy Reuters service, distribute it to local subscribers, and collect news themselves locally.

The first African-controlled news agency had been the Middle East News Agency, set up in 1956 by Egyptian newspapers, which felt that the country was not getting fair coverage by the international services—this was the year of Suez. M.E.N.A. was brought under direct State—or Party—control during the Press reorganisation of 1961, since when the Chairman and three members of the Board have been appointed by the Socialist Union and three elected by the agency staff. The agency is now the biggest national agency on the continent, with bureaux in London, Rome, Bonn, Paris, Geneva, Belgrade, Beirut, Damascus, Baghdad, Kuwait, Algeria, Morocco, Libya and Somalia, and thirty-five full-time correspondents abroad, including one each at Delhi, Kuala Lumpur and Addis Ababa. It also has part-time correspondents in Washington, New York, Havana, Dakar and Lagos. Internally, it has a staff of some 650, covering all main towns and regions, and serving press, radio and television. The agency's main operations have been in the Middle East, rather than in Africa, but operations in Africa are expanding.

Ghana followed, with the establishment of the Ghana News Agency in 1957, the year of independence, apparently largely on Dr. Nkrumah's personal initiative. Sir Christopher Chancellor, then Reuters General Manager, co-operated in the scheme, and arranged for Reuters to train Ghanaian journalists in agency work. The initial journalistic staff consisted of ten reporters and two sub-editors in Accra, and fifteen part-time reporters in the regional capitals. There were two teleprinter operators, one clerk and two despatch riders. One teleprinter carried home news to the Prime Minister's Office, Radio Ghana and the *Daily Graphic*; while the second carried Reuters news from London, which was received simultaneously by the three principal subscribers. Within weeks, the teleprinter service was extended to Kumasi, and soon to all eight regional capitals.

"I foresee the day," said the Prime Minister when he opened new offices for the G.N.A. in 1958, "when in the Press of the world, any news item warranted by the initials GNA will find an unchallenged place in any newspaper of standing wherever it may be."

Expansion came fast. The First Conference of Independent African States took place in Accra in 1958, and the All African Peoples' Conference at the end of the year; so heavy demands were made on the G.N.A.'s resources. It became a statutory corporation in 1960, with directors selected by Government and the main newspapers. It has an annual government grant, and is non-profit-making.

Today, the agency has come a long way towards fulfilling

the President's hopes for it. Apart from Government Ministries and Radio Ghana, it serves three newspapers by direct tele-printer link, and has other local subscribers served by courier, as well as subscribers abroad. It boasts 5,000 miles of teleprinter lines inside the country, and a staff of nearly 300, forty-five of them abroad. The agency has bureaux in London, Lagos, Nairobi and New York, and staff correspondents in Ouga-dougou, Abidjan and other African capitals. It transmits $6\frac{1}{2}$ hours daily to the London office, which re-transmits by radio beam to West and North Africa.

The G.N.A. in 1965 takes the services of A.F.P., the Arab News Agency (London), Middle East News Agency, D.P.A. (West Germany), Ceteka (Czechoslovakia), Tass, A.D.N. (East Germany), Tanjug (Jugoslavia) and Hsin Hua (China), by subscription or exchange, as well as Reuters.

The service itself is enterprising, detailed and highly pro-fessional. Mr. G. T. Anim, General Manager of the Agency, is one of Africa's most highly respected journalists, who was appointed first General Secretary, then Vice-President of the Union of African News Agencies. His policy is to provide a high proportion of African news, including fully documented reports of conferences, and of United Nations activities. Speeches by Ghanaian representatives are reported at length, but this 'formal' type coverage is not allowed to dominate political news from South Africa or Rhodesia, for example. International news still tends to stress British news.

The oldest of the other national news agencies in English-speaking Africa (as distinct from Ministries of Information functioning as news agencies for the purpose of distributing an international news service), is the Kenya News Agency. The K.N.A. was established in 1962, that is, before Kenya became independent, as the Kenya News Bureau. It had a staff of four local correspondents, and offered 6,000 words daily to East African, South African, Rhodesian, British and American newspapers. International news came from Reuters and A.F.P.

At the time of independence in 1963, the Minister of Inform-ation was Mr. Achieng Oneko, a man who had spent five years in detention following the Mau Mau rebellion, and understood very well the power of a hostile press. Backed on the one hand by his old colleague, the late Pio Pinto, and on the other by

K.A.N.U.'s information officer, an English journalist, Tony Hughes, he decided to set up a Government-controlled news agency. The local representative of Ceteka (the Czechoslovakia agency) was sympathetic, and was able to arrange for technical aid, and training of staff in Prague.

The agency was founded on the belief that however much any international agency may claim to be impartial, unbiassed and factual, none in fact is, and none selects news with a view to serving first the interests of Africa. This being so, the best chance of ensuring a fair service is to take more than one agency, chosen for their widely differing points of view, and combine them, by re-writing on the spot, "in such a way as to remove the bias from each."[1]

Accordingly, the first subscriptions were to Reuters, and Tass, though it is hoped to introduce more services in due course. Domestic news is collected through Assistant Press Officers in all seven provinces, but this aspect is not yet highly enough developed to provide a news service for sending abroad. Editorial staff in 1965 consists of one chief editor, one editor, and seven or eight sub-editors in the head office. But the agency does not expect to have its own foreign correspondents for a long time to come.

Although K.N.A. has exclusive rights over the services it buys from Tass and Reuter, it does not exercise a monopoly over other news, and papers are free to subscribe directly to any service—the *Nation* takes A.P., and the *Standard* Reuters World News Service. Even so, Mr. Hughes feels that, "the fact of our having the Kenya News Agency does constitute some kind of check to prevent items which might be detrimental to our national security and which might embarrass our international relations, from appearing, or at least from appearing without some observations by the Government."

Over the past few years, Reuters has prepared blueprints for several more countries planning to set up their own agencies, among them Nigeria, Malawi, Libya, Uganda, Tanzania and Ethiopia. Ethiopia's service, the Ethiopian News Agency, was already well established by the end of 1965, operated by the Ministry of Information, its main strength being an exceptional total of twenty-six offices in different parts of the country. The quality of the E.N.A.'s domestic service is of special significance

[1] The phrase is that of Mr. Hughes, in a letter to the writer, 20th May, 1965.

to Africa, since to it will fall the duty of a great deal of reporting on the Organisation of African Unity and the U.N. Economic Commission for Africa, both of which have their headquarters in Addis Ababa.

Like the other African agencies, E.N.A. gets its foreign news from international sources, mainly from Reuters, A.F.P., U.P.I. and occasionally from Tanjug, the Jugoslav agency. It complains, however, that these sources cannot possibly supply the African thirst for news of Africa. "So much news has been distorted, and so much has been seen through the eyes of the colonialist and the neo-colonialist, that it has been difficult to divorce fact from fiction, and wishful thinking from in-depth reporting."[1] Those responsible for the agency therefore strongly favour the development of a Pan-African News Agency to establish direct contact among African countries, and already the Director-General of E.N.A. has played a significant role in the setting up of the U.A.N.A., of which he was first Vice-President, and later Treasurer.

There are now, on paper, more than twenty national news agencies on the continent. Nine of them are in former French 'Afrique Noire', set up with the help of Agence France Presse. Between 1960 and 1961, after the dissolution of the French Community, the former Community members were anxious to demonstrate their formal independence of French ties, and national news agencies were established to replace the former A.F.P. bureaux in Cameroun (1960), the Central African Republic (1961), Congo, Brazzaville (1961), Ivory Coast (1961), Dahomey (1961), Gabon (1961), Guinea (1960), Mali (1961) and Senegal (1959). All of these except Guinea, which had technical advice and assistance from Tass, and Mali, which received aid from Ceteka, made contracts with A.F.P. And most of them not only received technical help and journalists on loan from the French agency, but actually inherited the existing A.F.P. bureau, the A.F.P. correspondent establishing himself elsewhere.

The constitutions of all the new agencies, save those in Guinea and Mali, are closely based on that of A.F.P. And the contracts with A.F.P. are all very similar, the most striking fact about them being a clause whereby the African agency undertakes "to

[1] Quoted from a memorandum prepared for the author by the Ethiopian News Agency, 1965.

distribute automatically and immediately, without omission or modification, the radio-teletype service received from A.F.P." A.F.P. therefore still has a virtual monopoly on foreign news distributed internally, for it sends out some 20,000 words a day to Africa, and if this service is to be distributed in toto, there remains very little transmission time, unless the agency is exceptionally well equipped, to distribute anything else, including, in some cases, the country's own domestic news! Most countries have since made subscription or exchange arrangements with other agencies, but the problem has been in most cases to make adequate use of them. Senegal receives Reuters, U.P., D.P.A., and A.P.; Congo (Brazzaville), D.P.A.; Dahomey receives D.P.A. and Reuters; Ivory Coast, A.P., D.P.A., Reuters, and has exchange agreements with all the 'Monrovia' States;[1] Gabon receives Reuters; and Guinea Reuters, U.P.I., Tass, and Hsin Hua. Mali takes A.F.P., Reuters, U.P.I., Tass, Ceteka, A.D.N., and Hsin Hua. Six French-speaking States, however,—Togo, Tchad, Somali (still a colony), Niger, Mauritania and Upper Volta have as yet no national news agency, and all except Togo (which plans a news agency, and now distributes a variety of services through the Government Information Office) still depend almost exclusively either on an A.F.P. bureau or an A.F.P. agreement with the Ministry of Information.

Thus the problem for the French-speaking States has been to free themselves from the confines which have made their national news agencies little more than local A.F.P. agents. Even A.P.S., Senegal, could not, as lately as 1963, afford to have its own regional correspondents within the country, and it depends on Government information services for news outside the capital, although it is one of the more richly endowed of the news agencies. Two States, however, have broken out of the strait jacket: the Ivory Coast (A.I.P.) and the Congo (A.C.P.), both of which called in Reuters to produce a plan for expansion of their services. Following adjustment to their transmitting equipment, both agencies are now able to transmit foreign and domestic news simultaneously, and thus free themselves to send out more material of their own choice. In both cases, it seems (1965), the 'monopoly' clause in the A.F.P. contract is being

[1] Cameroun, Central African Republic, Congo (Brazzaville), Dahomey, Gabon, Mauritania, Niger, Senegal, Tshad, Togo, Upper Volta.

dropped, and there seems a likelihood that other States will wish to follow their example.

It is not likely however, that any country will wish to break its links with A.F.P. altogether, for the Agence provides a comprehensive coverage on Africa of which it is justifiably proud.

There is one agency in French-speaking Africa that grew up, not as an offspring of A.F.P., but virtually in opposition to it. This is Algérie Presse Service, which was set up in Tunis in December 1961, as part of the information department of the Front de Libération Nationale, the F.L.N., aiming to give the world's Press the Algerian nationalists' point of view on the struggle for liberation. In Algeria, the Press was in the hands of French colons at the time, and news was heavily censored by the French authorities. But the A.P.S. developed its own network of military and political correspondents within the territory, and its roneoed bulletins were soon established as a major part of the F.L.N. propaganda programme. With liberation in 1962, the A.P.S. came home to a makeshift office in the Casbah of Algiers, and started a telegraphic service, followed in April 1963 by full telex facilities and a new office in the city. It has in 1965 a staff of about 150, eighty of whom are journalists. It has five bureaux abroad, the main one in Paris, where the international agency services are received (Reuters, A.F.P., U.P.I.), and others in Cairo, Tunis, Rabat and Geneva. Tunis Afrique Presse and Maghreb Arabe Presse reach Algiers by telex, and some twenty other agencies, including Tass, Tanjug, Prensa Latina (Cuba), Hsin Hua, the G.N.A., and MENA, are received on an exchange basis. A.P.S. has correspondents in New York, Brussels, Prague and Moscow, and early in 1965 was sending news out in French and Arabic, and hoping soon to be able to add services in English and Spanish.

The Algerians see the function of the mass media as a frankly propagandist one, a view underlined by the fact that the Press, and the national news agency, fall not directly under Government control, but under the Commission Centrale d'Orientation of the Bureau Politique of the F.L.N. Journalism is a political job, and it must be directed towards the political and cultural education of the people on the one hand, and serve the causes of national development, and of African liberation, on the other. The A.P.S. is therefore one of the most enthusiastic supporters of 'Africanisation' of news channels. It was an

Algerian, M. Muhammad Ben Mehal, who was elected first President of the Union of African News Agencies, when it was founded at the UNESCO-sponsored Tunis conference in April 1963.

The U.A.N.A. is a significant step on the way to opening up channels of communication for Africa. Although it corresponds to the Organisation of Asian Press Agencies, established with the help of UNESCO in 1961, its objectives are far more ambitious. Delegates to the Tunis conference were outspoken about the continuing colonial pattern of African communications, and demanded a concrete plan for altering it.

"The problem," declared Zein El Abdin Nagati, of MENA, "is rooted in the fact that in the past African news gathering and distribution was planned and implemented from the viewpoint of non-African interests." And he went on to complain of inequitable cable-rates affecting Africa: "It must be remembered that cable and telephone rates are arrived at by agreement between the sending and receiving countries. However, in the case of the former colonies of Africa there was the inevitable third party which demanded and received its share—the colonial power—thus pushing the rate up."

U.A.N.A.'s first aims are to strengthen existing national news agencies, to establish them in countries where none exist, and to examine problems of telecommunications as they affect the transmission of news. M.A.P. (Morocco), T.A.P. (Tunisia), A.P.S. and MENA all offered help in technical aid and training facilities for other African agencies.

The organisation held its first General Assembly in Algiers in December 1963, and it was here that a proposal from Ghana for a Pan-African News Agency was first mooted. The Executive was instructed to bring concrete proposals to an early session of the Assembly, and meanwhile to take all possible steps to encourage bi-lateral agreements among African agencies for the exchange of news.

The Statutes of the proposed Pan-African agency (PANAF) were finally adopted by the General Assembly of U.A.N.A. in Yaoundé, Cameroun, in December 1964, where it was also decided to set up an office for co-operation—Comité Africain des Moyens d'Information, or CAMI—comprising U.A.N.A., the Pan-African Union of Journalists and URTNA, to co-ordinate all efforts in the fields of mass communications.

The Educational and Cultural Commission of the O.A.U. had by late 1965 fully endorsed both the PANAF plan and CAMI, recommending that both be put into effect immediately they are accepted by the Heads of State.

The news agency project is probably the most ambitious and the most fundamental of all the projects for remaking the mass media on the continent. It would affect Press, radio and television alike, and make possible, for the first time, a full team of African correspondents and cameramen to cover news all over the world. As Radio Brazzaville picturesquely put it in greeting the decision in December 1964: "The imperialist and neo-colonialist Press is a giant mechanic of African brains which it unrivets and adjusts to make them receptive to certain distorted images of the world . . . The only way we can resist the imperialist Press is to supply Africa with the means of producing African news written by Africans."

The G.N.A. was no less enthusiastic, but it added the pertinent warning that, "Such a continental news agency can be most effective when it is under the political direction of a continental union government."

As Ghana recognises, the actual implementation of the project must encounter the same political obstacles as the effort towards African unity itself. To Ghana, unity is a prize to be seized by frontal attack, an urgent prerequisite to all other progress; to the more conservative African powers, it is a prey to be stalked warily, and without too much haste. M. Moulay Ahmed Aloui, Moroccan Minister of Information, opening an executive meeting of U.A.N.A. in 1964, described unity as "a concept that starts at the lowest levels of all populations, and works upwards, it cannot be imposed from the top downwards." Therefore, he felt, it did not matter whether PANAF was "achieved in five years or ten or more. What matters is that Africans are on the right road . . . Problems of personnel and telecommunications facilities are still considerable and need time for solution."

Problems of telecommunications and personnel are technical problems, the O.A.U., UNESCO and the I.T.U. are all committed to dealing with them, and most African States now see journalistic training as a priority. But the actual running of a Pan-African agency presents other problems. Its protagonists have two functions in mind for it: first, to centralise news from all national news agencies, and redistribute it to other African States; and second, and probably less immediately, to sell an All-African news service to the world agencies. The difficulties are obvious: the States of the O.A.U. agree on a minimum programme, but there are wide areas of disagreement which cannot help but be reflected in their news services. To compile a continental service fairly reflecting at once the views, say, of Algeria, Ghana, Tanzania and Ivory Coast, in such a way as would be acceptable to all of them, may prove a diplomatic task to try the skill of a Solomon.

The attitudes of the international news agencies towards PANAF vary considerably. Reuters are prepared to help in setting up the agency, and to buy its services. Patrick Cross understands that, in his own words, "it is mortifying for Africans that news of other African countries must reach them via white intermediaries"; and though he sees obstacles, he recognises that the very political inspiration behind the new agency may be its strength, producing a service different in spirit from the others, but one which the others will wish to buy.

Tass, according to its representatives in London, also welcomes the idea, and is prepared to collaborate with it, if desired to, both by offering technical help, and through exchange of information. It already exchanges news with fifteen African countries, and negotiations were proceeding, in May 1965, for exchange with two more. It has given technical help in the setting up of twelve agencies.

A.F.P. on the other hand, sees "some role" for PANAF, in distributing features and news commentaries, but mistrusts the idea of Government-controlled news. There is no doubt that A.F.P. would suffer perhaps more than any other world agency by the establishment of a really effective African agency; for it is at present in a strong position that it cannot hope much to better, and which unity would enable African states to undermine.

By the end of 1965, however, very few even of the new exchanges between agencies recommended by U.A.N.A. had in fact taken place. Ghana, Ivory Coast and the North African countries have some exchange agreements, but most of the other countries do not yet have sufficiently effective domestic news collection to justify offering their local service abroad. There is, in short, a great deal of building at national level to be done, before the dream can be realised.

CHAPTER 15

THE CONTINENT THAT GAGS ITS PRESS

AFRICA, ON THE one hand the world's most news-hungry continent, has also acquired for itself, in some quarters at least, a reputation as "the continent that gags its Press." The *Daily Mail*, London, in an article under that heading in August 1964, pointed to censorship in Ghana, attempts by the South African and Rhodesian Governments to suppress Press criticism, the deportation of journalists from Kenya, the banning of newspapers from Tanganyika, and censorship in the "leftish police states" of Guinea and Mali. Africa, declared the *Mail*, "will soon become a graveyard for the principle of free expression." Only in Nigeria, Senegal, the Ivory Coast and Malagasy did it find any crumb of comfort for the future.

It is in fact easy enough to come to the conclusion that most African States present a fairly bleak prospect for independent-minded editors. In Algeria, the U.A.R., Guinea and Mali the Government or the ruling political party are the only publishers of newspapers; in Ghana, all newspapers are run either by the party or by separate corporations under Government supervision, and outgoing Press telegrams have been censored since the attempt on the President's life in 1962. Rhodesia and South Africa have both suppressed opposition papers, and are arming themselves with a veritable arsenal of laws with which to defeat the Fourth Estate; and in Cameroun, Mauritania, Mali and Togo, copies of all newspapers must be lodged with the local administration two to four hours before publication—that is, there is an overt censorship. There is also censorship in the Portuguese colonies, where papers not infrequently appear on the streets with large blank areas from which a censored story has been removed. In addition, Gabon, Central African Republic, Congo (Brazzaville), Ivory Coast, Niger, Dahomey and Morocco boast Press legislation stringent enough to deter any editor, who hoped to survive, from any but the most punctilious adherence to Government policy. Morocco has had reason to use these powers, in banning effectively all those opposition papers which up to 1963 gave the Kingdom a reputation for tolerance; and Niger has banned all publications of the SAWABA opposition party. Africa, it would seem, would be no place for that eminent editor of *The Times*, who thundered at a past British Government: "We cannot admit that (the Press') purpose is to share the labours of statesmanship, or that it is bound by the same limitations, the same duties, the same liabilities as that of the Ministers of the Crown. The purposes and duties of the two powers are constantly separate, generally independent, sometimes diametrically opposite. The dignity and the freedom of the Press are trammelled from the moment it accepts an ancillary position. To perform its duties with entire independence, and consequently with the utmost public advantage, the Press can enter into no close or binding alliance with the Statesmen of the day, nor can it surrender its permanent interests to the convenience of the ephemeral power of any Government . . . We are bound to tell the truth as we find it, without fear of consequences—to lend no convenient shelter to acts of injustice and oppression, but to consign them at once to the judgement of the world."

Delane was laying down the principles of Press freedom and independence—the concept of the 'Fourth Estate'—as they are understood in the developed countries of the West today. This is a freedom of which the West is justifiably proud, and these are the principles on the basis of which criticisms of limitations on Press freedom in Africa are made. But they are not absolute, and it would be unjust to judge Africa by them without considering Africa's own case. The concept of freedom itself, for that matter, is not absolute, nor can be in any human society, for each man's freedom is limited both by physical environment and by the rights of other men. This all recognise. But there is a particular flaw in the Western concept of Press freedom that deserves to be examined. Newspapers are expensive to produce, and a modern daily can no longer be supported from sales alone. It must be subsidised. This subsidy can come from Government—in which case editorial is likely to be tied more or less closely to government policy. It may come from a political party, which would expect compensation for the inevitable economic losses, in political support. (No political party in Britain, for instance, has been prepared to shoulder the financial burden of a daily paper.) In a few rare cases, supporters of a paper may make up the losses by voluntary subscription. Or the subsidy may come from the sale of advertising space.

When in Europe, at the end of the last century, newspaper production costs rose to a level beyond which the individual newspaper proprietor, even a very rich one, could any longer expect to bear the risks himself, and ownership by joint stock companies was introduced, it followed logically that shares must promise a profit. The Press became at last an industry. It could not be adequately financed from sales, it would be subsidised by advertising. Advertisers would look for mass circulation; but mass circulation could be achieved only by expensive promotion. So started the scramble for circulation, the race for sensational and 'scoop' stories on the one hand, and on the other the rapid revolutions in lay-out, type-faces and use of photographs to make each paper more immediately attractive to the reader than the next.

The commercialisation of the British and American Press has without doubt brought enormous advances in technique and presentation, revolutions in production-methods that can only benefit the Press everywhere. It has frequently stimulated exciting and adventurous journalism—the 'exposure' story is a product of the circulation battle, as much as sex- and violence-mongering. But it has also brought serious disadvantages. In England, the Press has come to be divided. There are the few 'quality' papers, which because of the influential nature of their readership can still sell space on relatively small circulations; and there are a steadily diminishing number of mass circulation papers whose survival becomes questionable as soon as the A.B.C. (Audited Bureau of Circulation) figures hover below two million. The pressure on these papers is towards ever more sensational techniques, features and column-journalism, a basic vocabulary of fewer and fewer words (the *Daily Mirror* not only uses a large type and limited vocabulary, but insists on only one sentence per paragraph), and less and less hard news. What news coverage there is, may be chosen not so much for its political and social importance, as for its immediate 'human' interest. Thus foreign and political news may be sacrificed for a local sex drama, or the sure-fire success of a tale of cruelty to animals. The third consequence of Press dependence on the advertiser, and on profit, is something that Western journalists are often unwilling to concede, but are without doubt increasingly aware of. This is the built-in bias towards conservatism: advertisement is a capitalist technique, private profit is a capitalist motive. It is thus no accident that the Press in both Britain and America is basically a conservative Press, that accepts all the main assumptions of its society. It is true that the gigantic *Daily Mirror* group (I.P.C.) supports the Labour Party at election time—but one could read the *Daily Mirror* for weeks and its Sunday companion *The People* for months, without suspecting it, for neither paper is radical in any but the most humanitarian sense. They are commercial ventures with no fundamental desire to upset the society out of which they make their profits.

There are without doubt other and more direct and specific pressures on papers that make their profits from advertising: there *are* stories that are not printed because they may upset someone (an honourable editor may resist these pressures to the extent he can, but he has no answer to the argument: what do you want, a paper that compromises or no paper at all?). There are stories that are exaggerated because they suit the interests of financial backers, and others that are hidden away because they do not. But this is not the most important thing. What is important is that the overall consequence of a commercial Press is that it must go along with the free-enterprise society. The experience of those few newspapers that have attempted to challenge fundamentals bears this out. The old *Daily Herald*, the voice of Labour throughout the General Strike and the Depression, never found itself a penny of advertising. When it was eventually set on sturdier commercial feet by Odhams Press, its old campaigning nature had to change accordingly, and under the I.P.C. (Daily Mirror Group) the *Herald* died altogether. *Tribune* and *Peace News*, both left-wing and both challenging fundamental assumptions of capitalism, expect no real advertising either, and survive on subsidies from sympathisers. So does the communist *Daily Worker*, the only national daily that really challenges the assumptions of its society. It operates a complicated system of weekly guarantees from readers, and devotes a whole department of the paper to fund-raising through appeals, markets, and fairs run by Communist Party branches throughout the country.

A commercial Press is inevitably heavily biassed towards the commercial society that benefits its advertisers. Thus it cannot reflect primarily the convictions of its readers, nor offer them a real choice of editorial policy. There is no daily in Britain but the *Daily Worker* to question the fundamentals of capitalism— yet there are surely many people beyond the *Worker's* 25,000 readers who do question these values. There is no daily today that owes its loyalty to the Labour Party in the sense that the *Herald* did; but there are five—the *Daily Telegraph*, the *Daily Mail*, the *Daily Express*, *Daily Sketch* and *The Times*—to support the Tories. (Though *The Times* came out, before the 1964 election, with qualified support for Labour).

In a stable society, legal limitations, as opposed to commercial checks on Press freedom, may be relatively petty. But in explaining the stricter laws limiting the freedom of the Press in many African countries, Africans point out that a revolutionary society is not a stable one, and that most African societies, in the sense that they are in the process of rapid economic, social and political change, can be described as revolutionary. The conflict of forces generating, and being generated by change, may upset peace and order only too easily.

This argument may be used both by a Government genuinely attempting a programme of social progress, or equally by one that is resisting that progress. In its essentials, it is used by Algeria, for instance, struggling to build a socialist society, and by South Africa, trying to resist the forces of change. The apology can only be accepted if one is prepared to base judgement not simply on the law itself, but also on the cause in which it is imposed—the cause of suppression of popular aspirations, or of clearing the way for the fuller expression of these aspirations.

A closer look at the laws of a few countries will show whether this distinction is a real one.

In South Africa, there is no direct censorship, although the Press Commission which reported in 1964 proposed measures to censor outgoing press cables, and only the 'self-censorship' plan of the Newspaper Press Union forestalled a wider plan to control the Press itself. The N.P.U.'s 'Code of Conduct' adopted in 1963 contains one main controversial clause, which certain papers accepted only under protest, and the South

African Society of Journalists has consistently opposed. The disputed clause states that, "While the Press retains its traditional right of criticism, comment should take cognisance of the complex racial problems of South Africa, the general good, and safety of the country and its peoples."

The present Government has two main complaints against the Press—first, that it is dominated by the well-financed, high-circulation English-language newspaper groups, which do not support apartheid, and have a tradition of criticism; and second, that South African journalists, both through S.A.P.A. and individually as stringers for overseas newspapers, contribute to hostility to apartheid abroad by presenting it in a bad light. Several laws limit the freedom of newspapers to report and comment, and give Ministers power to suppress publications and ban journalists from writing.

Among these, the Suppression of Communism Act of 1950 empowered the Minister of the Interior to ban any periodical if he considers that it promotes the spread of communism, is published by an unlawful organisation, or serves mainly to express the views of such an organisation, or views calculated to further the achievement of any of the objects of communism. Under this act, the weekly *Guardian* was banned in 1952, and so were its successors *Advance* (1954) and *New Age* (1962). In 1962 an amendment to the act was passed enabling the Minister to demand a deposit of up to £10,000 against the registration of any new newspaper. And further amendments provided that anyone banned under the Suppression of Communism Act could also be banned from having anything to do with the publication of any newspaper or periodical, or from being quoted or published in the Press.

In addition to the Suppression of Communism Act, the Riotous Assemblies Act also affects the Press, in that it prohibits the publication of material likely to engender feelings of hostility between black and white. It was largely for fear of this act that editors in the daily Press gave the Sharpeville massacre in 1960 far less adequate coverage than it received abroad, and that the famous Sharpeville photographs have never been published in any South African newspaper. An eye-witness account of the shootings by a young white journalist working on the monthly *Drum* had to be sent abroad to find a publisher. Ambrose Reeves, former Bishop of Johannesburg, in his book *Shooting at Sharpeville*, commented afterwards: "I had the impression that the reports that *had* appeared (in the local Press) had largely relied upon statements made by the Police . . . even if my impressions were false, local editors were in the great dilemma that they might be accused of incitement."

Following a series of 'exposé' stories in South African papers about conditions in jails, the Government passed the Prisons Act in 1959 providing penalties of £100 fine or a year's imprisonment for "any person who, without the authority in writing of the Commissioner of Prisons, publishes or divulges any information concerning any prisoner, ex-prisoner or the administration of any prison." Hence the operations of the '90-day' clause of the General Law Amendment Act of 1963 (under which more than a thousand political suspects were held incommunicado for successive periods of three months) received virtually no coverage from the South African Press, until the victims eventually became the subject of Court cases. When in 1965 the *Rand Daily Mail* did finally publish an exposure on prison conditions, the Government retaliated by charging all those who had supplied information under the Prisons Act, or alternatively with perjury. The paper itself was threatened with action, and its courageous editor eventually "kicked upstairs" by Associated Newspapers.

Among the most recent of the Press laws is the 1965 amendment to the Official Secrets Act, which extends its provisions to include internal security matters involving the police. South African lawyers, and the daily Press, have warned that the Act is so framed as to prevent newspapers from publishing even the names of persons arrested for political offences, and the *Rand Daily Mail* alleged in an editorial that the act opens the way to a Secret police. The Newspaper Press Union, however, accepted assurances from the Minister of Justice that his powers would not be 'abused.'

The apparatus of South African Press law, then, taken as a whole, can be seen as designed not so much to suppress comment—though this too is advocated by the report of the Press Commission—as to suppress facts.

The principal Rhodesian law affecting the Press (before direct censorship was imposed after the illegal declaration of independence in November 1965) has precisely the same intention: the Law and Order (Maintenance) Act of 1962 provides for a mandatory prison sentence of up to seven years for publishing a false report "likely to cause alarm and despondency", and up to five years for publishing a "subversive statement." This is defined, *inter alia*, as one likely "to engender or promote feelings of hostility to, or expose to contempt, ridicule or disesteem any group, section or class in or of the community on account of race, religion or colour"; or "to have the effect of inducing any person or group of persons to resist, either actively or passively, any law or lawful administrative measure of Southern Rhodesia." The act empowers the Government to ban any publication considered a danger to law and security.

It was under this Act that the Thomson newspaper, the *Daily News*, Salisbury, was banned in August 1964, and its editor charged with publishing false reports. Eugene Wason, former editor of the *Daily News*, commented bitterly to the Assembly of the International Press Institute in London in May 1965 that, "if you report that at a meeting a bomb exploded, there was considerable damage and panic and thirty-four people were hurt, and if the Government considers the damage was not considerable, there was little panic and only thirty people were hurt, you can be charged under this section (34) of the Act."

The *Daily News* had been the only Rhodesian daily aimed primarily at African readers, and though it supported what it called "the legitimate aims of the African nationalists", had been at some pains strongly and often to denounce violence.

The effect on other newspapers of the Law and Order (Maintenance) Act, and the suppression of the *Daily News*, has been to discourage them from publishing any news of arrests, conditions in jails or detention camps, political acts of violence, or statements by African leaders, unless these are the subject of court proceedings or a Government announcement. After censorship was imposed in 1965, it became illegal for them to mention anyone restricted or imprisoned; and to their credit the Argus-owned dailies went out of their way to make fun of the regulations. They consequently often appeared with large blank white areas.

In the Portuguese territories of Angola and Moçambique,

all newspapers must be submitted for censorship before publication. There were until 1964 two independent daily papers in Lourenço Marques, *Nõticias* and *Tribuná*, which attempted to criticise Government policy. Both were taken over by the National Overseas Bank of Portugal (the B.N.U.) last year, and silenced. The proprietor and the editor of *Tribuná* were jailed. So was the editor of the weekly *A Voz Africana*, owned by the Bishop of Beira.

In independent Africa, practically every State guarantees freedom of the Press in its constitutions. Yet most states have also restrictive laws. The U.A.R. has a system whereby all newspapers must be registered by a Board appointed by the Arab Socialist Union (the national political party). Algeria's system is similar, the Press being run by a committee of the Political Bureau of the Front de Liberation Nationale (F.L.N.). In Somalia and Upper Volta a similar effect is obtained by licensing distributors of newspapers. In three countries—Mali, Mauritania and Togo—copies of all newspapers must be lodged with local officials some hours before publication. Normally, this does not involve pre-publication censorship so much as facilitate prosecution of editors and publishers for any offences committed. While in other countries, the law enables Government to seize, confiscate or ban local (as in the Central African Republic, Ghana, Mauritius, Congo Léopoldville, and Morocco) or foreign publications (as in Algeria, Senegal, Upper Volta, Gabon and Tshad). Togo appears to have had a regrettable record of persecution of journalists, under the regime of President Olympio, but all imprisoned journalists were released after the coup d'état in 1963, although, according to the latest report on Freedom of Information to the United Nations Commission on Human Rights, the laws themselves have not been changed.

What constitutes offences of the Press? Nearly all the French-speaking States base their law on the French law of 19th July, 1881, often with greatly increased penalties. Thus in Central Africa, Cameroun, Mali, Mauritania, Niger, Togo and Upper Volta (and also in Liberia and Somalia) almost identical laws provide for penalties ranging from eight days to one year in jail, or fines of between 10,000 and 10mn. Fr. C.A.F., for "defamation of the courts of law, army, public authorities and administration." The quotation is from the Act of 27th June 1963 in the Republic of Mauritania, but the principles are similar in the other States. In most of them, the protection is extended also to members of Government and the National Assembly, representatives of foreign governments, and Heads of State. Editors are also bound to insert replies of a similar length to the original article, within a period of days, if the defamed person was an official, and sometimes also if he was a private citizen. The penalties in Mali are more extreme than elsewhere, involving imprisonment for up to five years.

In several countries, including Mali, Mauritania, Somalia, Togo and Upper Volta, and, under Emergency Powers only, in Uganda, the publication of "false, exaggerated or tendentious news" (quotation is from the penal code of the Republic of Somalia) "as to disturb public order" is made punishable: by a fine of up to £150 or six months' imprisonment, in Somalia, and a fine of 1 mn. Fr. C.A.F. and/or three years' imprisonment in Upper Volta (up to five years if the report is "calculated to impair the discipline or morale of internal security forces"). Similar jail sentences may be imposed in Mali.

A third offence common to most of the former French States is that of publishing "any propaganda advocating racial or ethnic separatism or any manifestation of racial discrimination" (quoted from Article One of the Constitution of the Republic of the Congo, Brazzaville).

The terms of many of these laws are wide enough to enable governments to exert extremely strict supervision over the Press. Since October 1964, six newspapers have been banned in Morocco, including *Al Tahrir*, the organ of the opposition Union Nationale des Forces Populaires, and two papers of the Istiqlal Party, the political party which led the country to independence in 1956. In Niger, the opposition party paper *Sawaba* has been banned. Elsewhere, the law has been used more often to exclude foreign papers—Mali has powers to exclude all foreign papers, Algeria has periodically banned *Le Monde* and other French papers. The Algerians also eventually took over the assets of all those 'colon' papers that stayed behind after independence, not under a Press law, but under a general law authorising the nationalisation of foreign assets. While in the Ivory Coast, pressures arising from the very existence of the Press law led not to the banning of the French-owned *Abidjan-Matin*, but to its sale to the Government as a Government paper (now *Fraternité-Matin*).

Ghana, which has a reputation abroad as an enemy of Press freedom, has in fact banned only one paper, the *Ashanti Pioneer*, which, after a period under the censorship of the Minister of the Interior, was suppressed in 1961. There is also censorship of outgoing press telegrams, and several foreign journalists have found themselves summarily deported.

The banning of the *Pioneer* was attacked very sharply abroad. It has been a lone critical voice for four years (the *Graphic* had voiced some hostility too, but more cautiously), and it also commanded a great deal of affection among journalists for its long struggle for survival against great financial odds. The government replied that this was a period of great civil unrest in Ashanti, where the General Election of 1961 gave rise to violent attacks on C.P.P. meetings, assaults in the streets and the exploitation for separatist purposes of tribal emotions among the Ashanti, which could have been disastrous for Ghana's national unity. The *Pioneer* had been encouraging that opposition at a very critical time, and the Government felt that it had no choice but to act.

There are still a number of countries where private-enterprise newspapers or party publications coexist perfectly happily with Government—Congo, Léopoldville, is one, where Gabriel Makoso, editor of the main daily, *Courrier d'Afrique*, describes the press as "relatively free," and where seven daily papers are published, all owned by private companies, and expressing a variety of points of view. In Togo, there are currently three political parties, each of which publishes a newspaper. Nigeria has a wide variety of papers, in spite of a Press law passed in September 1964 which provides for up to three years in jail for anyone publishing *inter alia*, false reports, or reports "prejudicial to the defence of Nigeria, or to the public safety, public order, public morality or public health," and compels every editor to deliver to the Minister of Information a signed copy of every issue of his paper. But editors of papers unsympathetic to Government are increasingly uneasy, and the closing of the Amalgamated Press papers in November 1965 was probably not unconnected with the prosecution of one of their editors under the Press Act. In Senegal, Uganda, Tanzania, Kenya and Zambia, there are newspapers owned by missions, companies, and local settlers—but all are states dominated by a single political party, and none of these papers allows itself to forget the fact. The editor of *Dakar-Matin*, Michel de Breteuil, told me that he runs his paper "as if it were a government paper," that is, he comments only on foreign news and never on domestic policy.

In most of these countries, newspaper editors and proprietors have not so much existing laws to fear—Kenya has a sedition law, for instance, but it has never been tested in court in relation to the Press—as the introduction of new measures, should criticism from an independent Press seriously inhibit government policy. Tanganyika banned the Kenya-based *Daily* and *Sunday Nation* in 1964, after the 'mutiny' among Tanganyikan troops. The government subsequently lifted the ban, but made clear that it would welcome no further foreign-owned newspapers in Tanganyika. But on the whole newspapers in these countries do not expect any serious threat to their existence at present, provided, in the words of Kenya's Minister of Justice, Tom Mboya, they "write from a basic sympathy with the national effort."

On closer examination, does Africa deserve the label "the continent that gags its Press"? The only real generalisation possible seems to be that no African government, with one or two possible exceptions, seems to want a strong non-government Press in private, much less foreign, hands. Most governments, on the contrary, are struggling to set up some form of government-controlled or ruling-party-controlled, newspaper. But only a few governments, including those of the 'white' south, have a record of suppressing indigenously-owned newspapers. Newspapers have died in Africa in the past few years—but many more have been born, and a good case could be made for showing Africa as the continent of an expanding Press.

Maximum possible freedom of expression is undoubtedly a most desirable safeguard of democratic liberties, and also a stimulant to popular participation in nation-building. But one is also surely compelled to examine seriously the argument of the government that answers that there are other freedoms to be safeguarded first. The Republic of Mali submitted a report in 1964 to the U.N. Commission on Human Rights that sets out the case for control. "In December 1962," writes M. Aliou Demé, Procureur-Generale of the Supreme Court of Mali, "Mali was just entering on its third year as a politically independent state after nearly half a century of foreign domination. The end of the colonial regime was—and still is—too short in our memory for us not to seek how best to safeguard the *fundamental freedom* we had *just regained,* namely, *national independence,* for which lives and possessions were being sacrificed daily all over Africa.

"Mali's policy was therefore shaped by the need to safeguard that first of all freedoms, the freedom of the community as a whole . . .

"Every Malian realises that the nation's strength lies in the unity of its citizens, that it also depends on the community's economic development, that one of the essential pre-requisites for such development is increasing effort on the part of all, that all the country's vital forces and all the resources of law must be mobilised to that end, and that the primary means at hand is the dissemination of information, whether in spoken, written or pictorial form."

This is of course an exposition of the 'revolutionary' theory of the role of the Press. It is all the more strongly held because communications are at present so ill-developed, that it must be a primary task of Government to develop them, and to see that those that are developed serve the revolutionary purpose of Government. In detail, the Press shall be directed to encourage national unity (racial and regional propaganda is illegal), and political stability (insults to members of government and public officials are punishable, and so is the malicious publication of 'false reports'). The national Press shall be protected against foreign competition and foreign propaganda (by wide government powers to prohibit the entry of newspapers from abroad).

What has been called the 'revolutionary' theory of the Press, however, is not the only reason for the decline in Africa of Press freedom as the West knows it. There is a practical dilemma to be faced by any government of an independent State—and that involves the question of finance.

Four possible means of financing a newspaper were outlined earlier in this chapter: through government subsidy, a political party, donations from sympathisers, or advertising. The second method is open only to the few multi-party states in Africa, and few parties in any case could afford to shoulder the full subsidy required. The third requires a degree of prosperity among the sympathisers, which would be rare in an underdeveloped continent. Workers and peasants can barely afford the cost of buying a newspaper (in Nigeria, for example, circulations have been shown to rise at the end of a week or month, after pay-day, and to fall before the next pay-day). This leaves in practical terms a choice between subsidy by government, or by advertisement, or both.

There are two main objections to advertising as a means of subsidy. The first is that it places power in the hands of the advertiser. Only if all newspapers are government-controlled is this power entirely neutralised. It is true of course that few advertisers would risk offending a strong government by being caught exerting direct pressure on a newspaper. But they are likely to use what indirect pressures are open to them, in the direction, say, of a free enterprise economy, or of a policy encouraging imports from abroad, neither of which may be in the best interests of development. The conflict between the interest of the commercial advertiser and the national interest will be naturally greatest if the advertiser is a foreign company, which is usually the case. Ekani Onambélé, in his thesis already quoted, draws attention to the virtual monopoly of the great French advertising agency Havas-Afrique in French-speaking Africa. Havas is free to place its advertising as it sees fit. Yet under the five-year contracts it signs with African papers, it guarantees no minimum amount of advertising. It charges 40–43 per cent commission on foreign advertisements, demands an exclusive contract which precludes the newspaper from dealing with clients direct, and obliges it to make space available at any time. The proprietors must in addition indemnify the client in case of inability to fulfill the contract. "Such a contract," comments M. Onambélé, "is obviously an absolute weapon in the hands of the advertising agent, by which the newspaper is bound hand and foot." It is a "serious threat to freedom of expression." Some papers have broken away from Havas altogether since the appearance on the scene of a rival agency, Ouest Afrique Publicité, which does guarantee an annual minimum, though it extracts a compensatory 50 per cent commission. Algeria and Tunisia, and also the U.A.R., have established government advertising agencies of their own,

8

through which all advertising for their newspapers must be placed, to meet this very problem.

The second objection to commercial advertising in a developing country is an objection on grounds of economic policy. Press advertising, except when it is prestige advertising, directed mainly at Government, must be consumer advertising. And in an underdeveloped country, this only too frequently means advertising consumer goods, from motor cars to canned foods, that must be imported. Every African country, outside the Republic of South Africa, has problems of foreign exchange and balance of payments. None can afford, in the short or the long run, to stimulate internal demand for large rises in imports. Thus even if every advertiser were scrupulously to avoid any form of political pressure, his very existence may be a potential threat to the national interest.

Confronted with this dilemma, then, it is not remarkable if many African governments prefer to devote large sums from the budget to financing their own papers, rather than encourage the growth of an 'independent', commercially run Press. It is of course open to any government to give certain encouragements. Many African journalists who would like to see more newspapers, and who find themselves deeply frustrated by work on an inferior, uncritical government organ, advocate such measures as government investment in modern rotary presses which could be leased cheaply to independent newspapers; tax concessions for the Press; particularly on the import of newsprint; or even direct government subsidies to privately owned papers. But the conflicts are fundamental to the situation of any developing country, and they remain unresolved.

CHAPTER 16

BREAKING THE VICIOUS CIRCLE

WHAT THEN ARE the conditions required for mass media to develop? How can they best help the struggle to defeat poverty, ignorance and disease? How can radio, television and the Press be enabled to speak with an African voice, conscious of African priorities, rather than as loudspeakers for the voices of foreign news and features agencies, transcription services and television film-makers?

The first practical requirement is obviously an efficient postal, transport and telecommunications system for the continent. Member States of the O.A.U. are constantly pressing, through the International Postal Union, the International Civil Aviation Organisation, and the International Telecommunications Union, that the patterns of the past that centred all African communications in Europe should be broken, and direct trans-continental routes established. Since transit via Europe is likely to be profitable to Europe, in airport and post office charges, for instance, changes inevitably encounter resistance, and the process takes time. Africa, too, will need a voice in the evolution of new communication techniques, notably in the field of satellite communication. Seven African countries are already signatories to the forty-five-country agreement with COMSAT on the planning of a world satellite communications system; but inter-African co-operation will be required to provide capital for building earth-stations if adequate use is to be made of the new channels.

The second need is for training in all fields of communication, and initially for journalistic training for newspapers and radio, and production and programming for radio and television. It is only when sufficient local skill is available that dependence on tape and film and features from abroad can be reduced, and the real educational ambitions for the mass media be realised. The B.B.C. and OCORA both offer training for radio and television, and so does the Thomson Foundation's training school in England. Although Algeria, Ghana and the U.A.R.

each has a training school for broadcasting, there are however few facilities for training in Africa, and the shortage of professionals everywhere except in the 'white' countries is acute. OCORA still trains French students for senior posts in French-language stations. And many services are still actually managed by British companies, or by OCORA. Thomson Television International set up and provided senior staff for the services of Ethiopia, Sierra Leone and the Ivory Coast, and managed Kenya Television until it was nationalised in 1964; Rediffusion, through a local subsidiary, manages both television and radio in Liberia, and managed television in Western Nigeria until 1963; Granada Television manages Northern Nigeria Television, still with a largely ex-patriate staff; and OCORA participates in the management of the services of Gabon, Dahomey and the Ivory Coast. In most cases, local personnel have been or are being trained to take over production and technical posts, and in all cases final control rests with the Government concerned. But very important executive powers are in the hands of the companies, which are directly responsible to Government for programming and financial policy.

There are now at least five full-time training courses open to newspaper journalists in Africa: two of them are run by the International Press Institute and financed by the Ford Foundation of America. One school is in Lagos, and the other in Nairobi. The I.P.I.'s operation started in 1963, offering six-month courses in short-hand, reporting technique, sub-editing, lay-out, general knowledge and English language to journalists who have already had at least two years' experience on a newspaper. Mr. Tom Hopkinson, former editor of *Picture Post*, London, and *Drum*, Johannesburg, is in charge of the Nairobi school, and reports that 75 per cent of the students on his first course have been able to accept further responsibilities on their papers since their return. Ninety students altogether had passed through the courses by mid-1965, and a further 120 were expected to do so in 1965-66. A beginners' course was also to be started for women journalists, and other specialist schemes including training in picture journalism.

In addition to the I.P.I. schools, Nigeria has its Jackson School of Journalism at Nsukka University; Ghana has started a training school; and Cairo has a well-established University course for journalists. The International Organisation of

Journalists (headquarters in Prague) ran a course in Algiers in 1964; and short courses and seminars have also been run at Dakar and in Abidjan. UNESCO ran a course for about fifty Congolese journalists in Léopoldville in 1962/63; the International Federation of Journalists (headquarters in Paris) ran a four-month course in Conakry in 1964; but most of the remaining training offered has had to be abroad. UNESCO provides scholarships for several African journalists to attend the Journalism Centre of Strasbourg University, in France; many American universities offer places in their schools of journalism to African students; and several news agencies, including Reuters, Ceteka and Tass provide specialist training in agency work for experienced newspapermen.

There is one other project for training African journalists that deserves mention, if only as a warning that motives behind offers of assistance may not always be unmixed. This is a West German venture, privately sponsored by 'The Berlin Institute for Mass Communications in Developing Countries' (the main backer of which appears to be the Axel Springer group of newspapers, of which *Die Welt* is a member). Started in 1964, and claiming to be the first training school for African journalists outside the continent, the new school offers two four-month courses annually, for fifteen journalists. The first course comprised six students from Nigeria, two from Kenya, and one each from Cameroun and Mauritius. An eight-page broadsheet produced by the students at the end of the course suggests that West German policies will receive sympathetic treatment from them on their return to their newspapers. "All Germans hope for Unity" is the main story on page two; "Berlin's Way to Freedom—an interesting hour with the Governing Mayor of Berlin" on page three describes an interview with Herr Willi Brandt; and articles on the following pages are titled: "The Wall, a Symbol of Terror," and "Resigned, but Hopeful . . . Impressions of the People of Berlin." The stories themselves would do credit to the Federal German Information Office.

The total output of these various schools and course is already beginning to improve standards at sub-editorial level. The greatest remaining shortage is probably of suitable young men and women to enter the profession as trainees. In-service training is from many points of view the most effective: but few papers can afford a full-time training officer, such as the

Daily Mirror group and Thomson's have had in Nigeria. And the standard of secondary education is often so low that few trainee reporters can be expected to work without extensive supervision. There is clearly a need for more training for beginners, at least in general knowledge and in the 'political' techniques of journalism.[1]

The third essential for the African mass media is to tackle the problem of dependence on foreign sources for news and feature material. The main sources of information are at present the 'big five' news agencies, Reuters, A.P., U.P.I., A.F.P. and Tass, none of which is African. Although twenty-one African countries have their own national news agencies, only the Ghana News Agency, Algérie Presse Service and the Middle East News Agency (and of course S.A.P.A.) have their own correspondents abroad, and none of these has anything like adequate international coverage. M.E.N.A. and G.N.A. cover London and New York, A.P.S. covers Paris, Moscow, Prague and New York, and M.E.N.A. is well represented in the Middle East. But large areas of the world must go virtually unreported, except through non-African eyes. And so must Africa itself. G.N.A. now has offices in Lagos and Nairobi, and M.E.N.A. has correspondents in Lagos, Dakar and Addis Ababa; but most African agencies must depend either on occasional help from press attaches in their Embassies or High Commissions, or on the world agencies. The problem is made all the more acute because many agencies have not any real domestic news-collecting machinery to enable them to feed their own Press and offer a domestic service for sale or exchange abroad.

One of the dangers of this situation is that lack of indigenous material for Press, radio and television is a temptation to foreign propaganda and information services to flood the African media with their own material. The radio programme

[1] One journalist working in Africa wrote to me of the "shortage of people who can write anything that is not mere exhortation or declamation, frequently at a very high level of abstraction, and frequently one cannot help but feel in a language that is made deliberately pretentious; few have any understanding of the use of source material and facts, or of the art of using hostile sources as targets for polemic and as general sources of information; few have any appreciation of the continuity of news—in other words, that what happens this week must be related to what went before it if it is to have a meaning; few realise that the reader must be made to feel that he is drawing the conclusion which must automatically arise from the manner in which the facts are presented."

planner receives taped material in abundance, through the Transcription Services, for example, of the British Central Office of Information, which offers a free service, or the B.B.C., which provides up to 200 hours of taped programmes a month, in various languages, and at a nominal fee; the Packaged Programmes services of the Voice of America (about 72 hours a week, and also in several languages), and the Canadian Broadcasting Corporation; and the recorded material of OCORA. His counterpart in television receives the catalogues not only of the commercial agencies, offering film and video-tapes at rates bearing no relation to their original sale price in Europe or America; but from the C.O.I. (whose 'Films for Television' service includes C.O.I.-produced newsreels as well as independent programmes bought for free or low-cost distribution), and from the U.S. Information Agency (which claims that 10,000 hours of Agency-provided material was seen on television throughout the world in 1963).

To find itself the object of a series of major information and propaganda efforts by all the great powers is a mixed blessing for Africa. There are advantages—workers in the mass media can seldom complain that they are ignorant of the attitudes of the world powers to any problem, for briefings, texts of speeches and even television features see that they are not ignorant for long. Such background material may be of great value to an editor, and so may the 'non-controversial' material sent out by all the agencies: news photographs and fact papers from the U.S.I.A., cultural discussion programmes from the B.B.C., cartoon films from Czechoslvakia or Jugoslavia, popular science features from the Soviet Union. But Africa's principal need is for hard news, and for facilities to develop its own view of the continent and of the world. Here the efforts of the information services are not simply of little use. They may be an embarrassment. Political material which seeks to further the policy of a foreign State may seriously conflict with the non-aligned ideals of independent Africa. Or the more professional foreign productions may compete with the local product in such a way as to inhibit development.

Every news medium throughout the world may be subject to propaganda attempts to persuade it to adopt one line or another, and this is accepted as part of the consequence of living in an era of rapid communications. Editors after all are not normally compelled to make use of the material offered them. But in a situation where indigenous communication development is poor, where there is an acute shortage of journalists trained to distinguish fact from someone else's comment, and to recognise how selection can be used to slant a story, a bombardment of foreign information material may be so bewildering as to prejudice local enterprise.

A radio producer, for instance, who prefers to broadcast a highly professional recording of American jazz rather than spend money and energy on knocking an inexperienced group of local musicians into the shape of a creditable programme, may be exercising economy, but he is missing the real opportunities that radio offers him. And an editor who would rather publish a well-written analysis by a British journalist than wrestle with the fumbling efforts of his own staff, may be making an understandable choice; but it is a short-sighted one, not only because he is failing to encourage the indigenous product, but because the British journalist is selecting his facts from the stand-point of London, and not that of Nairobi or Lagos.

How hard foreign institutions are trying to influence the mass media in Africa can only be understood by taking a closer look at the information efforts. The following is a list of titles, unsolicited and received regularly by one East African periodical in 1964 and 1965.

From 'Western' sources:
Dateline. U.S.A. Published monthly by U.S.I.S., Kampala
The American Outlook Published monthly by U.S.I.S., Accra
AFL-CIO Free Trade Union News Published monthly by AFL-CIO, New York
News Features—Special Items of Interest to Students and Youth. Published monthly by Institute for International Youth Affairs Inc., New York
AMSAC Newsletter Published monthly by the American Society of African Culture, New York
Commonwealth Today Published monthly by C.O.I., London
Forum Service Published at least twice weekly by Forum Service, London
Comment Published weekly by Communist Party of Great Britain, London

Press and Radio Service Published weekly by International Confederation of Free Trade Unions, Brussels

The Bulletin Published weekly by Press and Information Office of Federal German Government, Bonn

From 'Eastern' sources:

Review of International Affairs Published fortnightly by Federation of Jugoslav Journalists, Belgrade

Commercial News Published fortnightly by Federation of Chambers of Commerce, Belgrade

Solidarity Illustrated Monthly Magazine for Czechoslovak-African Relations, Prague

Information Bulletin Documents of the Communist and Workers' Parties, Articles and Speeches, Prague

Trade Union Press Published fortnightly by World Federation of Trade Unions, Prague

China Reconstructs Illustrated monthly, published by China Welfare Institute, Peking

From African sources:

New Ghana Illustrated monthly published by Ghana Information Service, Accra

Ghana News Bulletin Published weekly by Ghana High Commission, Dar-es-Salaam

Uganda News Published weekly by Department of Information and Broadcasting, Kampala

Kenya Calling Published weekly by Kenya News Agency, Nairobi

African Association Review Published monthly by African Association, Cairo

This is not a complete list, since it was supplemented with other publicity material from abroad and from local embassies—special pamphlets, press releases, and photographs. But it does indicate the main facts about the operation of information services in most parts of Africa. It shows that foreign organisations are taking the continent very seriously; that Africa's own information effort is as yet comparatively small; and that the bulk of material comes from 'Western' sources, which supplied more titles, and more frequently, than the 'East.' Most of the 'Western' material was in fact specifically intended for Press, and sent by airmail.

By far the most professional of the publications listed is *Forum Service*, which is apparently a private venture on professional journalistic lines, like any commercial feature agency. Releases are interpretive, and usually consist of signed articles, profiles or columns commissioned from well-known journalists. In one fortnight in May 1964, for example, they comprised a profile of the President of the Indian Congress Party by the deputy-editor of *The Hindu*; two articles by an American journalist on the U.S. Civil Rights struggle; a 'viewpoint' column by a journalist on *The Economist*, London (items included an appreciation of President de Gaulle, the India-China border dispute, and problems of intellectuals in Poland); and an article by an exiled Spanish journalist on the trial of the poet Dionisio Ridreujo. What is remarkable is that so expensive a service should be made so widely available, free of any charge, and yet give no indication of its sponsorship. The letterhead gives an address, and the name of its editor, Mr. Murray Mindlin. Though the address is in London, Forum Service is in fact American-financed, and has close relations with the Congress for Cultural Freedom.

Only the rapid development of national news and feature agencies, as news collectors and not simply as agents for the sale of international services, can enable indigenous news and comment to compete with the highly skilful services already available. The financial investment necessary to establish adequate domestic and foreign coverage, let alone the additional tape and film material required by radio and television, is beyond the resources of most African States, and the only solution possible is co-operation, by the exchange of news and feature material, joint financing of foreign correspondents, and the eventual emergence of a Pan-African News Agency. The concept should be planned from the beginning to include a radio and television section—M.E.N.A. already acts for U.A.R. radio and television, usually by commissioning coverage of events by commercial agencies, through its offices abroad. This is an expensive plan, but it is the only possible plan if media in Africa are not to increase, rather than reduce, their dependence on foreign material in every field.

The fourth and final major problem confronting the mass media, the problem underlying all others, is that of finance. Who is to finance them, as they develop? Radio is everywhere (except in the Portuguese colonies) a State or State-chartered concern; and so is television,[1] although in several countries foreign companies are contracted to manage it and thus exert considerable influence over policy. But the question arises mainly over the Press.

There are still several African countries, including six French-speaking States and the three High Commission Territories in South Africa, without any daily newspaper. Here the problem is clearly an economic one, for the small States without a daily are also without a literate population big enough to support one, or even rich enough, perhaps, to buy a newspaper every day. Finance by circulation, and its twin, advertising, is therefore impossible. Even in Niger and the Ivory Coast, where the French Société Nationale des Entreprises de Presse has undertaken the management of papers, losses are reported to have been sufficient to deter the organisation from embarking on similar ventures in other less developed societies. Are these countries to remain without newspapers? Must mass literacy campaigns come first? Gabon has television—a powerful instrument in a literacy campaign—and no daily paper. So has Congo-Brazza. Theirs may indeed be examples of the use of the newest of the mass media to create conditions for the establishment of the oldest. But for such a plan to succeed, development must depend upon Government's looking on the mass media as public services, in which it is compelled to invest for no immediate return.

In the majority of countries where a daily Press has developed, newspapers fall into two main categories: those financed by governments or ruling political parties (*The Ghanaian Times* and its sister papers in Ghana, the *Morning Post* and its Sunday in Nigeria, *The Nationalist* in Tanzania, *L'Action* in Tunisia, *The Ethiopian Herald*, *Fraternité-Matin* in the Ivory Coast—financed in this case with outside help—*Togo-Presse*, *Horaya* in Guinea, *L'Essor* in Mali, and all the Algerian and U.A.R. papers); and those owned by foreign companies, and in a few cases by local Europeans. With a very few exceptions— the *West African Pilot* in Nigeria, *Ngrumo* in Tanzania, and the Congo papers (though their position too involves strong participation of foreign capital)—there are no independent

[1] In both Rhodesia and Zambia, where television had been run by private companies, steps were being taken by Government in 1965 to assume control.

dailies in Africa financed by local African capital. The choice is between government, or party, and foreign finance. What then are the present sources of foreign investment, and which are the firms that play a major role among the mass media in Africa?

They are mainly British firms (Thomson; International Publishing Corporation—the Daily Mirror group; Rediffusion Ltd.; Granada Television; Lonrho; and Television International Enterprises); French concerns (de Breteuil in Senegal and Cameroun, HAVAS the great advertising agency, and governmental organisations such as OCORA and SNEP); and South African, or more accurately, companies belonging to the complex of Rand-Copper-Belt mining interests that involve capital from South African, British, United States and Belgian sources, and are concerned through the Argus group with newspapers in South Africa and Rhodesia (which up to 1965 controlled the major share in Rhodesia Television), through the Union Minière with the Katanga Press, and through Lonrho with the *Times of Zambia*, *Zambia News* and Zambia Television.

Thomson's is the most diffused enterprise, for it controlled in 1965 twenty-two newspapers and sixty-four magazines in the U.K., and was associated with thirty-eight newspapers in Canada, twenty-one in the United States, three in the West Indies, one in Liberia (*The Star*), and, until November 1965, two in Nigeria, the *Daily Express* and the *Sunday Express*. It owns two publishing companies in South Africa,[1] and eight in Rhodesia and Malawi. It owns Scottish Television Ltd. (a "licence to print money" Lord Thomson once called his contract with the Independent Television Authority), and through its subsidiary Thomson Television (International) it runs or helps to run television stations in fourteen countries, including Ethiopia, Ivory Coast and Sierra Leone; and is associated with three television companies in Canada and one in Trinidad, and with five radio companies in Canada and one in Trinidad. Profits for the year 1964-65 amounted to over £6mn. Thomson had shares in Rhodesia Television, and made several attempts to acquire newspaper interests in East Africa. For a time his organisation had a share in the *Nation* in Kenya,

[1] Lord Thomson said of these in his Chairman's Review for 1964 that they had had "an excellent year's trading and I confidently predict that these investments will become increasingly valuable in the years ahead."

whose television system Thomson's incidentally set up. Thomson's is thus involved in all the areas of English-speaking Africa, and has begun to make an entry into French-speaking Africa as well.

Lord Thomson is down on record as believing that the Press "must operate as a business on good business principles."[1] In his British operations, he insists that his newspapers make a profit, and has closed down papers that did not. But it seems that the requirement has been relaxed as far as his newer interests in the 'developing areas' are concerned. "In these areas," he told his shareholders in 1964, "the profits we hope to achieve are less than they would be for comparable enterprises in Britain, but we feel it right that we should play a part in the expansion and progress of the developing countries."

In fact, Lord Thomson, although he prides himself on not interfering with local management or editorial policy in any way, takes his responsibilities in international mass communications very seriously. He talks of his 'stewardship' over the newspapers he owns. And he is not without political ideas. He expressed some of them at a Press conference in Ontario, Canada, in December 1964, when he said that he believed that African countries lacked the necessary background and training to be allowed to use the Press. "Use of the Press results in much irresponsible criticism of the government in local African newspapers," he said, and he added that African politicians were "peculiar people. Unless they have their name in large type on the front page they think you are against them."[2] In more serious mood, he explained to his shareholders his motives in entering the field of television in the developing countries: "It is clear that were it not for what is essentially S.T.V. Ltd.'s initiative in this field, a number of the newly formed nations of the world would have been obliged to turn for assistance to members of the Communist bloc, who do not share our view that the provision of technical services should not be regarded as a lever for interference in the political affairs of the countries concerned."[3]

Mr. James Coltart, deputy Chairman of the Thomson

[1] Speaking at the Ninth Commonwealth Press Conference in 1961.

[2] Reported in *The Star*, Johannesburg, 2nd January, 1965, and subsequently attacked in *The Nationalist*, Dar-es-Salaam, in an editorial.

[3] Chairman's Annual Review, The Thomson Organisation, 1964.

Organisation, and reputedly the financial wizard behind the empire, told me in 1964 that far from merely making less profits than in Britain, Thomson was making very considerable losses on the *Daily Express* in Nigeria, and was making losses on the *Daily News* in Salisbury before it was suppressed. I asked why, in view of Lord Thomson's belief that newspapers should be economically viable, he carried on publishing. "My dear," said Mr. Coltart, "have you ever considered how much the Americans spent on building roads and hospitals in Cuba? And how little Krushchev had to spend in training Castro? And where are the Americans in Cuba today?" Mr. Coltart is a strong supporter of Moral Re-armament, and refers frequently to the struggle for "men's minds." To my knowledge, none of the Thomson newspapers or television networks in African has been accused of giving undue publicity to M.R.A., though the charge has been levelled in Britain against S.T.V. and against the *Scotsman*.[1]

The International Publishing Corporation, which entered West Africa as the *Daily Mirror* Group in 1947, is now perhaps the biggest publishing corporation in the world. It has ninety-one subsidiary and associated companies in the United Kingdom (including Associated Television, one of the largest of the commercial television companies), Australia, New Zealand, Barbados, British Guiana, West Germany and Italy.

Unlike the Thomson papers, the *Daily Times* of Nigeria has been making a steady profit (£72,638 in 1963-64). In fact, the *Daily Times*, the *Daily Mail* in Sierra Leone, and the former I.P.C. paper, the *Daily Graphic*, in Ghana, are the most profitable, if not the only profitable, newspapers in West Africa. Also unlike Thomson, I.P.C. does not seem to have made any recent move to expand its interests in West Africa.

Rediffusion and Granada are two of Britain's largest television companies, each of them controlling a network of subsidiary companies. Rediffusion Ltd. controls twenty-five companies, including electronic firms, television set rental and radio-diffusion companies. It runs both television and radio systems for the Liberian Government, and radio-rediffusion in West Nigeria and in Orlando township, Johannesburg.[2] The

---

[1] cf. Tom Driberg, *The Mystery of Moral Rearmament*, 1964.
[2] Which pipes the government's apartheid propaganda over Bantu Radio to the African people.

Granada Group Ltd., whose subsidiary runs Northern Nigeria Television, owns or controls thirty-six cinemas in the U.K., has interests in eleven others, and owns all shares of Granada Television Network Ltd., and five other companies. Authorised capital of the group is £7,100,000 (1965 figure).

Another small but important British company with interests in African mass media is Television International Enterprises Ltd., which buys television programmes abroad for Ethiopia, Sierra Leone and Kenya Television, as well as for other stations in developing countries. The company was founded with a small nominal capital in 1959, by Colonel David Stirling, who still owns the largest single block of shares. Colonel Stirling was from 1947 to 1959 President of the Capricorn Africa Society, which sought to stem the tide of African nationalism in Central and East Africa by urging Europeans to concede partial voting rights to Africans, on educational and other qualifications. And amongst the directors of the firm is Aidan Crawley, Conservative Member of Parliament for West Derbyshire, a former Under-Secretary for Air in the 1945 Labour Government, who crossed the floor in 1957. Mr. Crawley is a specialist on the subject of communism in Africa. He told an audience at the Royal Commonwealth Society early in 1965 that Africa presented a depressing prospect for the West, but that "we have to go on giving aid and investing, but I hope with a little more discrimination. I really do not think it is sensible to give extensive help to rulers who are doing their utmost to undermine other African rulers who are our allies and our friends. I think we have to continue to struggle with our own problems here, and I think above all, we have to give up having a guilty conscience.

"People are still speaking as if the colonial period was a contemptible period; I have no hesitation in saying it was a great period . . .

"Only if we produce a mental and moral renaissance in Europe, are we going to be looked to by the emerging nations for true inspiration. I do not believe—and I say this with the utmost affection and respect—that the Americans can do this. I believe it can only be done in and through Europe, and if the Commonwealth is to mean anything in the future, it will only, in my opinion, do so if we lead Europe."

Lonrho, formerly London and Rhodesian Mining, which

owns the *Times of Zambia* (*Northern News*), the *Zambia News*,
and a share in Zambia Television, is also a London-based
company, but it belongs in the Southern African complex of
mining and land companies that, through the Central-Mining-
Rand-Mines Group, exerts a large measure of control over the
Argus Printing and Publishing Company, which in turn
controls the Rhodesian Printing and Publishing Company;
and through its connection with the Union Minière du Haut
Katanga, influences *L'Essor du Katanga*. Lonrho was established
in 1909, and has sixty-three subsidiary and associated companies in Central, East and Southern Africa. The Hon. Angus
Ogilvy, cousin by marriage to the Queen, and director of
thirty-seven companies, is a director, and Mr. Harold Drayton,
the City of London financier who controls extensive interests in
the Republic of South Africa, is a major shareholder. But the
largest single shareholder listed (apart from two blocks of
shares held by the Standard Bank as nominees) in 1965, was the
British South Africa Company. B.S.A.C. is Rhodes' original
Charter Company, that administered Southern Rhodesia until
1923, owned all mineral rights there until 1932, and until the
eve of Zambian independence in 1964, all mineral rights in
Northern Rhodesia. Former directors include Lord Salisbury,
and 1965 directors Lord Malvern (first Prime Minister of the
Federation of the Rhodesias and Nyasaland), Sir Charles
Hambro of Hambro's Bank and the Union Corporation, and
Mr. Harry Oppenheimer.

B.S.A.C. has for some time had links with the Anglo-
American Corporation in South Africa, but a development in
1965 formalises the connection. According to Mr. Oppenheimer's annual review as Chairman of the Anglo-American
Corporation (published on June 1st, 1965), the Corporation's
main investment company in London, Consolidated Mines
Selection Company, had been amalgamated with B.S.A.C.
and the Central Mining and Investment Corporation, as
Charter Consolidated Ltd. "Charter", said Mr. Oppenheimer,
"will invest chiefly outside South Africa, and to a certain extent
outside the African continent." Through B.S.A.C., then,
Charter has a major interest in Lonrho, and thus in Zambia's
Press. Central Mining, on the other hand, is part of Central-
Mining-Rand-Mines which in turn is the major investor in the
Argus group of South Africa and Rhodesia. Thus Anglo-

American, if indeed it had no direct interest in Argus before 1965 (and the fact that Rand Mines and Anglo-American shared four key directors, and some with Argus Printing and Publishing itself, suggests that it did), it is now a major shareholder. There is some irony in the fact that *The Northern News* was sold out of the Argus group a year previously, almost certainly because the group's South African origin might be embarrassing in an independent African State. The *News* was not an unprofitable venture.

Whether the *Times of Zambia* will now be operated, as H. Lindsay Smith in 1946 accused the Argus of operating, on the premise that "what is good for the gold (or copper) mining industry is good for the country," remains to be seen. The relationship between owner and editorial policy is rarely a simple one, in any large newspaper concern. Both Thomson and I.P.C. pride themselves on refraining from interference with the day-to-day policies of their editors, and Michel de Breteuil, son of the founder of the de Breteuil papers in West Africa, and now editor of *Dakar-Matin*, so far from using his paper to intervene in local politics, says that he refrains from comment on internal affairs altogether. Peter Enahoro, editor of the *Daily Times*, Lagos, apparently finds no contradiction in being the African editor of a British-controlled paper, and is far more disturbed by the policies of African governments, which he accuses of "trampling freedom under foot." Hilary Ngweno, former editor of the *Nation*, Nairobi, feels that management and editorial posts in African hands are sufficient guarantee that a foreign-owned paper will speak with an African voice.

The real significance of foreign ownership for African news media does not lie in the danger that day-to-day policies will be dictated from abroad. It lies in something less concrete, and more pervasive, in the general orientation of the media (dictated in part by where they buy their material, and how they train their journalists,) and in the 'cast of mind' of editorial staff, which in turn influences that of the reader. The fact that the British Foreign Office sets great store by the presence of British personnel in key training and administrative positions in the Africa media tends to underline the political significance of these enterprises; and there is no doubt that the companies themselves recognise a political role in helping to mould public opinion, or even simply in providing investment which otherwise might come from sources 'hostile' to the West.

From the point of view of some African States, however, the inevitable built-in conservatism of foreign free-enterprise may be less attractive than to the former colonial power. Although editors may be African, and given a freer hand in fact than many of their colleagues working for Government newspapers, and although the Thomson papers in Rhodesia and Nigeria were on occasion bold in their criticism of the regimes under which they worked, there are certain things which foreign papers cannot do. Just as the Argus has never seriously criticised the South African mining industry, so British-owned papers will be unwilling to question the basic assumptions of capitalism, or of Western defence strategy against 'communism.' But these are the very assumptions that Africa finds itself questioning, through the O.A.U. and in its campaign for the liberation of the remaining African colonies.

A second, and related, ground for conflict between the interests of newspaper-owner and those of national policy, arises from the fact that foreign-owned papers are all commercial papers, depending on mass sales, and on advertisement, to keep them alive. On the one hand the urge for profit brings in its wake technical accomplishments, professionalism, variety of coverage and imagination of presentation that can only benefit the African Press as a whole. But on the other hand it brings a tendency to stress the 'entertainment' rather than the educational aspects of newspaper publishing. The *Daily Times* often reports local court cases to the virtual exclusion of foreign news, and M. de. Breteuil says that he would take the foreign news off his front page at once, since "local news sells papers," were it not for pressure from influential Senegalese readers. The *Nation* has good news coverage, but it feels compelled to feature 'pop' charts rather than the more earnest preoccupations of adult education.

The tendency towards the trivial is most serious when there is no strong African newspaper able to do the educating; in which case, a commercial Press may well be an obstacle to progress. Its competition is likely to overwhelm new and under-capitalised ventures. Increase Coker quotes an example from Nigeria, where distribution is a major difficulty, since railways are inadequate. The *Daily Times* can afford to run its own fleet of lorries, each expected to last a mere six months, to carry its papers to each of the three regions. The *Daily Express* did the same. Indigenous papers, however, are forced either to abandon a comparable national sale, or to invest in fleets of lorries themselves. "Several attempts were made in the past," writes Mr. Coker, "to form a distribution company owned jointly by the newspapers and taking over the distribution of all publications . . . No positive step has however been taken to form such a company, partly because the other foreign-financed newspapers do not seem enthusiastic about it."

Those governments that aim at a 'crash' programme of economic development in which they hope to enrol the mass media as instruments of their campaign, will be the most likely to find themselves intolerant of a competitive and commercial Press, especially when that Press is foreign-owned. The problem for countries planning a socialist pattern for their society is accentuated because private enterprise, and above all commercial advertising, is likely to conflict with such a policy. And if foreign enterprises are difficult to compete with now, they are likely to be virtually impregnable in the future. We are on the verge of technical developments in newspaper production that will revolutionise the Press throughout the world—web-offset machines can already reduce capital outlay and running costs dramatically, picture transmissions will be made eventually cheap and easy by satellite, and transmission of whole pages by satellite has already been achieved. For Africa, these developments could help the rapid and imaginative growth of the indigenous Press; but they could also be used by the great international companies to carry them away out of all reach of competition, and even, conceivably, to reduce the Press in the developing countries to the wholesale reproduction, perhaps with local variations, of papers put together in Paris or London or New York. It seems that the choice between heavy 'public service' investment in mass communications, or reconciliation with indefinite foreign domination of the mass media, is being forced on Africa now.

The cost, for the present, it must be admitted, may be the sacrifice of a certain amount of freedom of expression, and of a certain degree of variety in the Press and in broadcasting. The pace of development, on the one hand, and the relative stability or instability of the Government and the wisdom of its leaders on the other, will determine the degree to which this is necessary. What is certain is that *if the sacrifices are genuinely made in the cause of social development,* and actually lead to improvements in educational and economic opportunities, social advances will themselves produce a public to demand freedom and variety. And a watchful public is really the only guarantee of any democratic right.

There is after all a vicious circle to be broken. Mass media cannot flourish until mass literacy and a new level of mass education have been achieved; but mass education programmes need the media for their implementation. Economic development is necessary to provide capital for the expansion of education and of the mass media; but economic development can move fast only when communications have been established and the general educational level raised. A 'new' country has to start somewhere: it seems that it must start with communications.

POSTSCRIPT: JUNE 1967

THIS BOOK was finished in December 1965, and within three months there had been no fewer than seven *coups d'état* in Africa. Among them was the military coup in Ghana that swept from power President Nkrumah and the Convention People's Party; and the coup led by General Ironsi in Nigeria, in which the Federal Prime Minister and the strong man of the North, the Sardauna of Sokoto, lost their lives. In June 1967, Africa is in many ways a changed continent. General Ironsi in his turn has been killed in a second coup (July 1966), and the Nigerian Federation itself disintegrated with the secession of the East Region as the independent state of Biafra (May 1967). In Sierra Leone a military coup has unseated civilian government (March 1967). Yet, while violent change rocked independent Africa, the white south has remained apparently unshaken. Dr. Verwoerd has gone, but apartheid continues, and expands, under Prime Minister Vorster. The United Nations has resolved on economic sanctions against Rhodesia—but Ian Smith, whose prospects of survival seemed in December 1965 to be measurable in "weeks rather than months," continues to rule.

These developments do not alter the basic argument of this book; but they have naturally had their effect on the mass media, particularly in West Africa. In Ghana, Nigeria and Sierra Leone newspapers and journalists have fallen casualties to the coups. In Sierra Leone, all newspapers were banned when the military government took power, except the government-owned *Daily Mail* (which was taken over from its British owners towards the end of 1965). In Nigeria, the Lagos-based *Morning Post* and *Daily Times* have been banned from the Eastern Region (now Biafra) since January 1967, and the Eastern papers that used to circulate in the Midwest banned in their turn. Easterners employed on Lagos papers have long joined the refugees on the trek for home. Journalists have been arrested, including the editor of the *West African Pilot*, Stephen Iweanya, in June 1966, for breach of a public order banning the display of signs, symbols, slogans or flags of any of the dissolved political parties; and the editor of *Tribune*, Ibadan, in May 1967. In Ghana, editors of all the main newspapers, together with the Director-General of Broadcasting, were among the mass arrests of the military régime when it assumed power in February 1966. Some were released early in 1967—only to be swept up once more in the detentions that followed an attempted counter-coup in March, and as far as is known at present, all are still in prison, and none have been brought to trial. Most of the main papers have continued to publish, under new editors and in some cases with new staff, but the *Daily Gazette*, *Sunday Punch* and *The Spark*, together with all publications of the Bureau of African Affairs, have disappeared.

In Ghana and Sierra Leone severe Press Laws, and in Nigeria a State of Emergency, restrict the publication both of news and comment. Decrees on the "Prohibition of Rumour" passed by the Ghana National Liberation Council in October 1966 make journalists and editors liable to arrest for up to twenty-eight days without trial, and to jail sentences of up to three years, if they publish anything likely to "cause alarm and despondency," to "disturb the public peace," or to "cause disaffection against the N.L.C."[1] The Sierra Leone Newspaper Law of March 31, 1967, makes every publisher of a newspaper publishing any reference to "any political party or organisation which was in existence before 23rd March 1967," liable, if found guilty, to not less than two years' or more than five years' imprisonment; and to similar penalties for "defaming" any member of the National Reformation Council. It is no defence if the report is true, and false statements, rumours or reports "calculated to bring into disrepute any person who holds office under the Constitution in the discharge of his duties" carry punishments of up to £250 fine or up to two years' imprisonment or both.

[1] In spite of these ferocious limitations, the N.L.C. government is anxious to present itself as favouring Press freedom, and three days after the coup Col. Afrifa, N.L.C. member, congratulated the *Ghanaian Times* for criticising the new régime. A year later he was actually lamenting the lack of Press criticism. There have indeed been genuine instances of criticism both of members of the special commissions set up by the military government (for instance, the *Ghanaian Times* has attacked Dr. Busia, Chairman of the Political Commission planning a new constitution); and even members of the N.L.C. itself. But what no newspaper has done is to offer a single word in defence of the former régime, of President Nkrumah or any of his colleagues, or of any of his policies. Indeed, no newspaper is complete without at least one attack on the former President. It seems that in effect the Press is 'free' as long as it supports the present government—a conclusion confirmed by General Ankrah himself only a few weeks ago, when he warned that newspapers were not giving enough attention to the achievements of the N.L.C.

Newspapers must be officially registered, and may be suspended for up to six months. Nigeria, on the other hand, was relatively free of Press Control under the first six months of military government, and in 1966 a genuine and outspoken political debate on the future of the Federation took place. In the second half of the year, however, comment became less and less outspoken, and information to be gleaned from the broadcasting services, both of the Federation and the Regions, more limited. With the State of Emergency declared on May 27, 1967, full-scale censorship in the Federation was imposed, including a ban on all unapproved political news and comment. There is at present no formal censorship in Biafra, but if there is any significant opposition to Lt. Col. Ojukwu's policy, it is not expressed in the newspapers. The Government's paper, the *Nigerian Outlook*, is now the *Biafra Sun*, and the East Nigeria Broadcasting Service has been renamed Voice of Biafra, under the control of the Department of Information.

All these developments, however, may be said to arise out of "emergency" situations. They may be temporary, because the emergencies may give way to more stable conditions. In the long term, it is the change in Ghana that is likely to prove most important, both for that country and for media development on the continent as a whole: since there a fundamental policy of national investment in, and control of, the mass media has been abandoned. In January 1967, the N.L.C. announced that the publicity committees in charge of the Press, the Ghana News Agency and the Broadcasting Corporation had been reconstituted. In February the Director-General of the G.B.C., W. F. Coleman, declared that commercial radio and television services would be launched before the end of the year. The only new paper that has been established since the 1966 coup is a privately owned one—*The Ashanti Pioneer*, revived after its suppression in 1961. Present policy appears to be to encourage the mass media to find backing from private, probably foreign, enterprise though no foreign capital has so far come forward to take over any of the national newspapers. The present instability of the country is unlikely to encourage foreign investment, but the change of attitude is already reflected in the newspapers themselves, in increased sports coverage, women's fashion, beauty contests, "pop" features: the effect is more various and more entertaining than in the past, but in the spirit of commercial "popular" journalism rather than that of social education.

Elsewhere in Africa, too, recent moves have tended to increase foreign intervention in the Press. During 1966, Lonrho, the great British land and investment company which already owned Zambia's only daily newspaper, and a Sunday, acquired two new papers, the *Livingstone Mail* and the *Financial Mail* (now *Business and Economy*), and thus a position of overwhelming domination in the country, challenged only by the Government's *Zambia Mail*, still a weekly. Then, in a surprise move in mid-1967, Lonrho gained a 51 per cent interest, through its subsidiary African Investment Trust, in the company (Consolidated Holdings) which owns the most influential newspaper chain in East Africa—including the *East African Standard*, Nairobi, the *Uganda Argus*, Kampala, and the *Standard*, Dar-es-Salaam. Lonrho, connected in no way with the Press three years ago, is now one of the biggest newspaper proprietors on the Continent, and with Thomson's, probably the foreign concern with the biggest stake in Africa's mass media. What is more, it is a particular kind of foreign company, one with historic links with the Rand mining complex of South Africa (the British South Africa Company, now part of the Anglo-American empire, sold its considerable holdings in Lonrho in 1965), and close present involvement in white Southern Africa as a whole—for instance, through its joint ownership of the Beira-Umtali oil pipeline.

It is too early yet to predict what effect the takeover will have either on the policy of these long-established dailies in East Africa, or on the East African Press as a whole. It will certainly considerably strengthen foreign interests, in an area where the indigenous Press is still very weak. But it is worth noting that in Kenya, home of Consolidated Holdings, the conflicts generated by foreign domination of the Press are beginning to cause the Government some concern. Several Ministers saw fit to comment on the *East African Standard*'s vicious attacks on the U.A.R. government at the time of the Middle East war, and it is clear that Kenya is now feeling particularly keenly the lack of any major African-owned newspaper.

The developments of the past eighteen months have thus brought little progress as far as the liberation of the news media is concerned, from either foreign control or local restriction.

Nor has there been the hoped-for expansion—in fact, the latest
figures published by UNESCO, in 1965, actually reflect a drop
in the total number of daily newspapers since 1962 (220 to 200),
and in the ratio of copies per hundred of population (1.1 in
1964, 1.2 in 1962). Figures for broadcasting transmitters and
receivers have improved, however—there were 550 radio transmitters on the continent in 1964 (400 in 1962), 3.7 receivers per
hundred of population (2.3 in 1962), 58 television transmitters
(25 in 1962), and .16 television receivers per hundred of
population (.07 in 1962). And in the field of news collection and
distribution, Tshad, Libya, Malawi, Somalia and Upper Volta
have all started national news agencies, or information services
planned as the basis of full-scale news services. News exchange
agreements among existing agencies have also been regularly
reported, though the vast majority are still between African
and non-African countries. Two new television services are
planned, in Libya in 1968, and in the Central African Republic
(assisted by Israel).

There is one field, however, in which progress has been
steady, and that is the field of telecommunications. Lines of
policy have now been laid down, among African states and
between them and the International Telecommunications
Union, for the building of a modern inter-African network
directly linking all main centres, and linking these centres with
the outside world. Already, many of these links are in operation,
and more are being opened month by month, enabling news
and information to travel faster, and more cheaply, than ever
before. This is the spadework without which none of the more
dramatic projects—PANAF, or the exchange and pooling of
broadcast programme material—will be possible.

The Organisation of African Unity held a joint conference on
telecommunications with the Economic Commission for Africa
in March 1966, and adopted a ten-year continental development programme to cost more than £360m, and involve the
eventual adoption of a system of satellite communications,
microwave, and cables. All countries were to make planning
surveys by September 1966. In June and July the Afro-
Malagasy Posts and Telecommunications Union, too, considered an international telecommunications network including
satellite communications. And in January 1967 the I.T.U.'s
Regional Telecommunications Planning Committee met at last

in Addis Ababa, with thirty African countries represented, together with experts from France, the U.K., U.S.S.R. and the United States, to draw up a plan for the north, west and central areas of Africa for the period 1970–1975. It was decided to establish main routes via overhead carrier lines, underground cables and radio relay, and to retain the present H.F. links only as stand-by. The goal of twenty-four-hour direct traffic between all countries was adopted; and all rates were examined in order to achieve eventual standardisation. And most recently, U.R.T.N.A. (African National Radio and Television Union) met in April 1967, gave priority to the building of a technical centre on broadcasting at Bamako, and charged the Director of the new centre with contacting the I.T.U. on the use of artificial satellites in the development of African broadcasting.

Africa is thus coming increasingly to see the use of satellites as essential to its communications in the future. A feasibility study has already been taking place on the building of a ground station in East Africa, and earlier this year the Federal Military Government of Nigeria contracted a United States firm, Telecom Incorporated, as engineering consultants for a satellite ground station, to cost over £2m. It is only when Africa has its own chain of ground stations, of course, that the continent will be able, for instance, to take advantage of the growing system of satellite communications being developed by the U.S.-dominated international consortium INTELSAT, whose Canary Bird satellite (companion to the Atlantic Early Bird) was launched over West Africa in March 1967.

And what of the future? It is my own hope that some progress will be made in two directions, in the years before 1970: in the establishment of a Pan-African News Agency, and the harnessing of all the media, particularly television, to the needs of literacy and social education. The first project may have to await a return to some kind of political stability, especially on the West Coast, where among others the Secretary General of the Pan-African Union of Journalists and Secretary of CAMI (the O.A.U. sub-committee charged with setting up PANAF) is currently in jail—Kofi Batsa of Ghana—and governments are at present far too internally preoccupied to devote enough attention, let alone finance, to inter-African projects. As for the second project, some Governments are already keenly aware of the contrast between their hopes of three years ago, and the realities of television programming today.[1] When programme and managements contracts come up for renewal, as some of them will very soon, changes may be expected. A few real educational projects are under way, including a pilot scheme in educational television at Dakar, run by UNESCO, and the unique educational television service set up by the Zambia Government, and run through the extra-mural department of the University of Zambia.

* * * * *

This is not a book by an "expert", nor is it a thorough survey of its subject. Thorough surveys, it is hoped, will come later, based on studies on the spot, such as I would have liked to have been able to undertake myself. I have concentrated on the situation in English-speaking Africa, which I know best, and where in general Press, radio and television are most highly developed. There, the problems raised by dependence on foreign sources of news and programme material are most complex. What I have done is little more than point to the difficulties—the solutions will come from Africa.

I have many people to thank for their help. Some of them are mentioned in the text, but many more are not. Their contributions were not therefore less valued or less substantial, and I am deeply grateful.

ROSALYNDE AINSLIE.

Note: After this book was printed, the names of the principal Congo cities Leopoldville, Elizabethville and Stanleyville were changed (July 1, 1966) to Kinshasa, Lubumbashi and Kisangani.

---

[1] Current programme schedules for radio and television in Zambia reveal a contrast repeated all over the continent. Radio uses ten languages, including English. It broadcasts Zambian music daily, programmes of news and comment, including wide African coverage; African plays and short stories; and women's magazine material ranging from local history to baby care. Television offers practically no live or locally made material except religious services, news and sport. It is a dreary catalogue of Danger Man, Meet the Wife, Ben Casey, Peyton Place—even Match of the Day is British, not Zambian, football!

A SHORT BIBLIOGRAPHY of Published and Unpublished Material on Press and Broadcasting in Africa

BOOKS AND DOCUMENTS

The Press in Africa, Helen Kitchen: Ruth Sloan Associates, 1956.

Communications Fact Books for African Countries: U.S.I.A., 1960–66.

Communication in Africa: a Search for Boundaries, Leonard W. Doob: Yale University Press, 1961.

Sound and Television Broadcasting in the Overseas Territories: Colonial Office Handbook, London, 1963.

UNESCO PUBLICATIONS

Mass Media and National Development: the Role of Information in the Developing Countries, Wilbur Schramm: Stanford University Press and UNESCO, 1964.

Radio in Fundamental Education in Undeveloped Areas, J. Grenfell Williams, 1950.

Legislation for Press, Film and Radio, Fernand Terrou, 1951.

The Problems of Transmitting Press Messages, 1956.

Mass Media in the Developing Countries (Reports and Papers on Mass Communication, no. 33) 1961.

Developing Information Media in Africa (Reports and Papers on Mass Communication, no. 37) 1962.

Space Communications and the Mass Media (Reports and Papers on Mass Communications, no. 41) 1963.

Report on the Meeting of Experts on the Development of News Agencies in Africa, held in Tunis, April 1963: May 1963.

East Africa: Mass Media Training Needs: August 1964.

Documents of the Meeting on the Introduction and Development of Television in Africa, Lagos, September 1964: November 1964.

World Communications: a UNESCO handbook, 1964.

UNITED NATIONS:

Annual Reports on Freedom of Information, U.N. Commission on Human Rights.

SOME PERIODICAL ARTICLES

The Nigerian Press 1900–1950, Ernest Ikoli: *West Africa Review*, June 1950.

Information Media in Mali: *Africa Report*, September 1960.

Press and Radio in Post-Independence Africa, Robert E. Hartland: Background Book, *Africa and the U.S. Images and Realities*, the 8th National Conference of the U.S. Commission for UNESCO, Boston, October 1961.

Press and Radio in Africa: *Africa Report*, February 1964.

Work of the Plan Committee in the Intercontinental Sphere: *Telecommunications Journal*, April 1964.

Space prevents the inclusion of less readily available books and documents but a list of these can be obtained from the publisher: Walker and Company, 720 Fifth Avenue, New York, 10019.

African Broadcasting Stations, News Agencies and Daily Newspapers, June 1967

Country	Population[1]	Illiteracy[2]	Radio	Television	News Agency	Daily Papers
Algeria	10,975,000	81% (1954)	Radio-Télévision Algérienne (Government)	R.T.A.	Algérie Presse Service	Al Moudjahid Al Nasr (both published under direction of F.L.N.)
Angola	5,084,000	97% (1950)	Emissora Oficial de Angola (Government) 12 radio clubs 1 mine station 1 religious station	None	Lusitania and A.N.I. (both Portuguese)	Diário de Angola Diário de Luanda O Comércio A Provincia de Angola
Botswana	543,000	79·5 (1946)	Radio Botswana (Government) B.B.C. Relay Station	None	None	None
Burundi	2,500,000		Radio Burundi (Government) Radio Cordac (religious)	None	None	None
Cameroon	5,103,000	90–95% (±1950)	Radio Buea Radio Douala Radio Garoua Radio Yaounde (all Government)	None	Agence Camerounaise de Presse (Government)	La Presse du Cameroun (foreign owned) The Cameroon Times
Central African Republic	1,320,000		Radio Bangui (Government)	Planned, with aid from Israel	Agence Centrafricaine de Presse	None
Chad	3,300,000		Radio-diffusion Nationale Tchadienne (Government)	None	Agence Tchadienne de Presse	None
Congo (Brazzaville)	826,000		Radio Brazzaville (formerly R.T.F.) Radio Congo (both now Govt.)	Télévision Congolaise (Government)	Agence Congolaise d'Information	None

[1] Mid-1964 estimates, United Nations Statistical Yearbook, 1965.

[2] UNESCO Handbook on World Communications, 1964, and UNESCO Statistical Yearbook, 1965.

Country	Population	Illiteracy	Radio	Television	News Agency	Daily Papers
Congo (Kinshasa)	15,300,000	84·6% (1955–57) (African pop. only)	Radio-diffusion Congolaise (Government, 6 stations) Radio Collège (religious) Radio UFAC (religious)	Planned	Agence Congolaise de Presse	Kinshasa: Le Courrier d'Afrique L'Etoile du Congo Le Progrès Actualités Africaines Présence Congolaise La Tribune Lubumbashi: L'Essor de Katanga La Voix de Katanga La Dépêche Kisangani: La Gazette
Dahomey	2,300,000		Radio Dahomey (Government)	Télévision Dahoménne (run by OCORA)	Agence Dahoménne de Presse	None
Ethiopia	22,200,000	95–99% (±1950)	Radio Addis Ababa (Government) Radio Voice of the Gospel (religious)	Ethiopia Tele-vision (run by Thomson Tele-vision Inter-national)	Ethiopian News Agency	Addis Ababa: Addis Soir Addis Zemen Ethiopia Dimtz Voice of Ethiopia Ethiopian Herald Eritrea: Il Quotidiano Eritreo Giornale dell'Eritrea Hebret
Gabon	459,000	87·6% (1960–61)	Radio-Télévision Gabonaise (Government)	R.T.G.	Agence Gabonaise d'Information	None
Gambia	324,000	95–99% (±1950)	Radio Gambia (Government)	None	None	Gambia News Bulletin (3–4 times weekly) The Ghanaian Times
Ghana	7,537,000	75–80% (±1950)	Radio Ghana (Government)	Ghana Television	Ghana News Agency	The Evening News (owned by Government-controlled corporation) Ghana Graphic (independent trust) Ashanti Pioneer (local private ownership)

Country	Population	Literacy	Radio	Television	News Agency	Press
Guinea	3,420,000		Radio-diffusion Nationale (Government)	None	Agence Guinéenne de Presse	Horaya (Government)
Ivory Coast	3,750,000		Radio Abidjan (Government) Radio Bouaké (Government)	Télévision Côte d'Ivoire (run by Thomson Television International)	Agencie Ivoirienne de Presse	Fraternité-Matin (Government owned, run by Société Nationale des Entreprises de Presse)
Kenya	9,104,000	75–80% (±1950)	Voice of Kenya (Government)	Kenya Television	Kenya News Agency	East African Standard (foreign capital) Daily Nation (foreign owned) Taifa Leo (foreign owned) Kenya Daily Mail None
Lesotho	733,000	65·1% (1946)	Radio Maseru (Government)	None	None	None
Liberia	1,041,000	91·1% (1962)	Liberian Broadcasting Corporation—ELBC (Government) Voice of America ELWA (religious)	E.L.T.V. (run by subsidiary of Rediffusion, London)	None	The Daily Listener Liberian Star (run by Thomson Organisation, London)
Libya	1,559,000	87·1% (1954)	Libyan Broadcasting Service (Government)	Planned for 1968	Libyan News Agency	Taraboulous al Gharb Fazzan (Government) Al Raqeeb Giornale di Tripoli None
Malawi	3,900,000	93·5% (1945)	Malawi Radio (Government)	None	Malawi News Agency	None
Mali	4,485,000		Radio Mali (Government)	None	Agence Nationale d'Information	L'Essor (ruling party)
Mauritania	900,000		Radio Mauritanie (Government)	None	None	None
Morocco	12,959,000	86·2% (1960)	Radio-Télévision Marocaine (Government) Voice of America Relay Station	R.T.M.	Maghreb Arabe Presse	Al Alam Al Anbaa Al Massa Al Muharir (NUPF opposition)

Country	Population	Illiteracy	Radio	Television	News Agency	Daily Papers
						Le Petit Marocain (foreign) La Vigie Marocaine (foreign) Maroc Informations L'Opinion (Istiqlal party) España (foreign owned) Diário de Africa (foreign owned)
Moçambique	6,872,000	98·5% (±1950)	Radio-Club de Moçambique (state-subsidised) Radio Beira (private club) Radio Pax (religious)	None	Lusitania and A.N.I. (both Portuguese)	Notícias (Portuguese owned) Notícias da Tarde (Portuguese owned) Tribuna Diário de Moçambique Diário
Niger	3,250,000	99·1 (1960)	Radio Niger (Government)	None	None	Le Temps du Niger (Government owned, run by Société Nationale des Entreprises de Presse)
Nigeria[1]	56,400,000	88·5% (1952–53)	Nigerian Broadcasting Corporation (statutory corporation) operating Federal and three regional stations 3 commercial stations—one in each region	Federal, and 3 regional networks, all Government controlled but run by foreign companies	None	Lagos: Daily Times (foreign owned) The Morning Post (Federal Government) West African Pilot (Zik group) Daily Telegraph Enugu: Nigerian Outlook (East Government) Eastern Guardian (Zik group) Onitsha: The Spokesman (Zik group) Ibadan: The Daily Sketch (West regional Govt.)

The New Nigerian (North regional Govt.) (Main papers only listed —there are nearly 20 dailies in Nigeria)

Country	Population	Literacy	Broadcasting	Television	News Agency	Press
Rhodesia	4,140,000	75–80% (±1950 all pops.)	Rhodesian Broadcasting Corporation (statutory corporation)	R.B.C. (run by Rhodesia Television, a private company)	Inter-African News Agency (subsidiary of S.A.P.A.)	Salisbury: Rhodesia Herald; Bulawayo: The Chronicle
Rwanda	3,018,000		Radio Rwanda (Government) DeutscheWelle Relay Station	None	None	None
Senegal	3,400,000	94·4% (1961)	Radio-diffusion du Senegal (Government)	Unesco is running a pilot educational project	Agence de Presse Sénégalaise	Dakar-Matin (foreign owned)
Sierra Leone	2,200,000	90–95% (±1950)	Sierra Leone Broadcasting Service (Government)	S.L.B.S. (run by Sierra Leone Television Ltd., in which Thomson Television International, Television International Enterprises and National Broadcasting Corporation of America, all have interests)	None	Daily Mail (Government owned)
Somalia	2,350,000	95–99% (±1950)	Radio Mogadicio Radio Somali (both Government)	None	Somali National News Agency	Corriere della Somalia
Sudan	13,180,000	88% (1956)	Sudan Broadcasting Service (Government)	S.B.S.	Sudan News Agency	Al Rai al A'am; Sawt al Sudan; Al Sudan al Gedid; Al Ayam; Al Zaman; Al Alam; Al Jamaheer; Morning News; Vigilant; An-Neel

Country	Population	Illiteracy	Radio	Television	News Agency	Daily Papers
Swaziland	288,000	77·2% (1956)	Radio Mbabane (Government)	None	None	None
Tanzania	10,325,000	90–95% (±1950)	Radio Tanzania Voice of Zanzibar (both Government)	None	None	Standard (foreign owned) The Nationalist (ruling party) Uhuru (ruling party) Ngrumo
Togo	1,603,000	90–95% (±1950)	Radio-diffusion du Togo (Government)	None	None	Togo-Presse (Government) La Verité Togolaise Togo-Matin (independent)
Tunisia	4,565,000	84·3% (1956)	Radio-Télévision Tunisienne (Government)	R.T.T.	Agence Tunis-Afrique Presse	L'Action (ruling party) Al Amal (ruling party) Essabah (independent) La Presse de Tunisie (foreign owned) Le Petit Matin
Uganda	7,367,000	74·9% (1959)	Radio Uganda (Government)	Uganda Television	None	Uganda Argus (foreign owned) Taifa Empya (foreign owned) Munno (mission owned) Omukulembeze (Government owned)
United Arab Republic	28,900,000	80·5% (1960)	U.A.R. Broadcasting Corporation (Government)	U.A.R.B.C.	Middle East News Agency	Al Gomhuriya Al Akhbar Al Shaab Al Ahram Le Progrès Egyptien La Bourse Egyptienne Egyptian Gazette (Main papers only listed —there are some 30 dailies in the U.A.R., all published under the supervision of the ruling party)

Country	Population		Radio	Television	News Agency	Press
Upper Volta	4,750,000		Radio Haute Volta (Government)	Télévision Haute Volta	Agence de Presse Voltaique	None
Zambia	3,600,000	75–80% (±1950) (African pop.)	Radio Zambia (Government)	Television Zambia—TVZ Separate educational service	None	Times of Zambia (foreign owned)
South Africa	17,474,000	68·5% (1960) (African pop. only)	Radio South Africa (South African Broadcasting Corporation)	None	South African Press Association (owned by newspapers)	Bloemfontein: The Friend, Die Volksblad — Cape Town: Cape Argus, Cape Times, Die Burger — Durban: Natal Daily News, Natal Mercury — East London: Daily Dispatch — Johannesburg: Rand Daily Mail, The Star, Die Transvaler, Die Vaderland, The World — Kimberly: Diamond Fields Advertiser — Port Elizabeth: Eastern Province Herald, Evening Post — Pretoria: Pretoria News (Main papers only listed—there are more than 20, including 2 in South-West Africa)

INDEX